The CELL PHONE

ITS USE (AND MISUSE!) THROUGH THE AGES

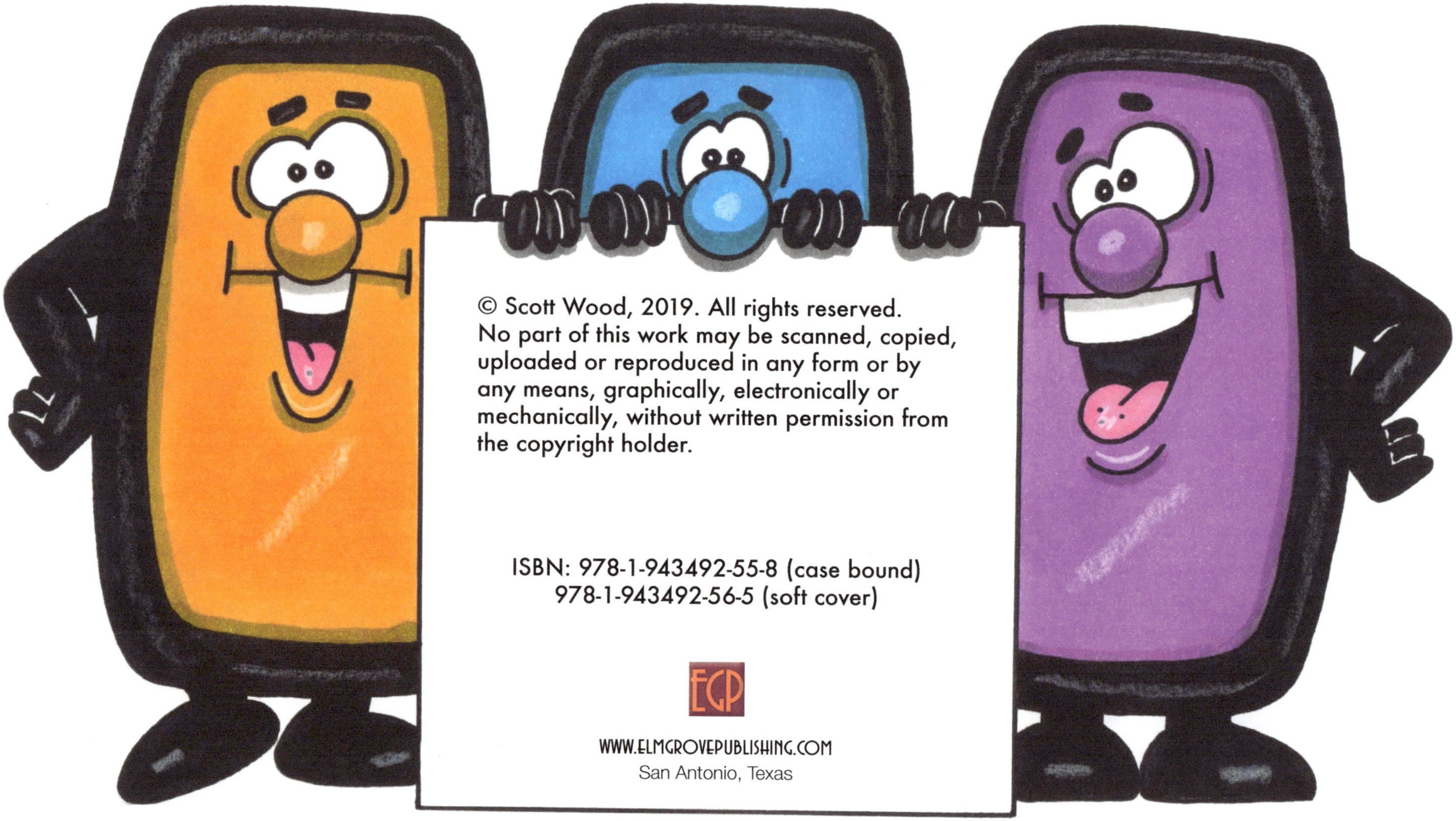

ISBN: 978-1-943492-55-8 (case bound)
978-1-943492-56-5 (soft cover)

WWW.ELMGROVEPUBLISHING.COM
San Antonio, Texas

Book design by: **designpanache**

The CELL PHONE

ITS USE (AND MISUSE!) THROUGH THE AGES

ORIGINAL CARTOONS BY

SCOTT WOOD

CONTENTS

Foreword..................6

In the Beginning..................7

The Dating Game..................24

At Work... 32

...Or Play..................48

Life's Little Moments..................54

The Animal Kingdom..................81

Out There..................100

And Finally... 108

FOREWORD

It's hard to believe the cell phone is almost 50 years old. The first cell phone call was made on April 3rd, 1973, and it started a revolution in personal communications which is still ongoing.

For anyone who remembers those first cell phones, they were heavy, cumbersome and clunky. Texting hadn't been invented yet, and there was no video or music to download, it was strictly voice only. But it was a way to stay in touch, anywhere, anytime (provided you kept your enormous battery properly charged!) and people couldn't seem to do without them.

How the cell phone changed history!

Cell phones, for better or for worse, have become part of our lives. In some cases, it seems as though they might actually control peoples' lives.

Internationally known cartoonist Scott Wood, famed for his *Quibbley* cartoon strip in the European issue of *Stars and Stripes*, as well as his work for luxury car manufacturer Porsche, takes a fun and nostalgic look at those early cell phones and how they changed our lives… and how they might have changed history if they'd been invented 100 or even a million years ago.

We've come a long way, Mr. Bell… Enjoy!

In The Beginning

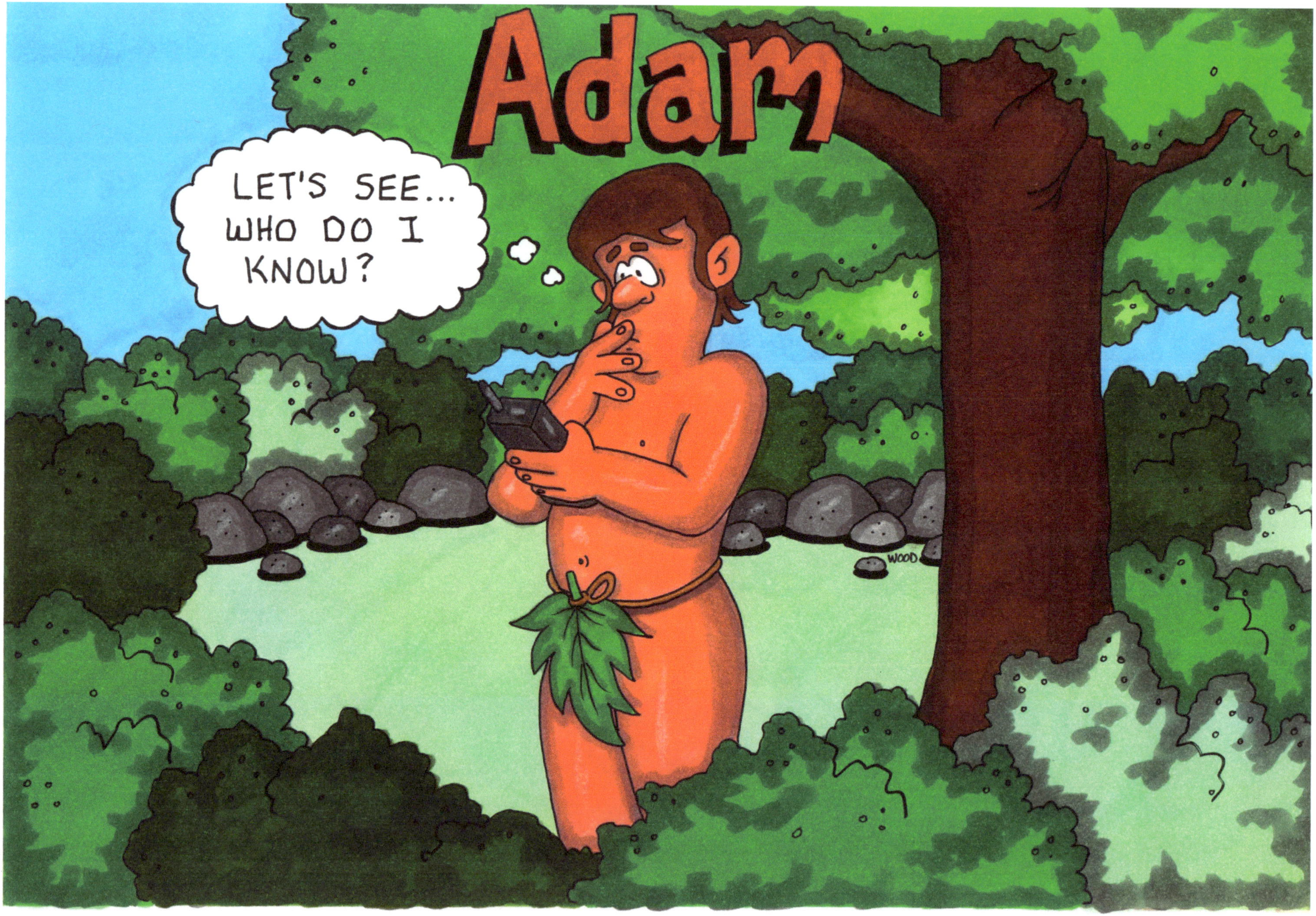
Adam
LET'S SEE... WHO DO I KNOW?
WOOD

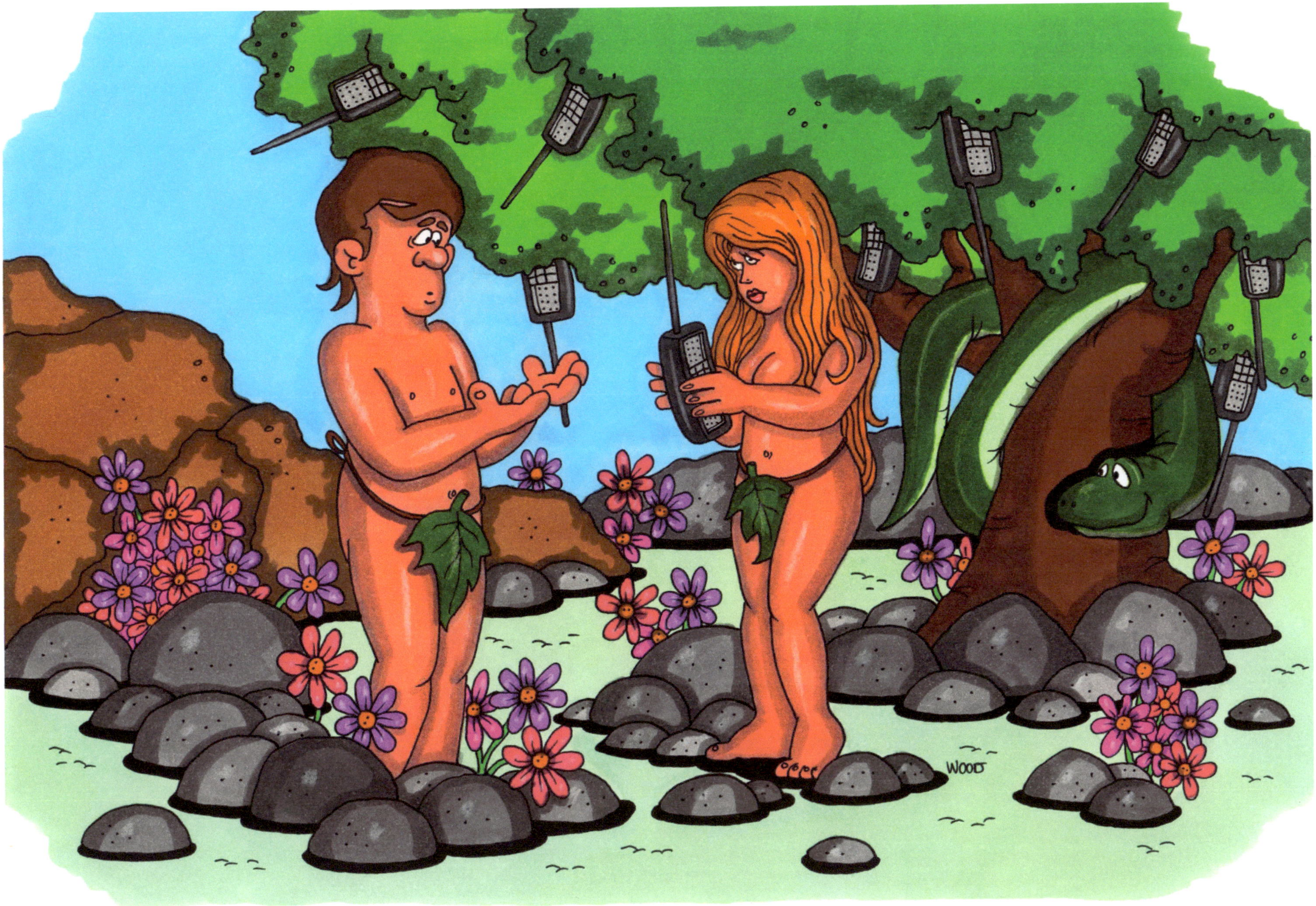
WOOD

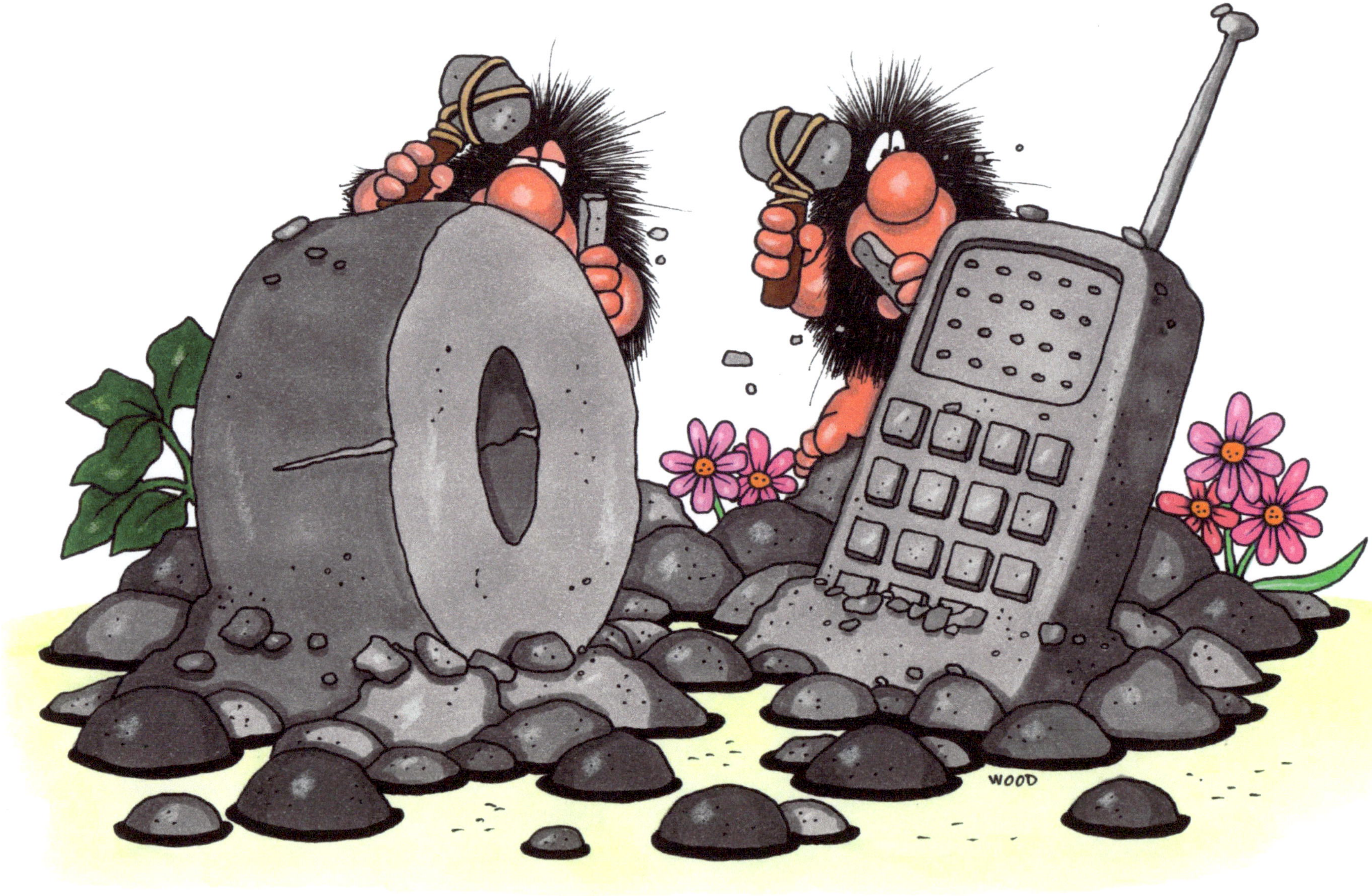
WOOD

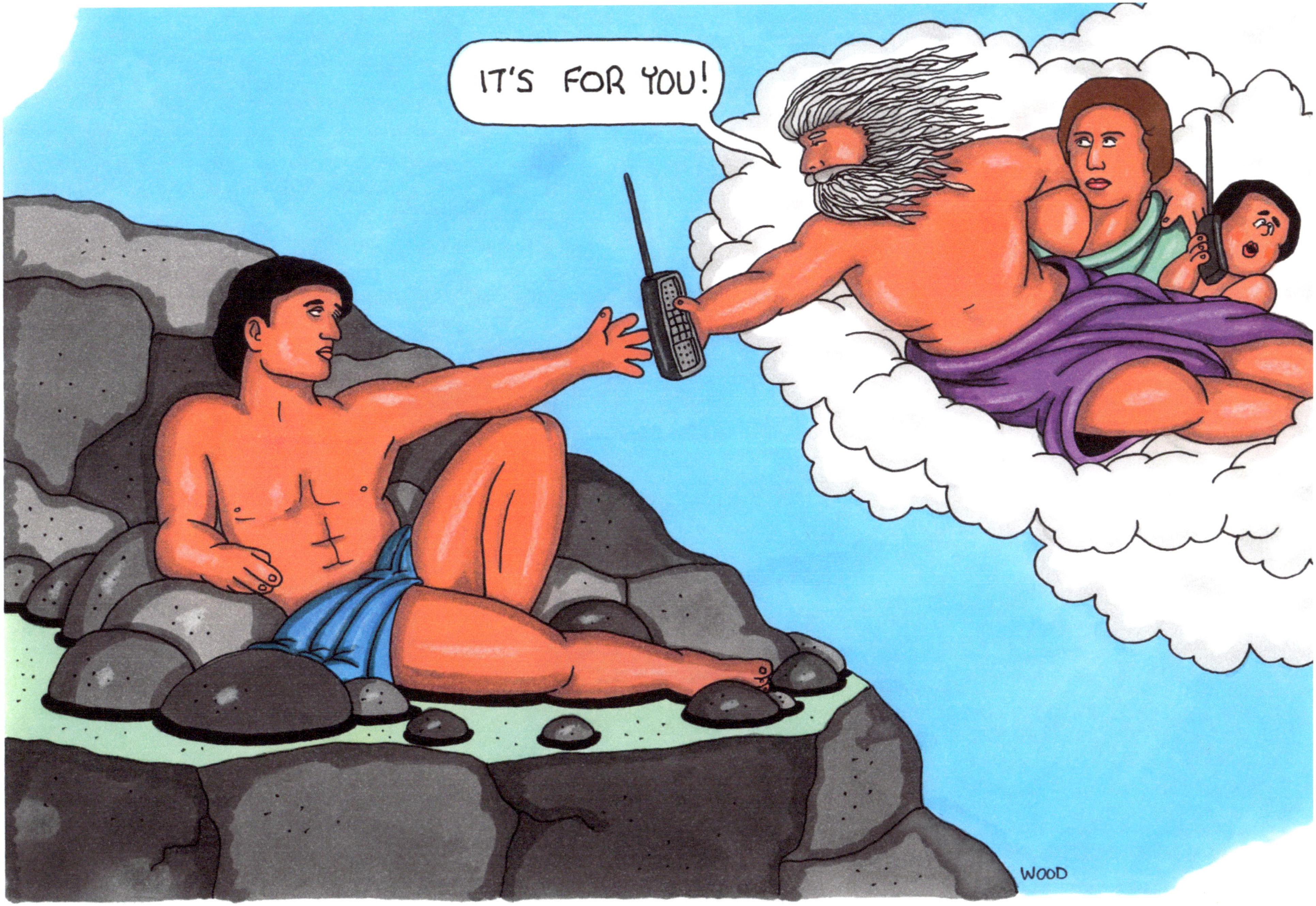
IT'S FOR YOU!
WOOD

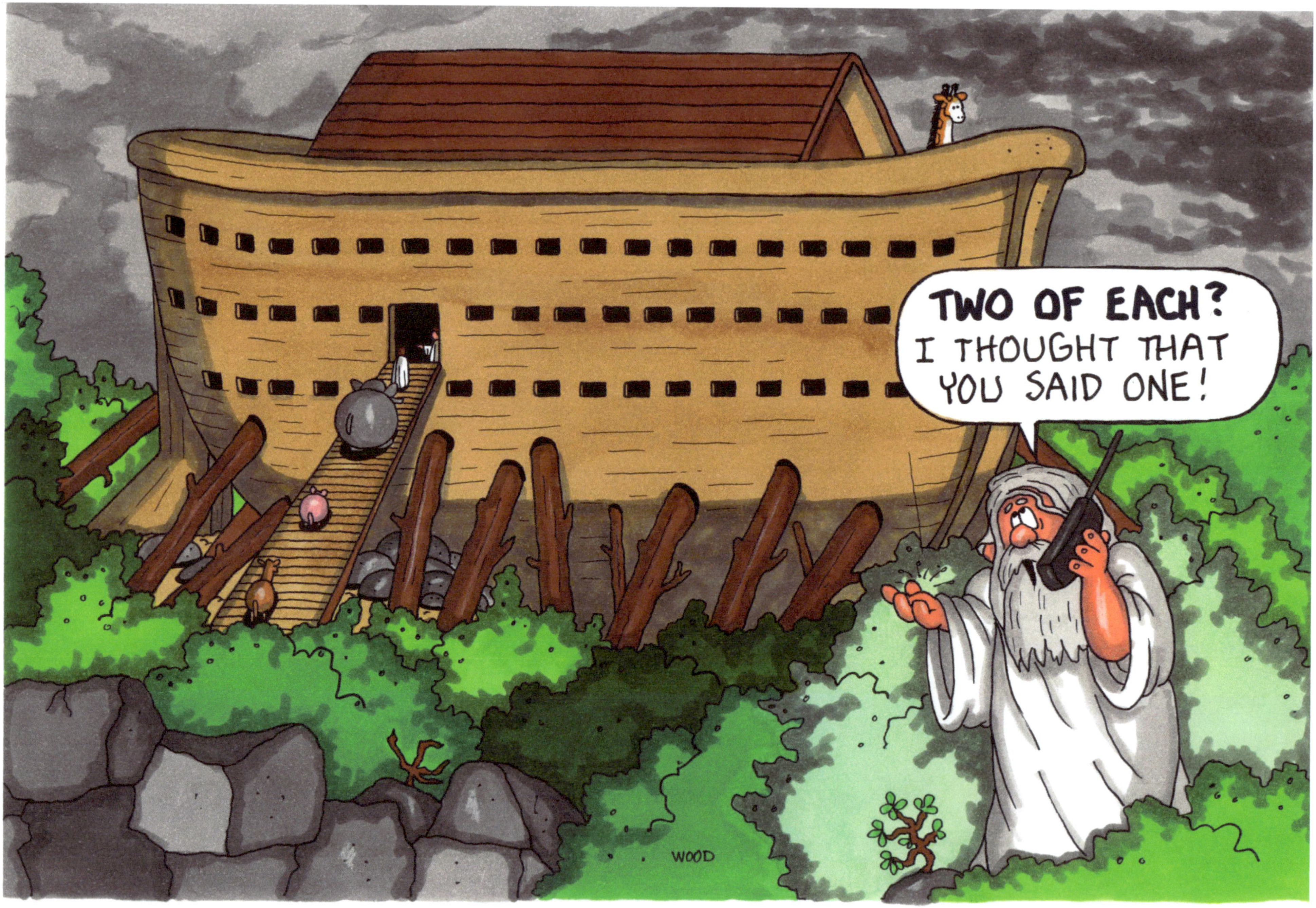
TWO OF EACH?
I THOUGHT THAT YOU SAID ONE!
WOOD

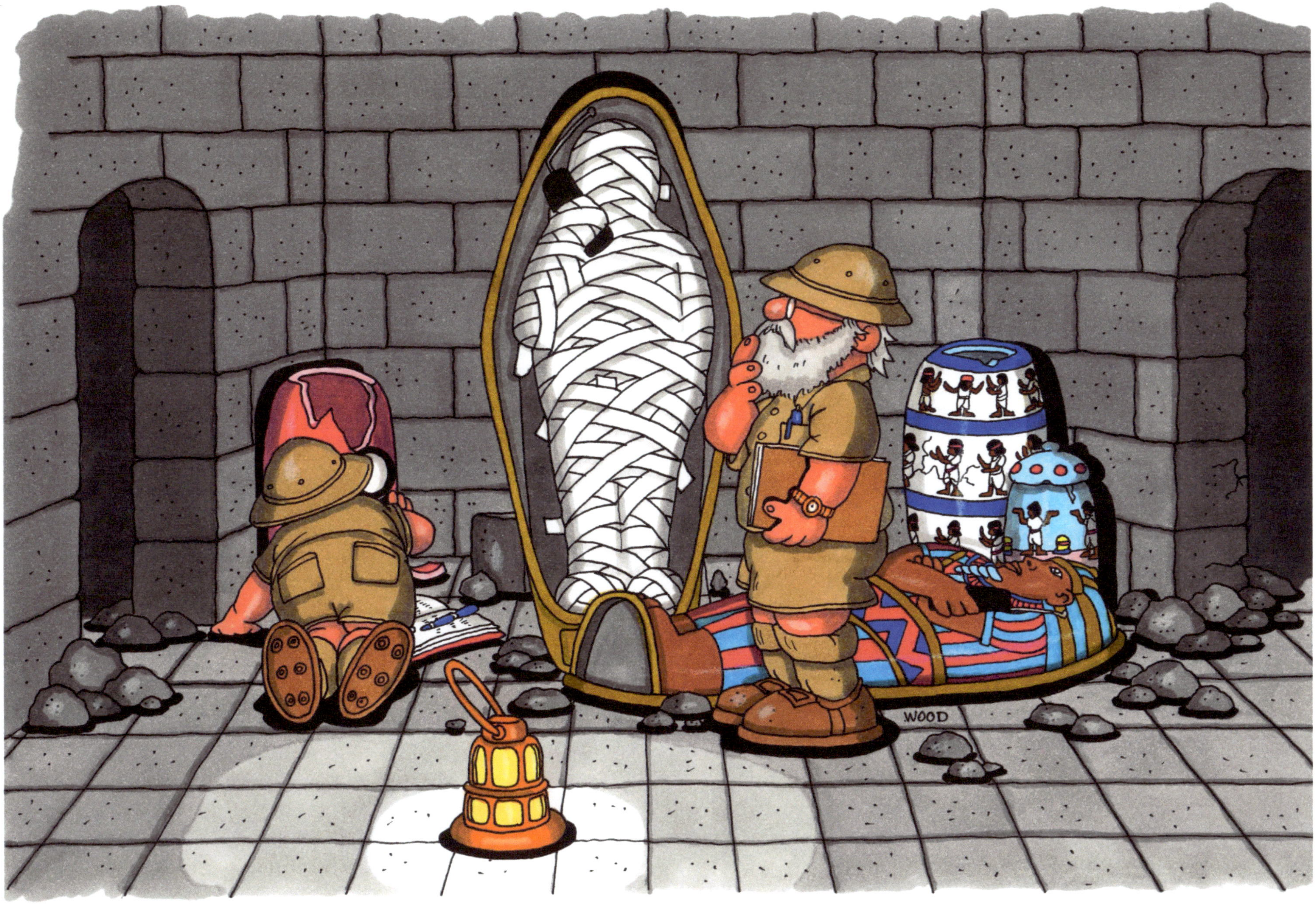
WOOD

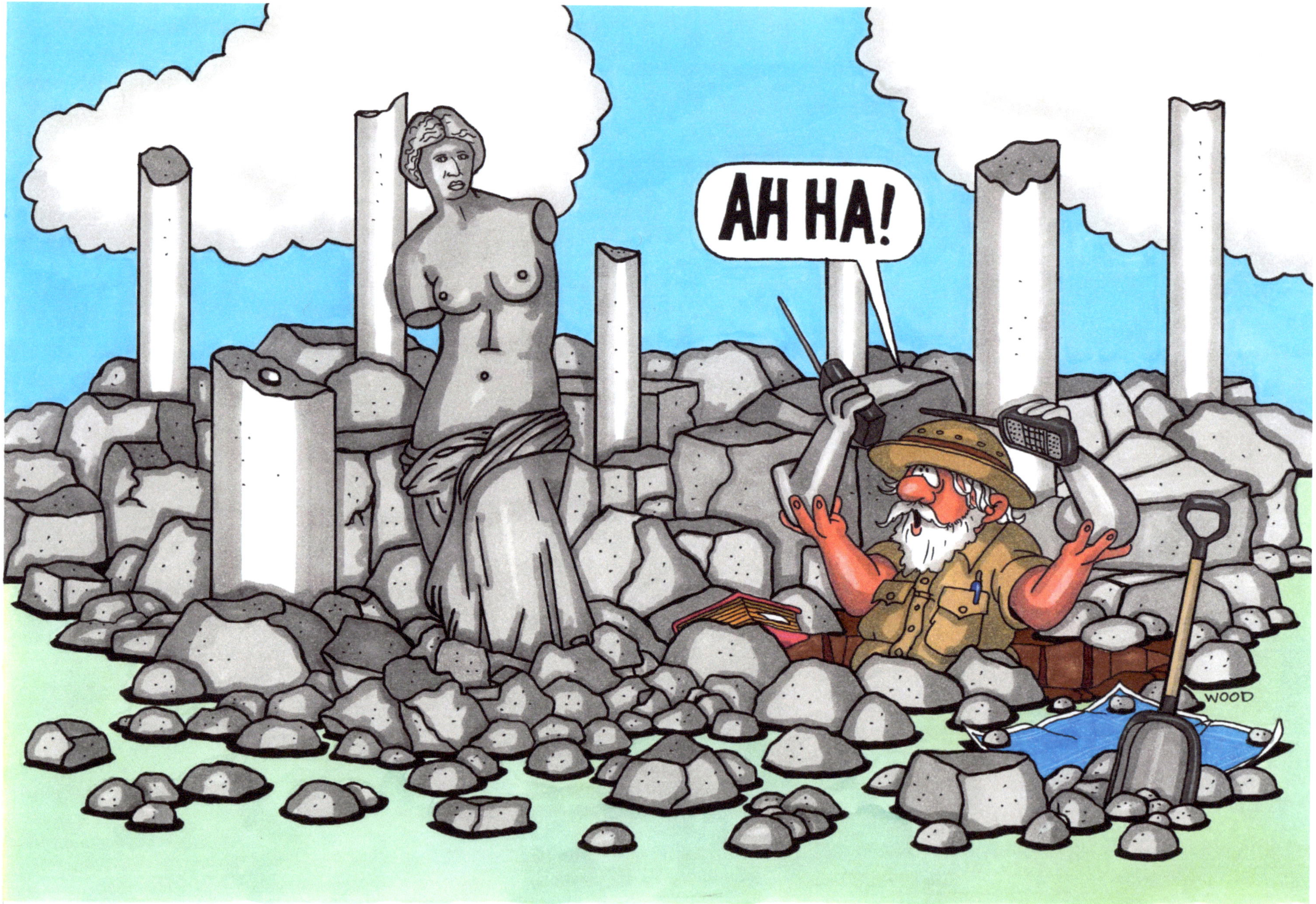
AH HA!
WOOD

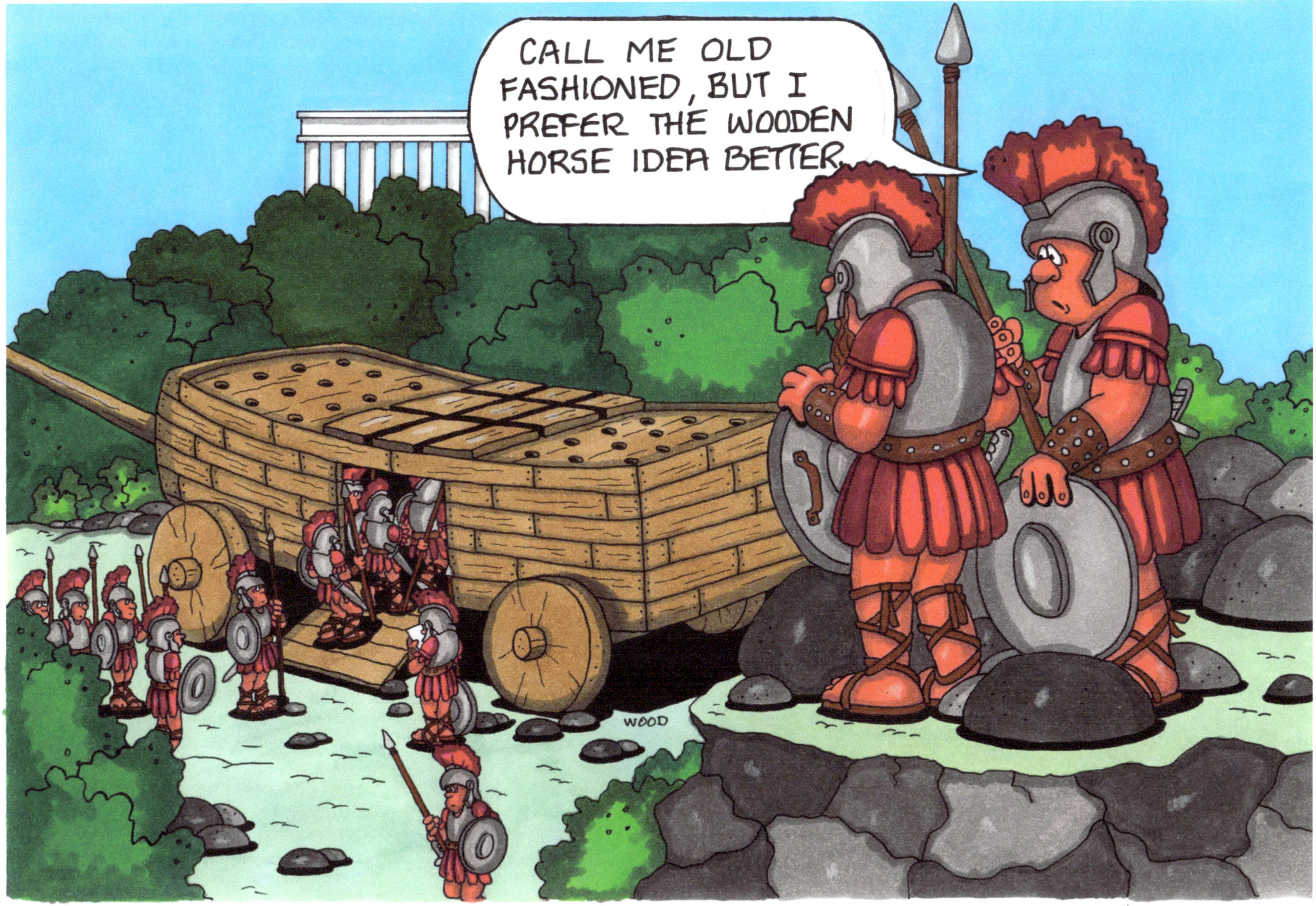
CALL ME OLD FASHIONED, BUT I PREFER THE WOODEN HORSE IDEA BETTER.
WOOD

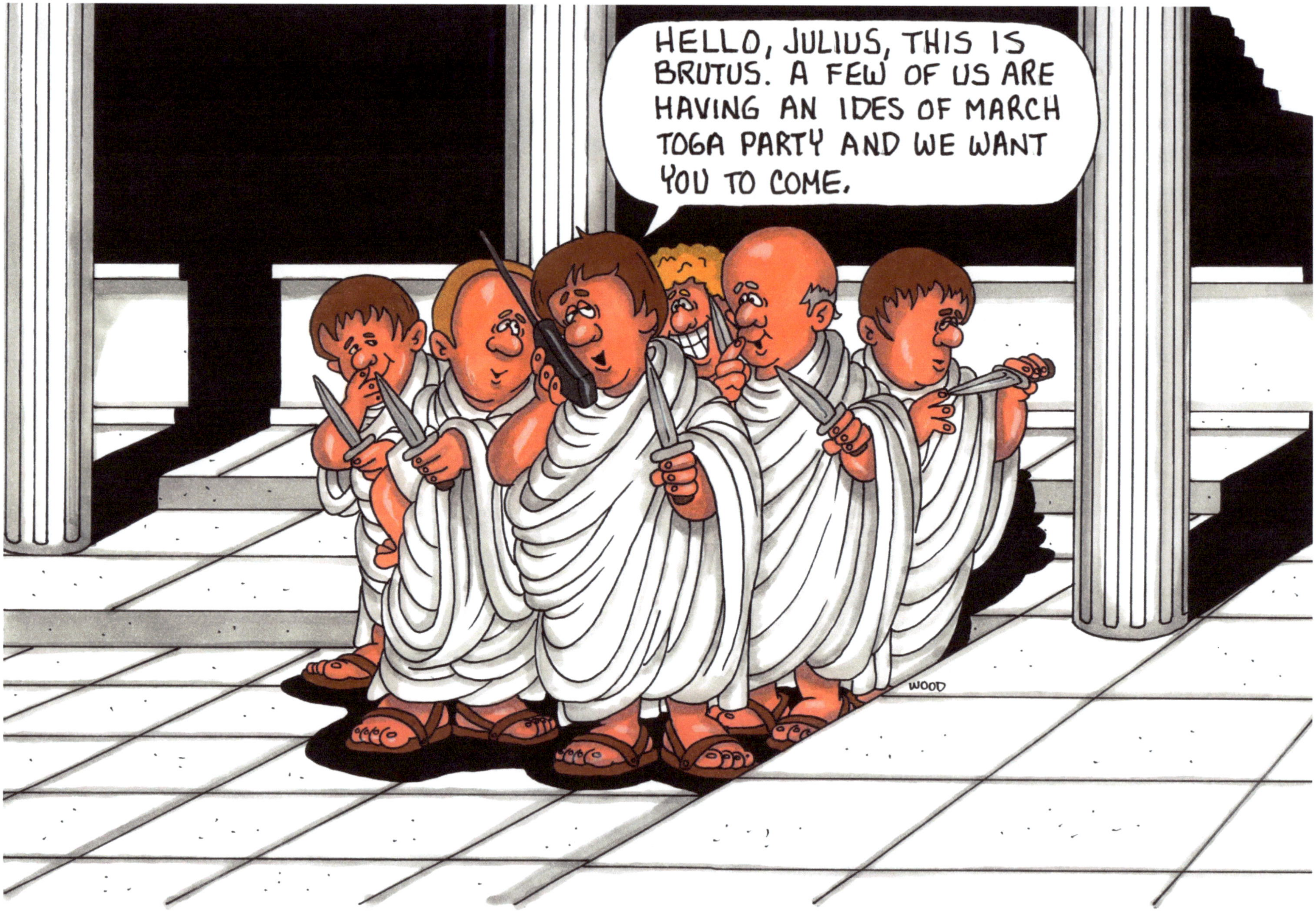
HELLO, JULIUS, THIS IS BRUTUS. A FEW OF US ARE HAVING AN IDES OF MARCH TOGA PARTY AND WE WANT YOU TO COME.
WOOD

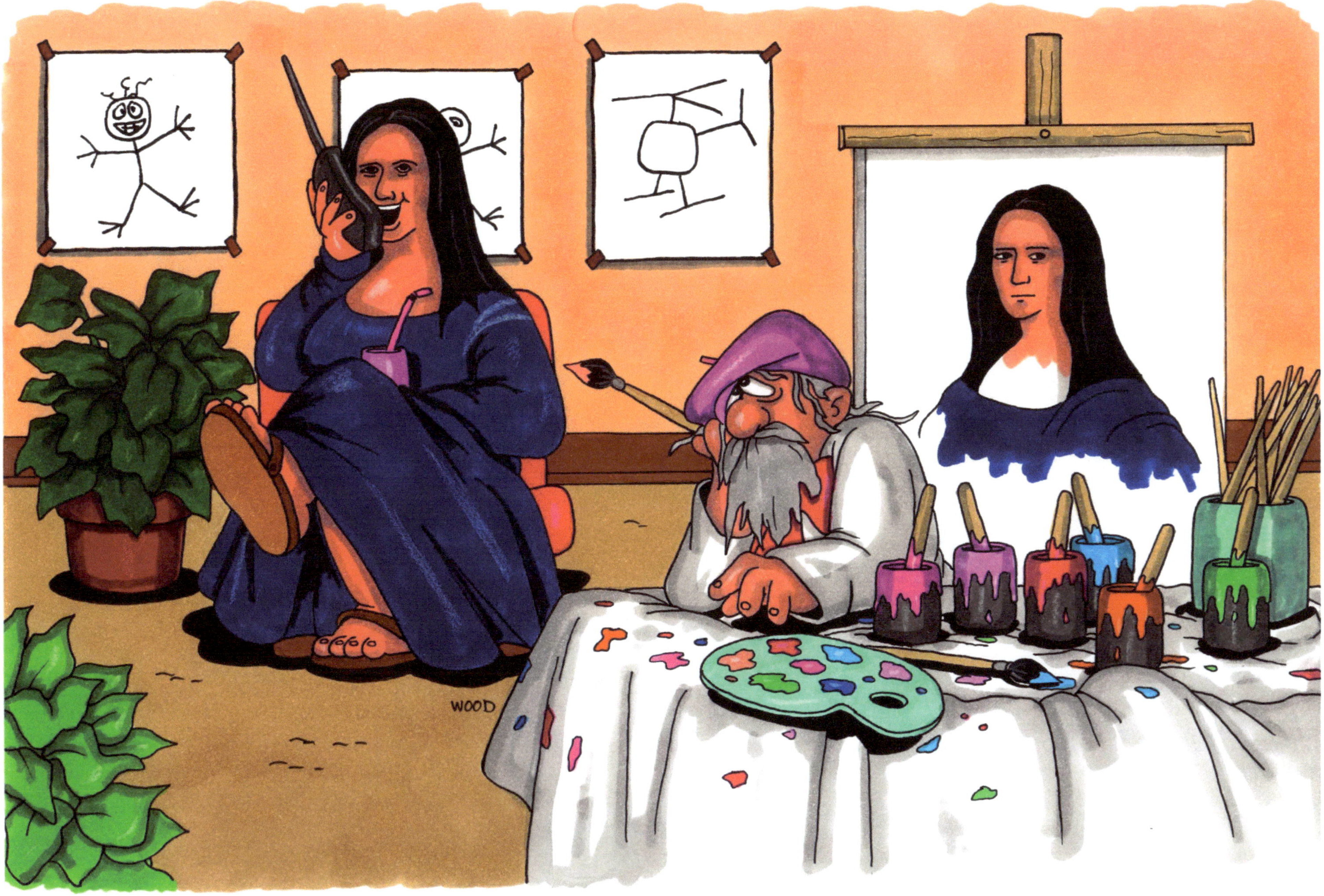
WOOD

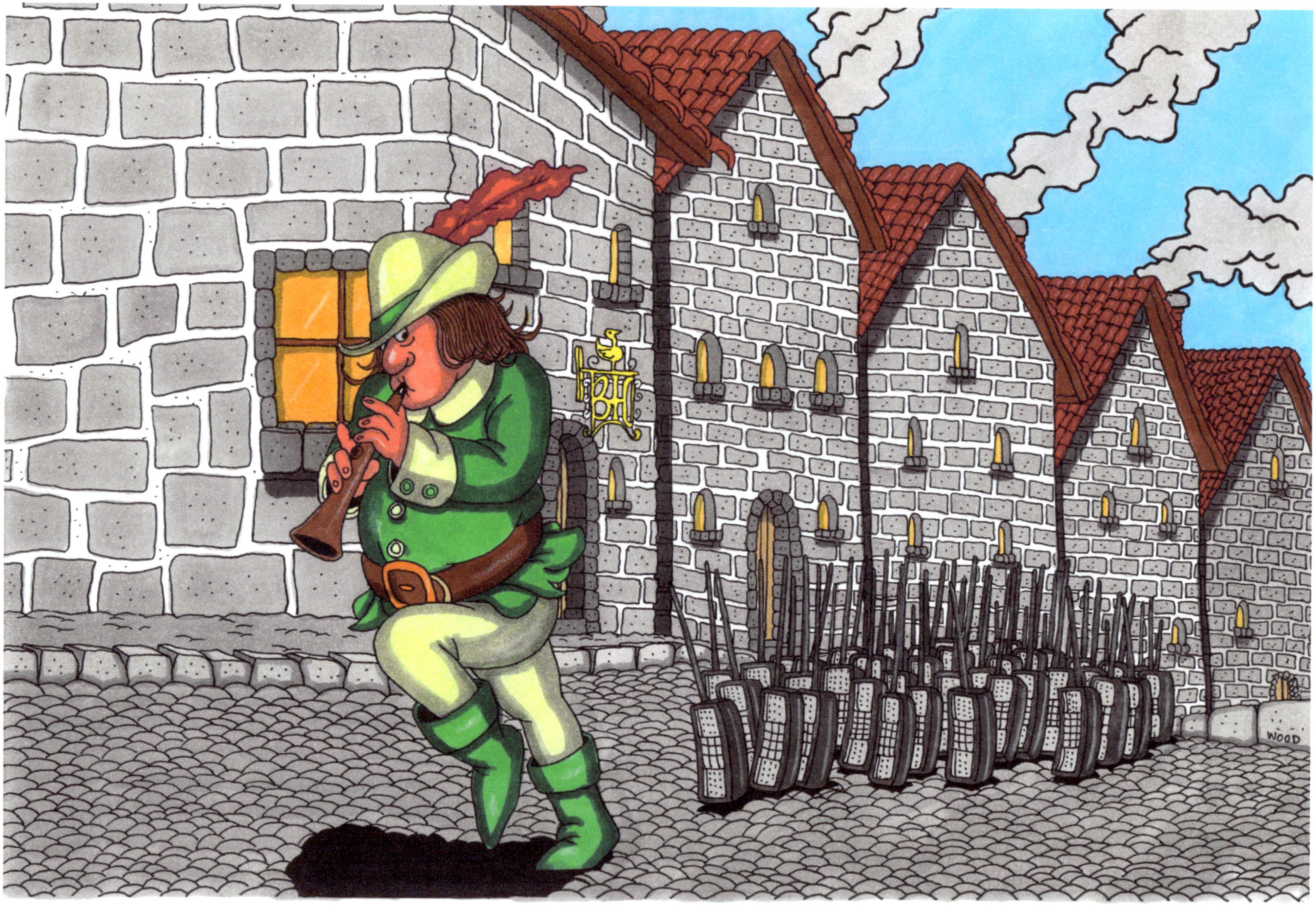
WOOD

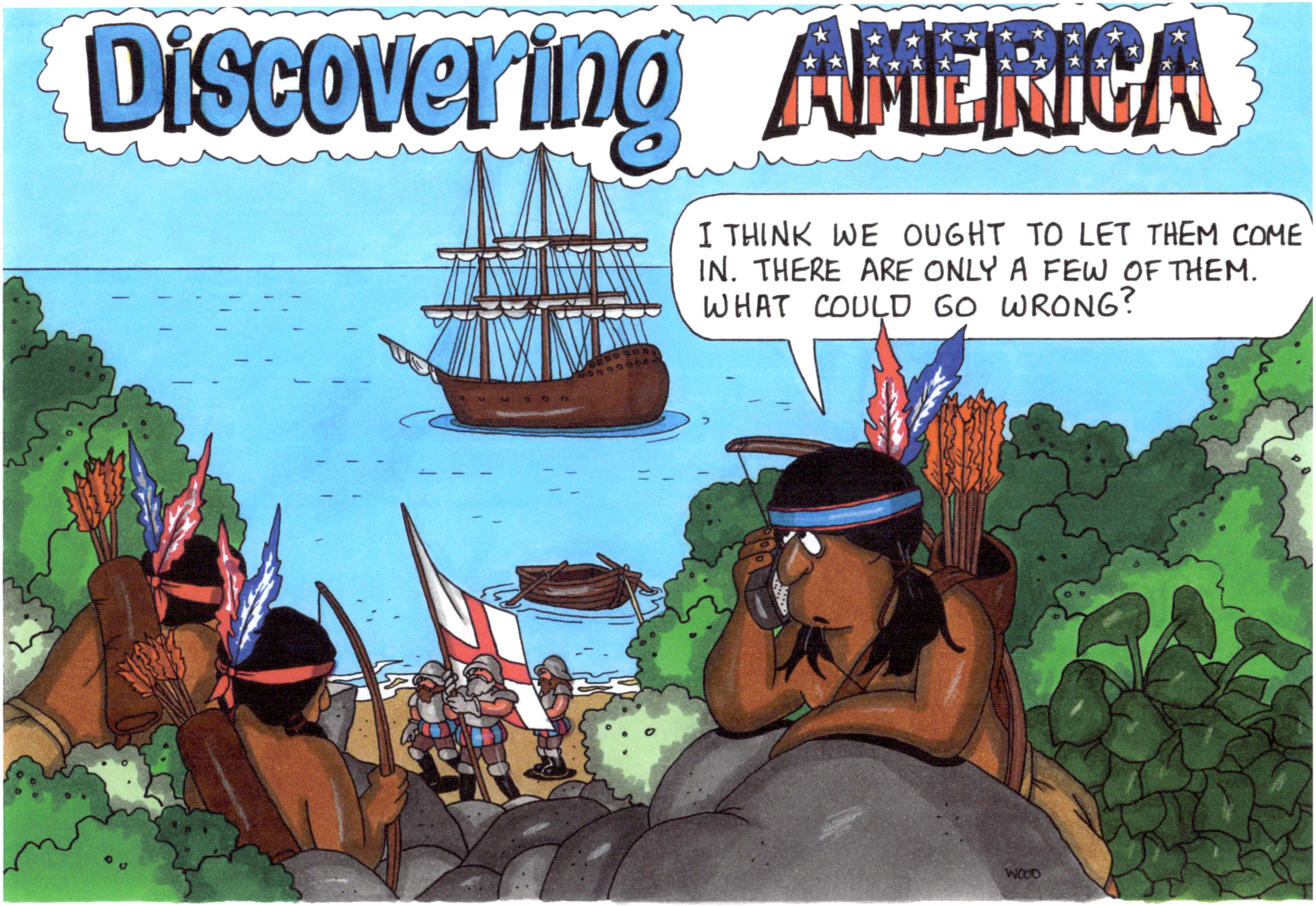
Discovering AMERICA
I THINK WE OUGHT TO LET THEM COME IN. THERE ARE ONLY A FEW OF THEM. WHAT COULD GO WRONG?
WOOD

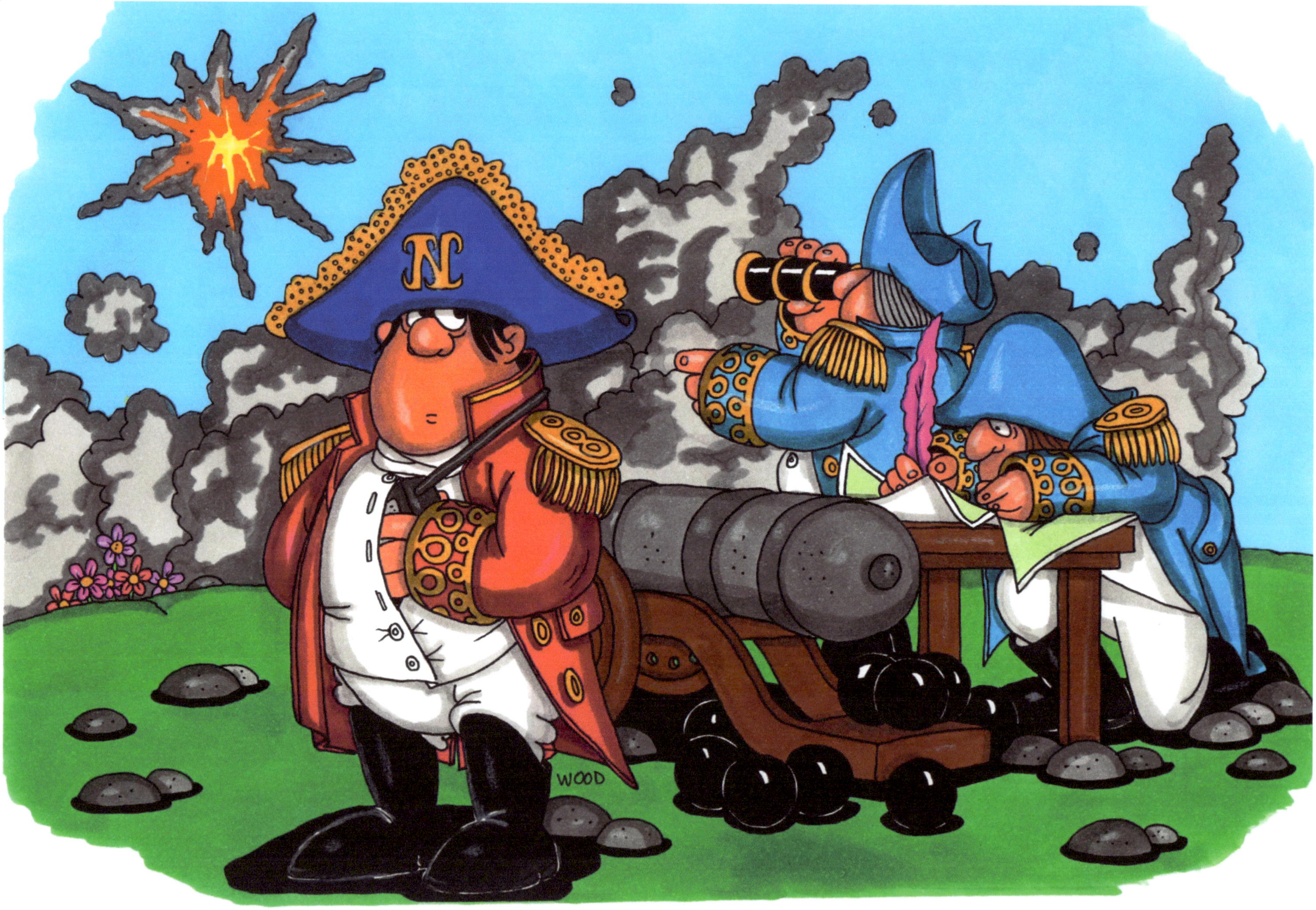
N
WOOD

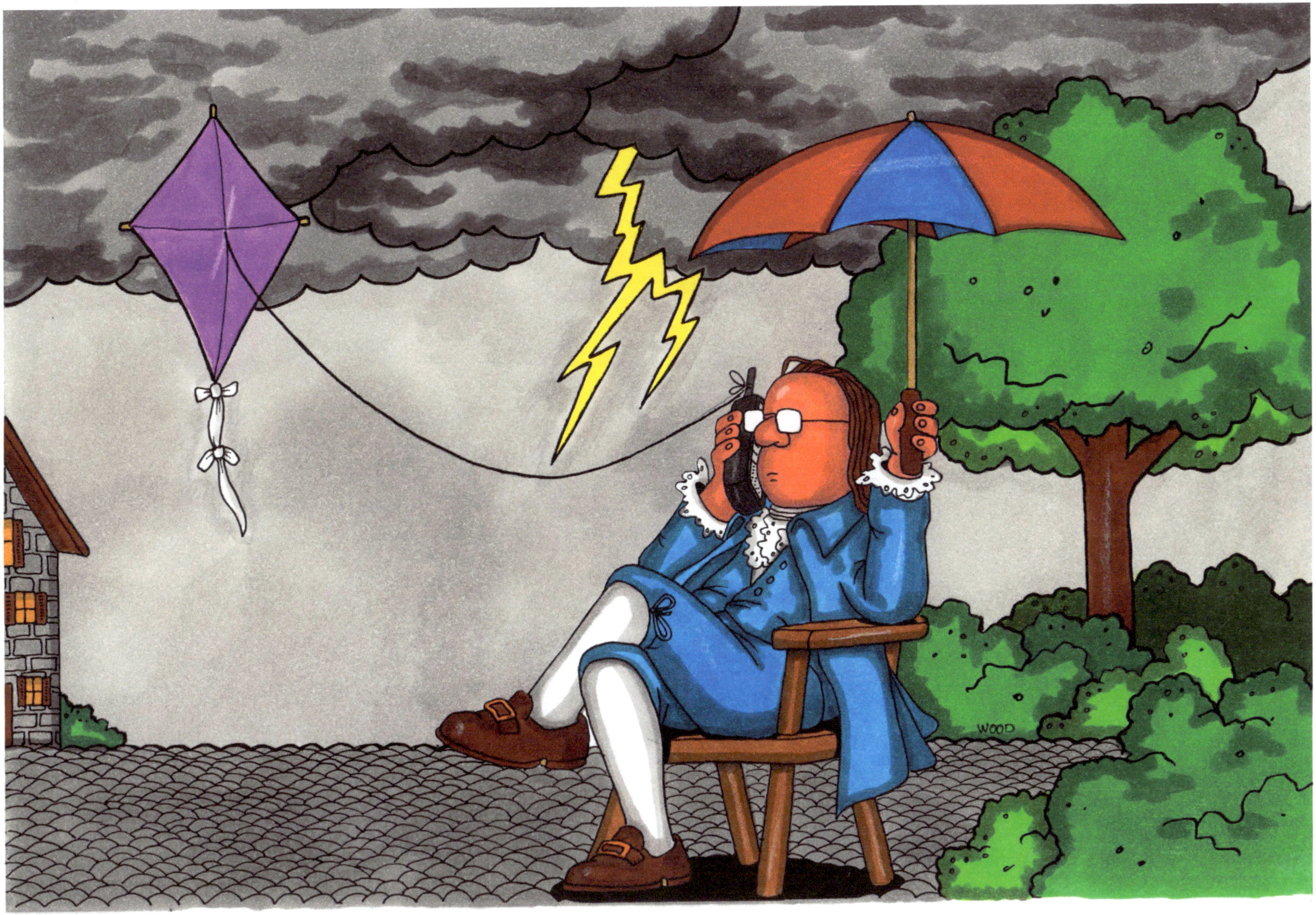
WOOD

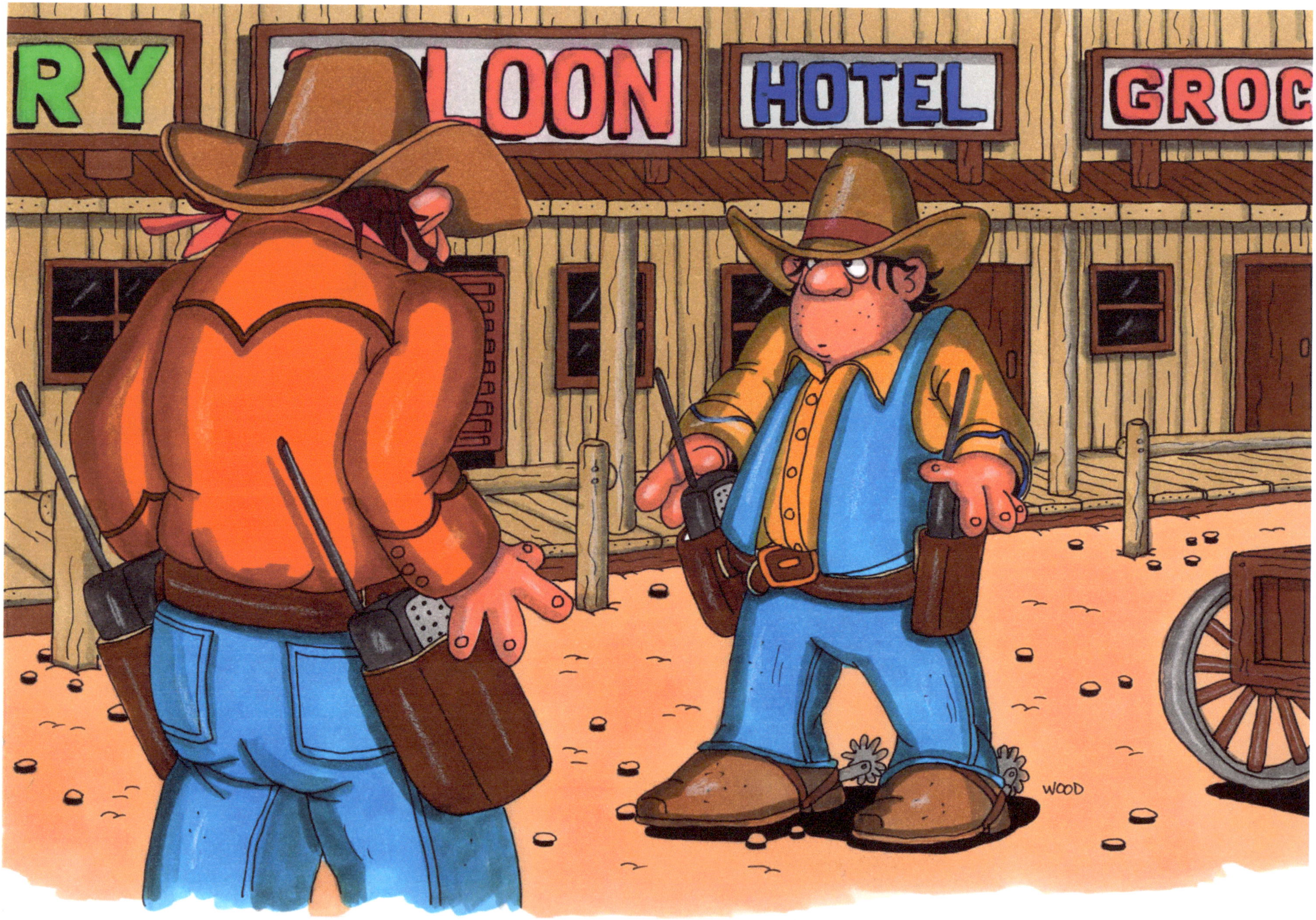
RY
LOON
HOTEL
GROC
WOOD

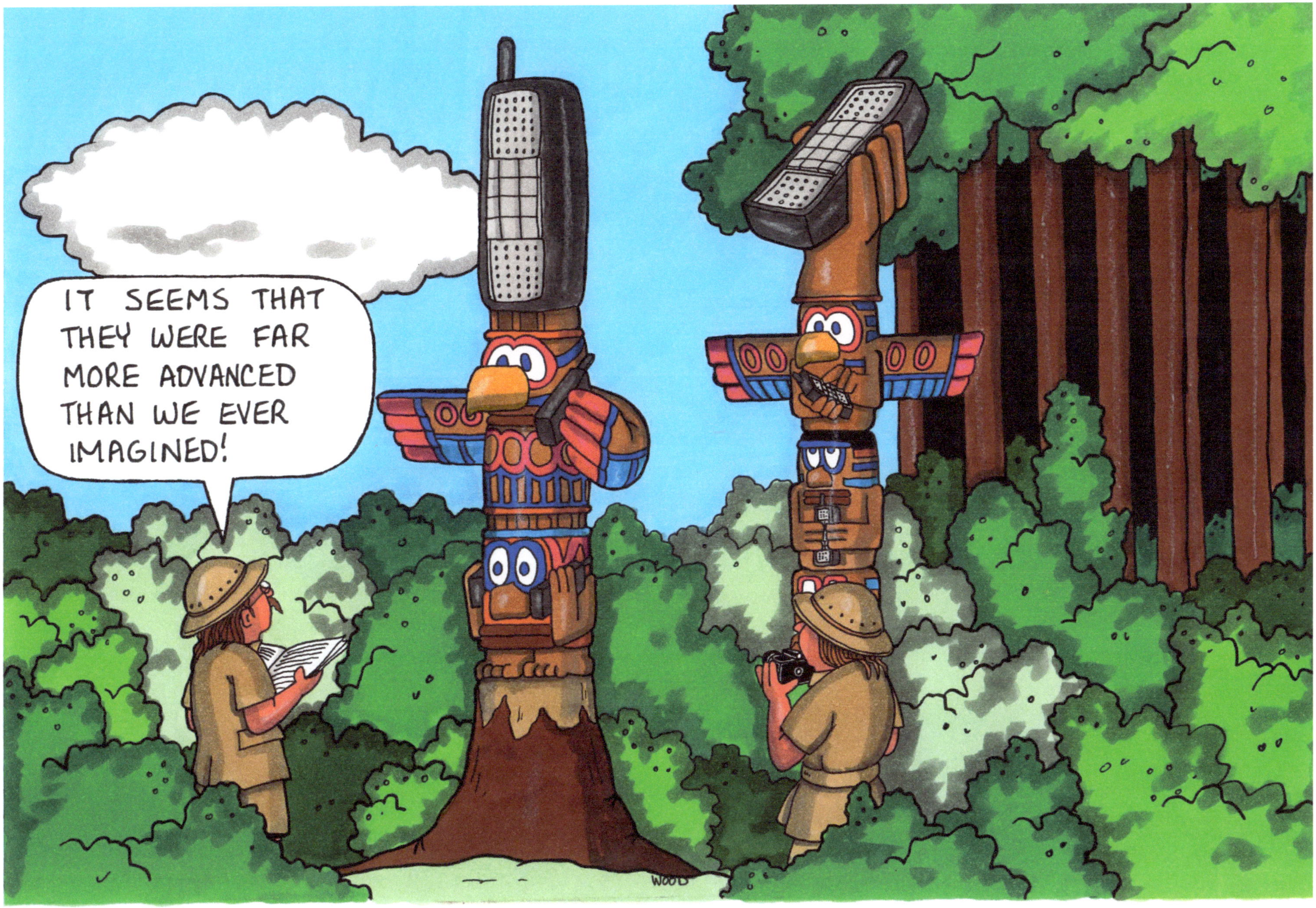
IT SEEMS THAT THEY WERE FAR MORE ADVANCED THAN WE EVER IMAGINED!
WOOD

The Dating Game

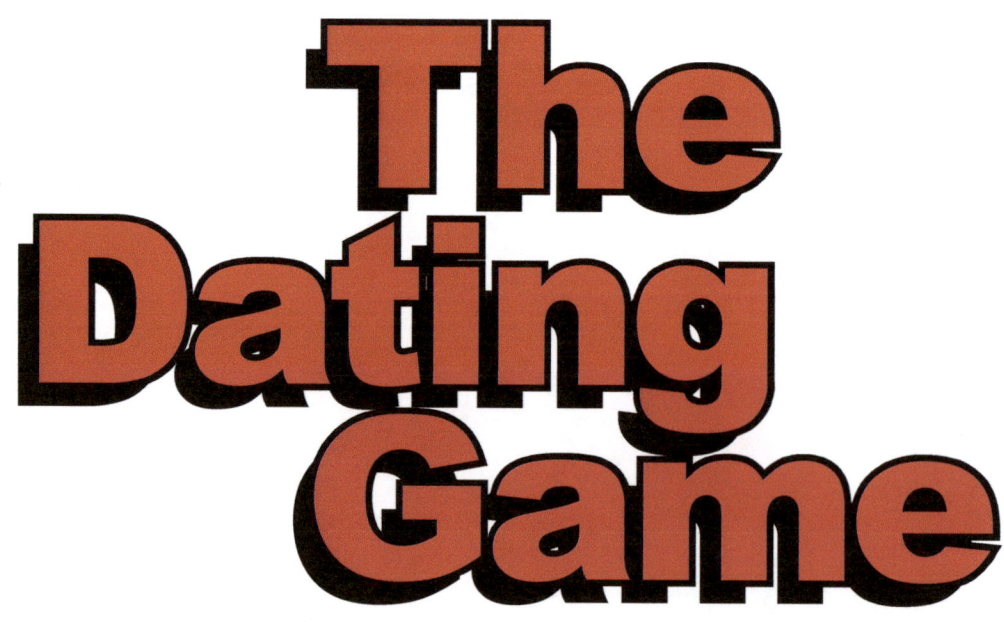

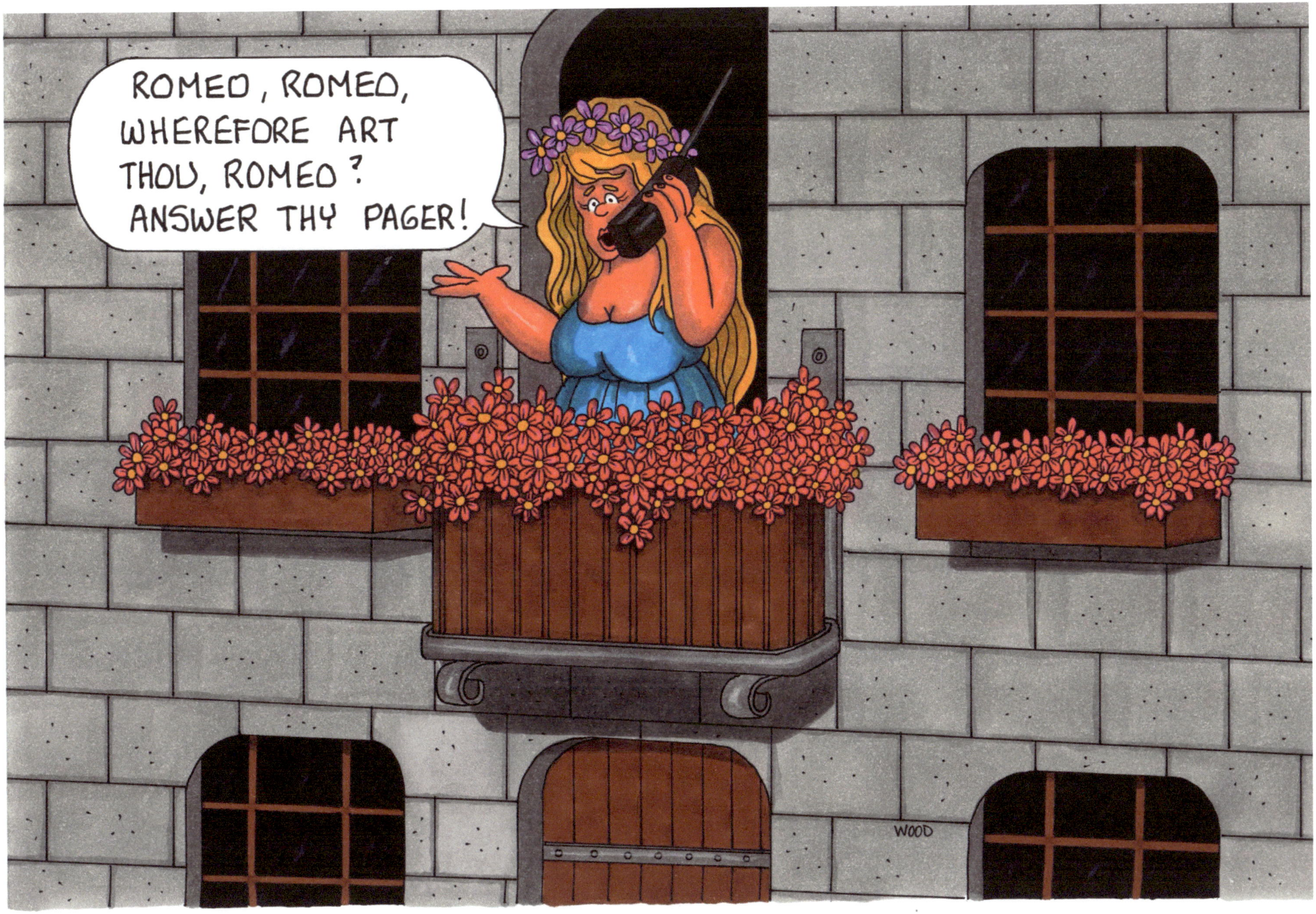
ROMEO, ROMEO, WHEREFORE ART THOU, ROMEO? ANSWER THY PAGER!
WOOD

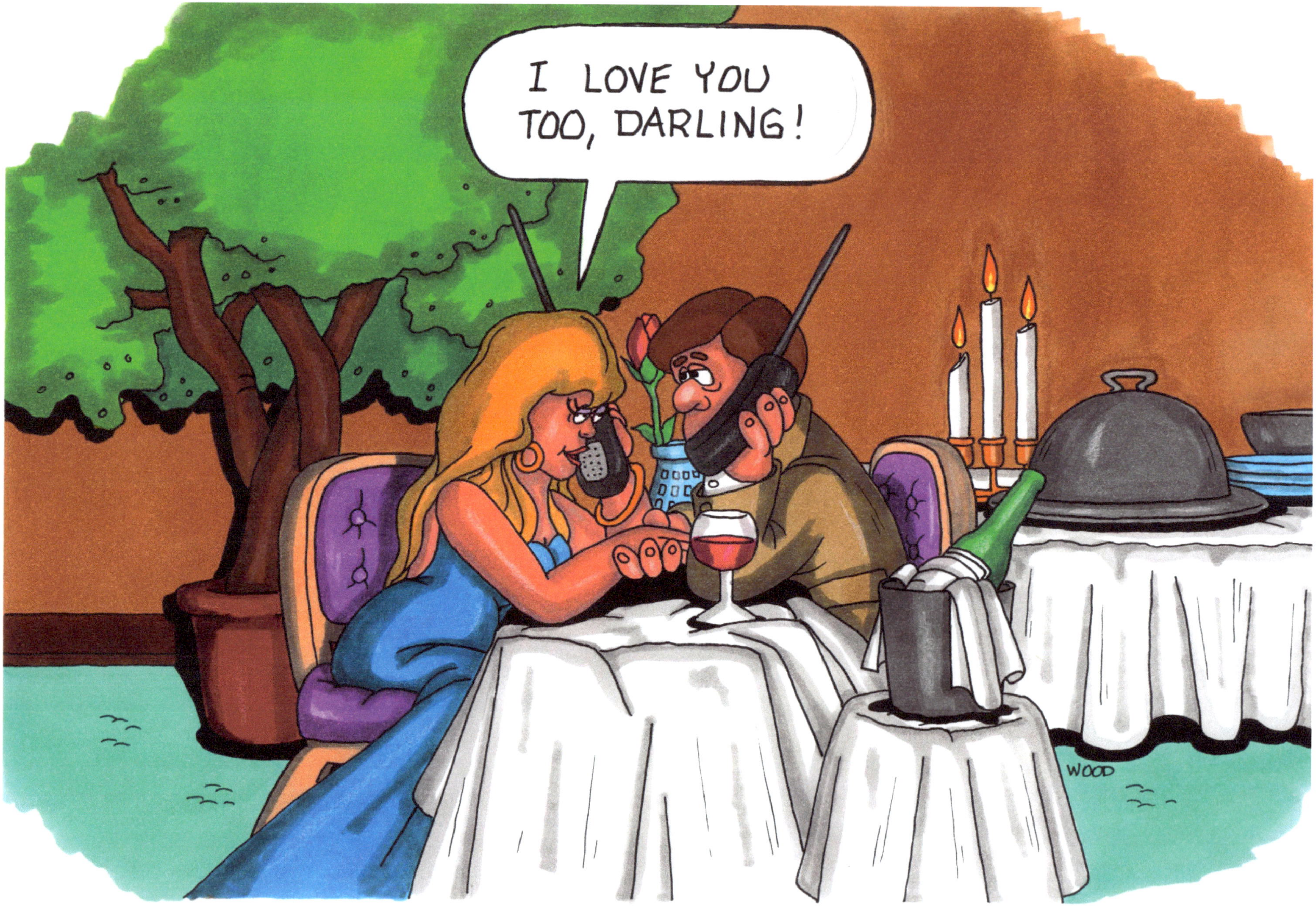
I LOVE YOU
TOO, DARLING!
WOOD

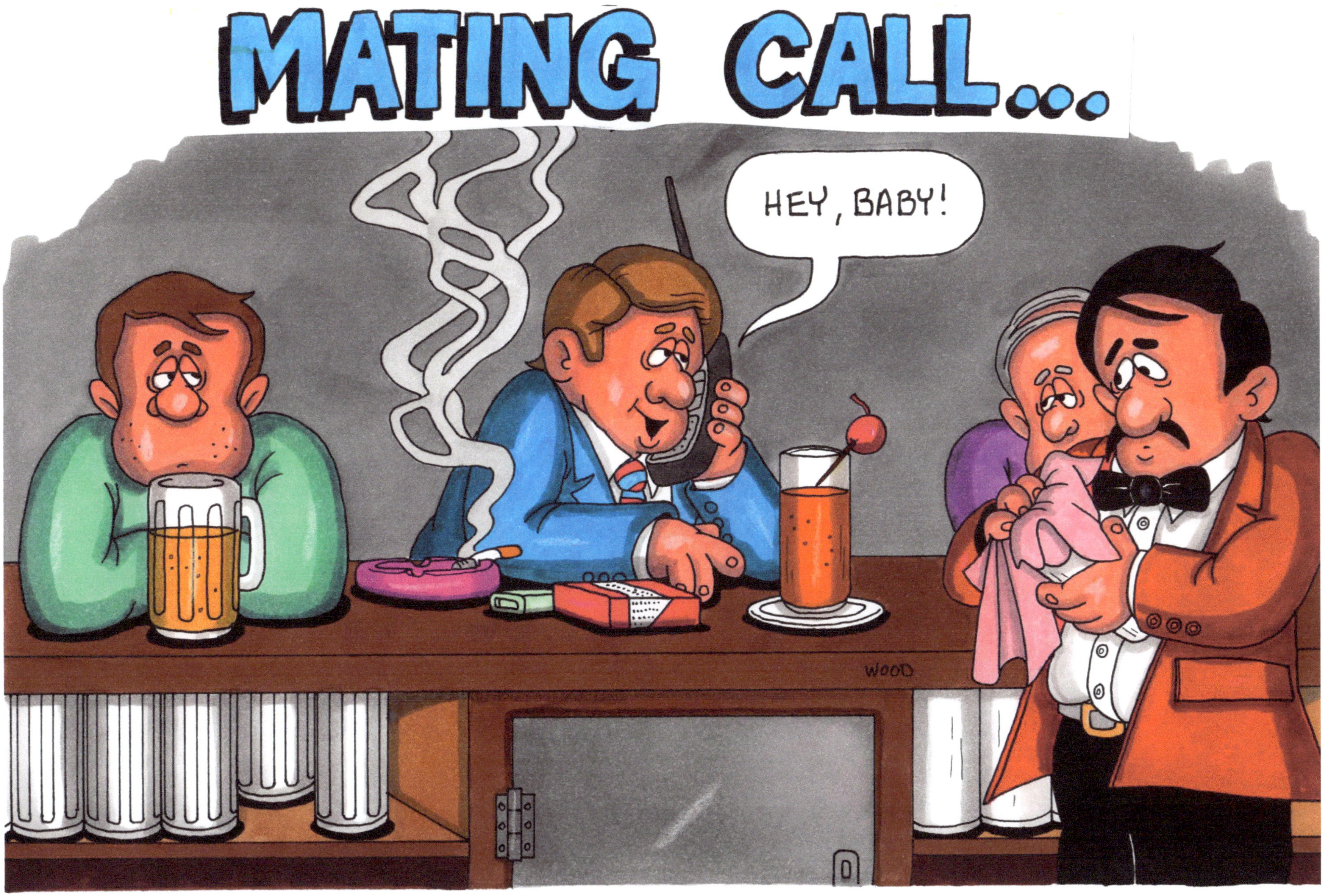
MATING CALL...
HEY, BABY!
WOOD

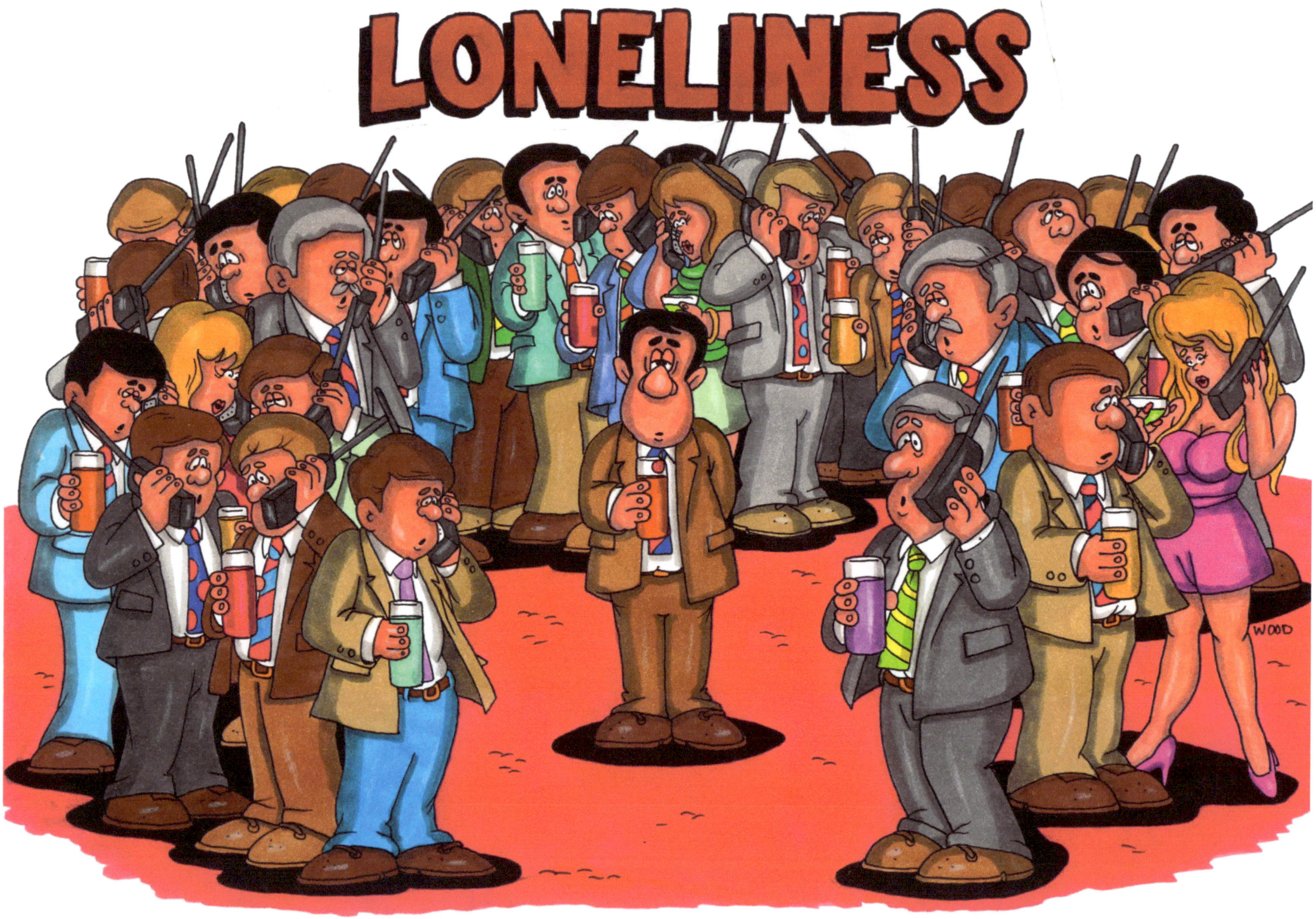
LONELINESS
WOOD

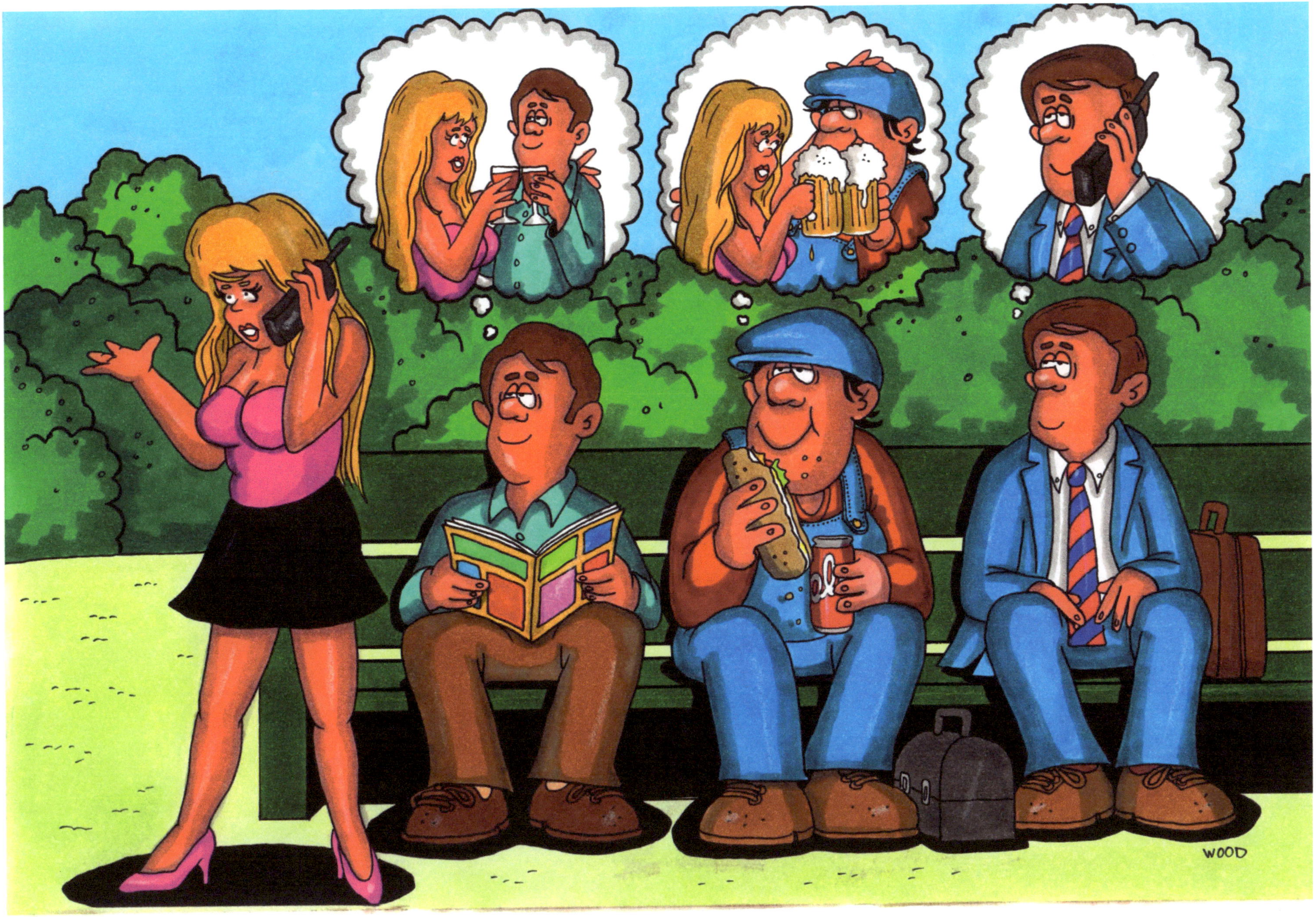
WOOD

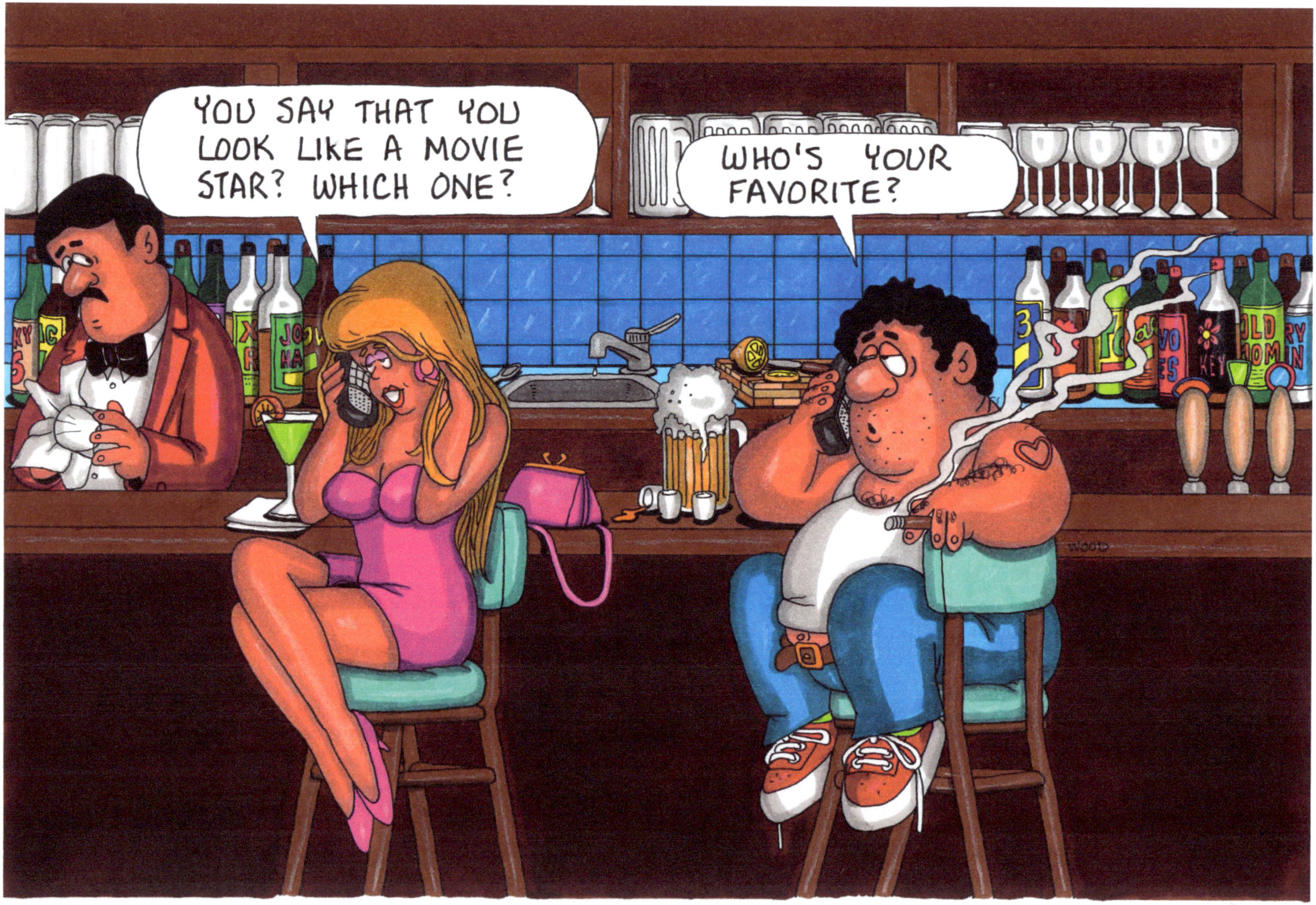
YOU SAY THAT YOU LOOK LIKE A MOVIE STAR? WHICH ONE?
WHO'S YOUR FAVORITE?

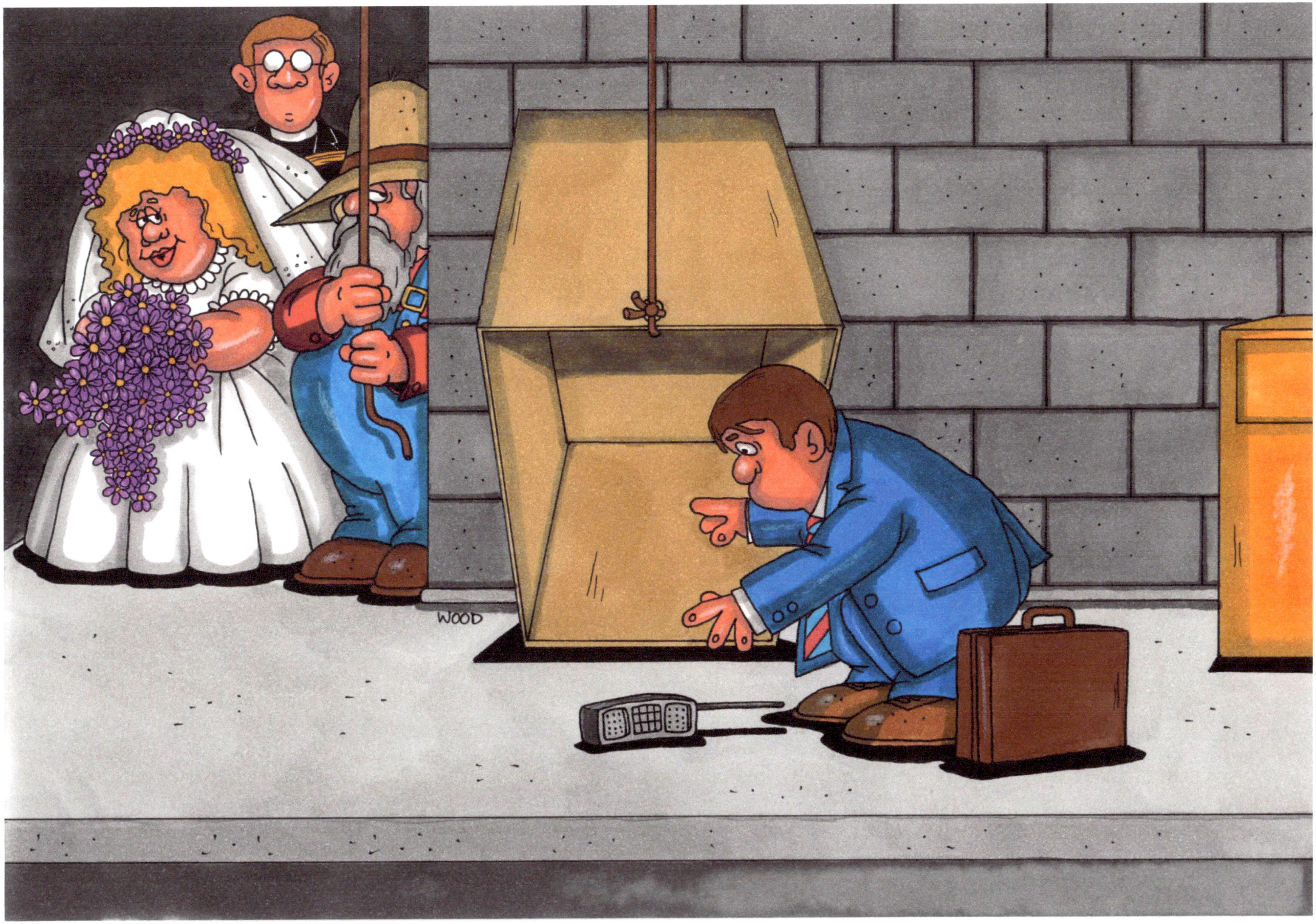
WOOD

At Work...

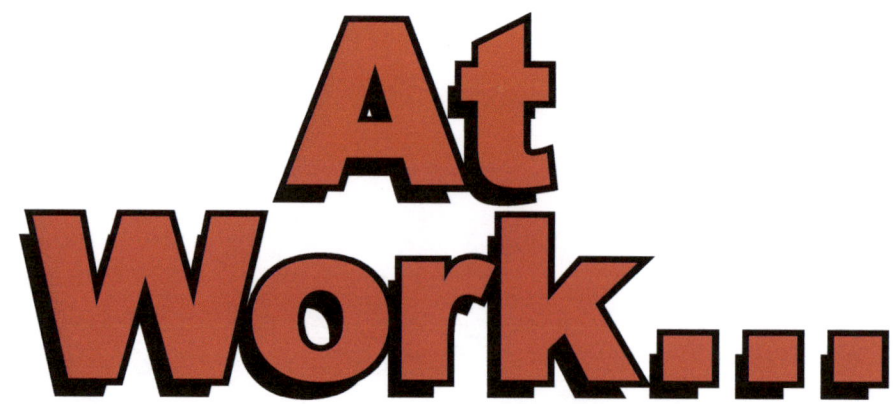

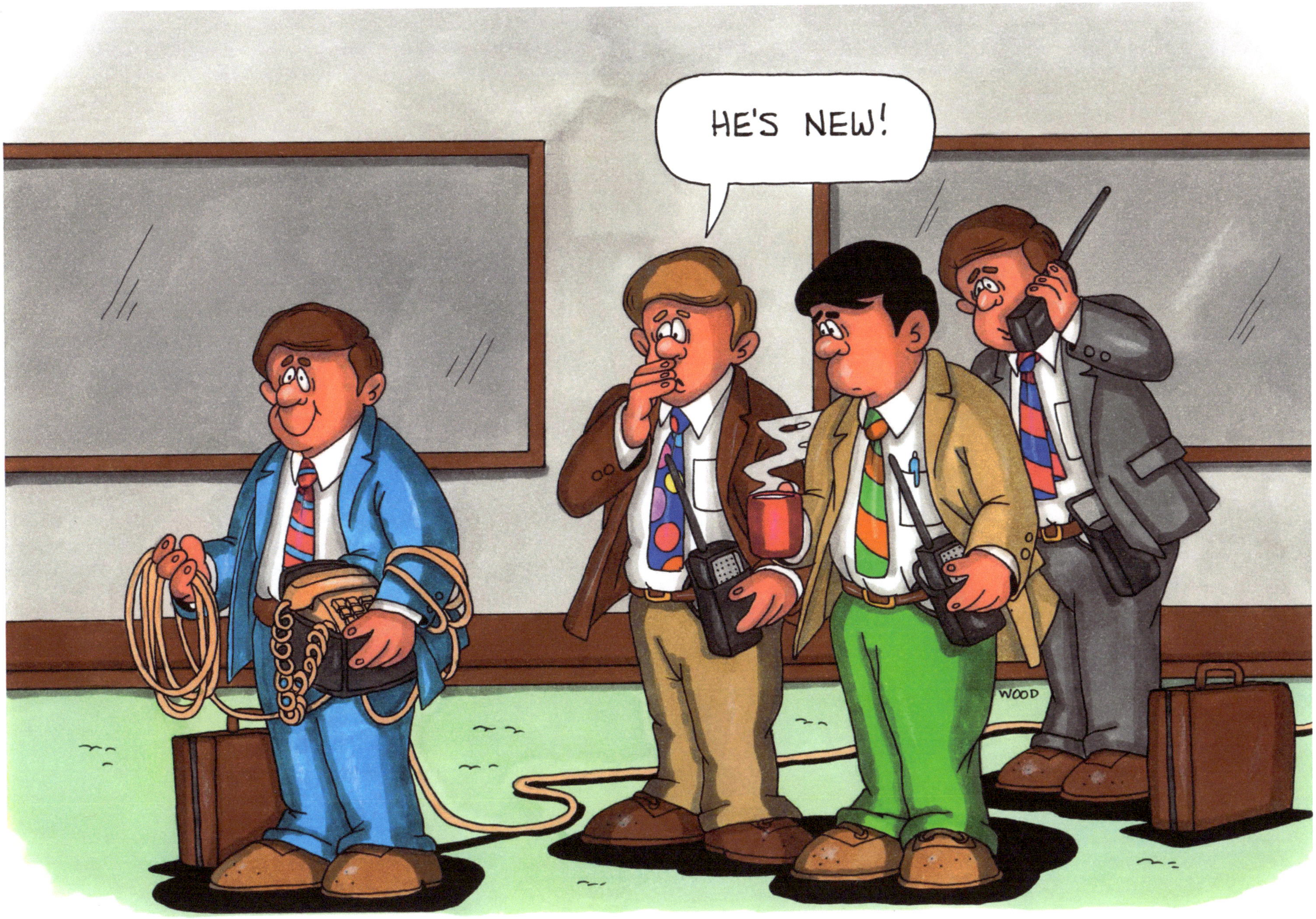
HE'S NEW!
WOOD

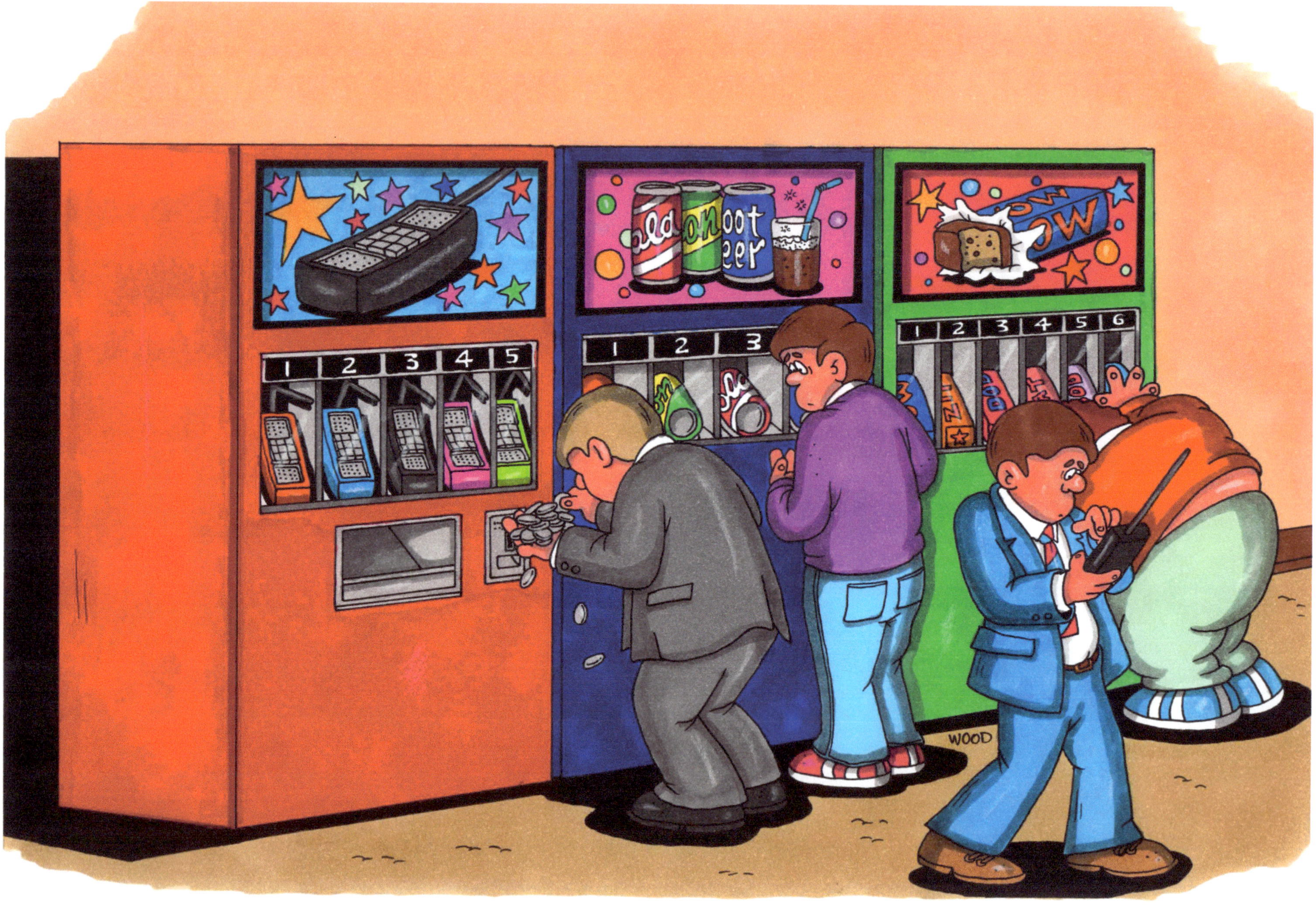
1 2 3 4 5
1 2 3
1 2 3 4 5 6
WOOD

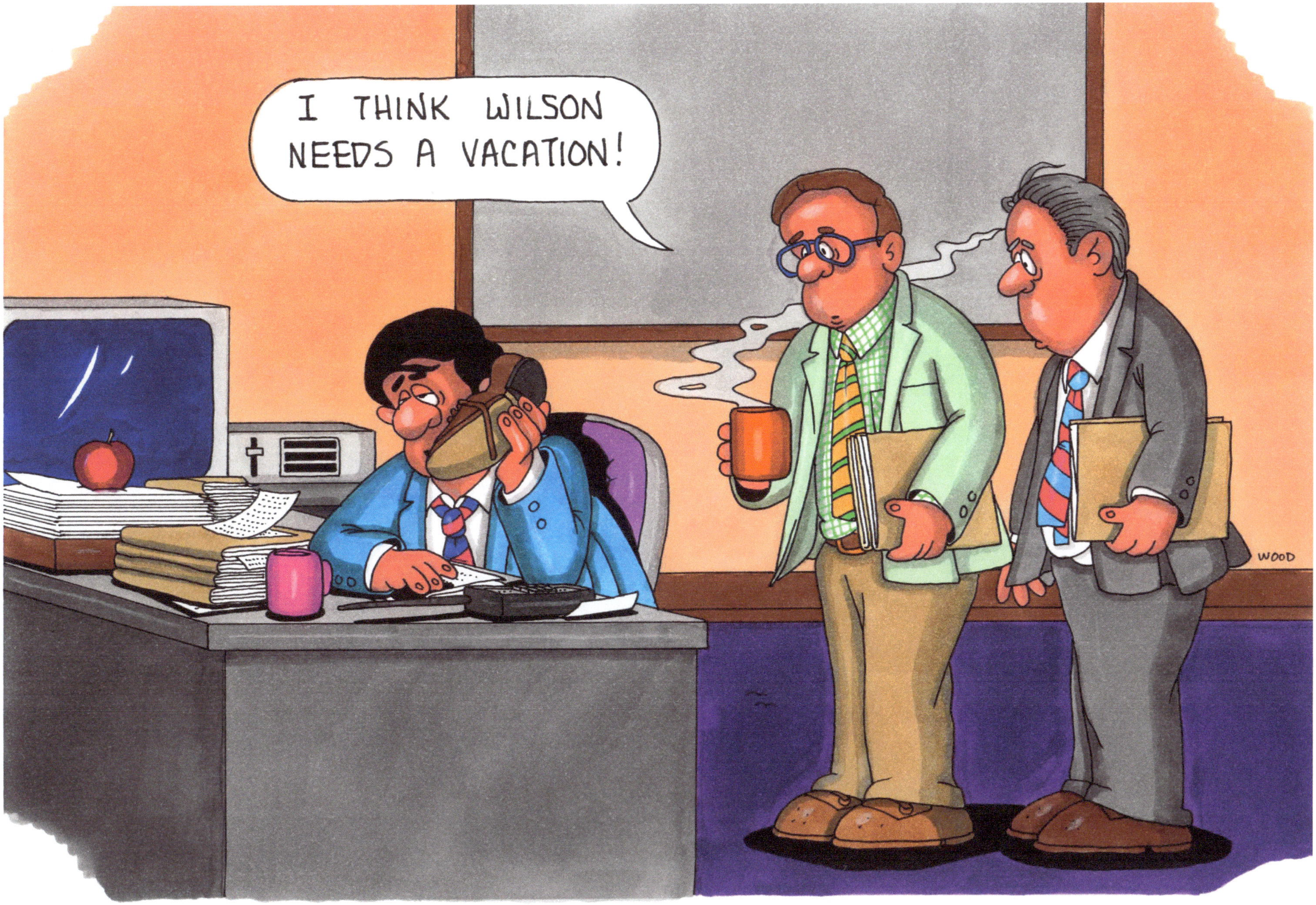
I THINK WILSON NEEDS A VACATION!
WOOD

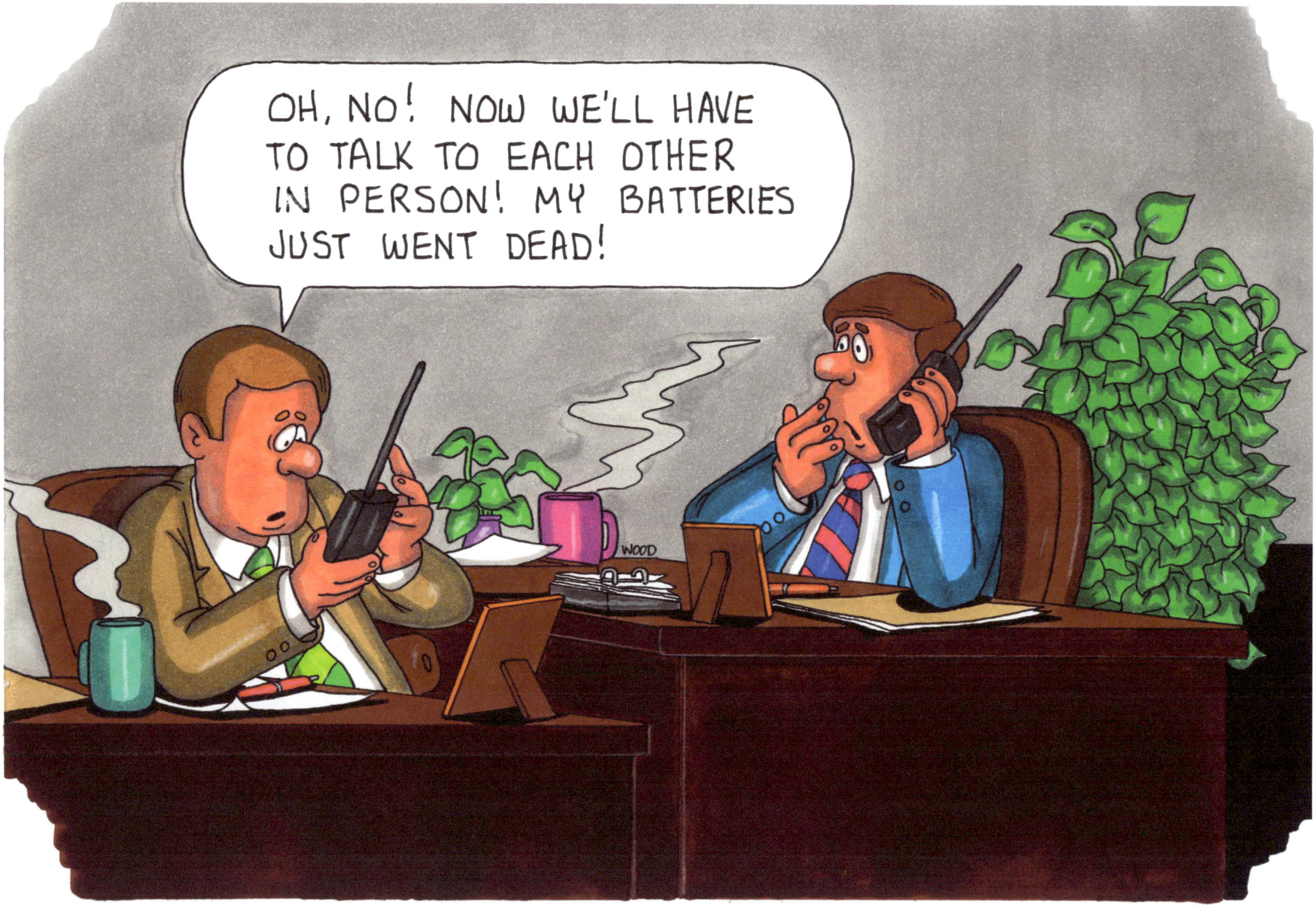
OH, NO! NOW WE'LL HAVE TO TALK TO EACH OTHER IN PERSON! MY BATTERIES JUST WENT DEAD!
WOOD

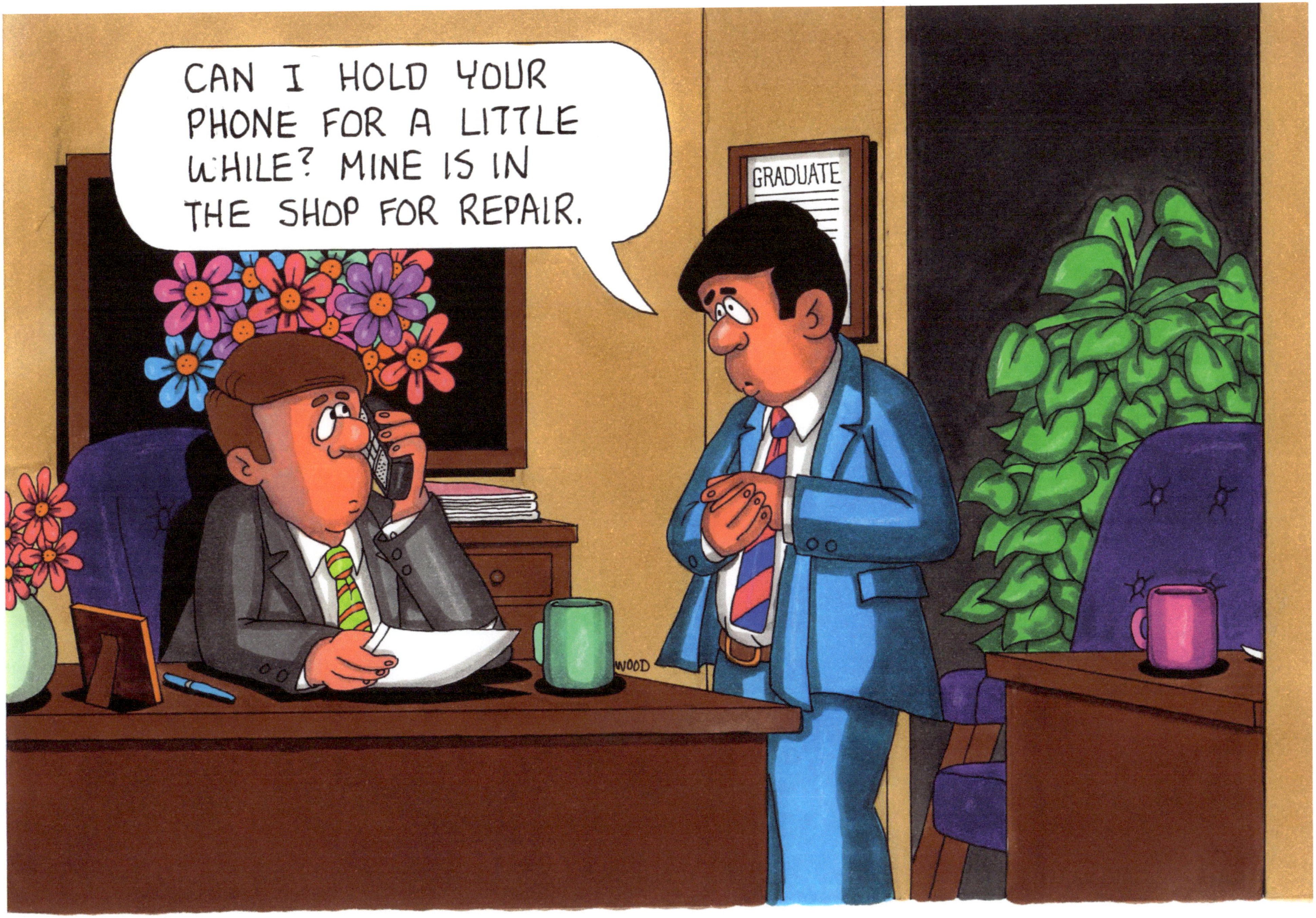
CAN I HOLD YOUR PHONE FOR A LITTLE WHILE? MINE IS IN THE SHOP FOR REPAIR.
GRADUATE
WOOD

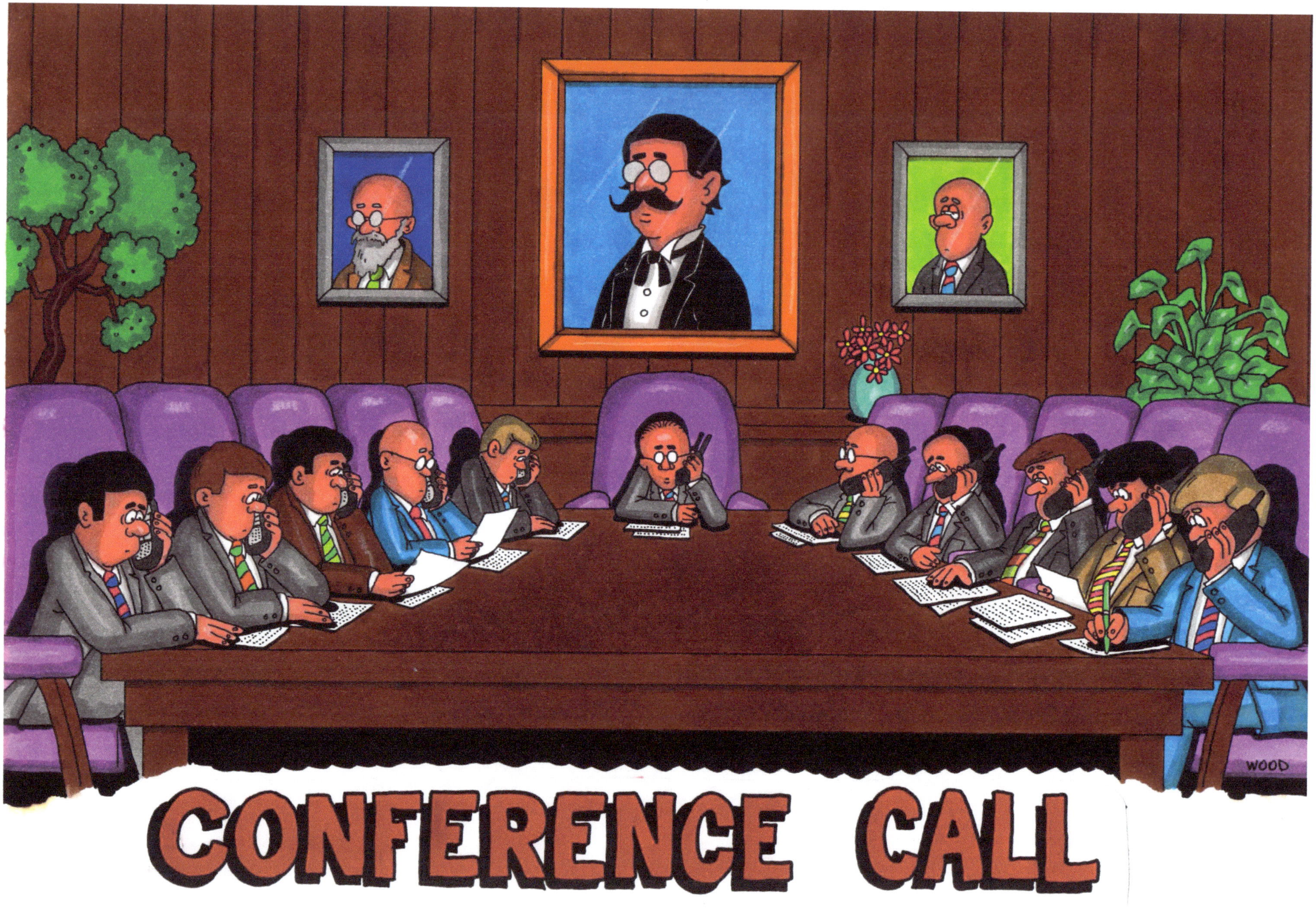
WOOD
CONFERENCE CALL

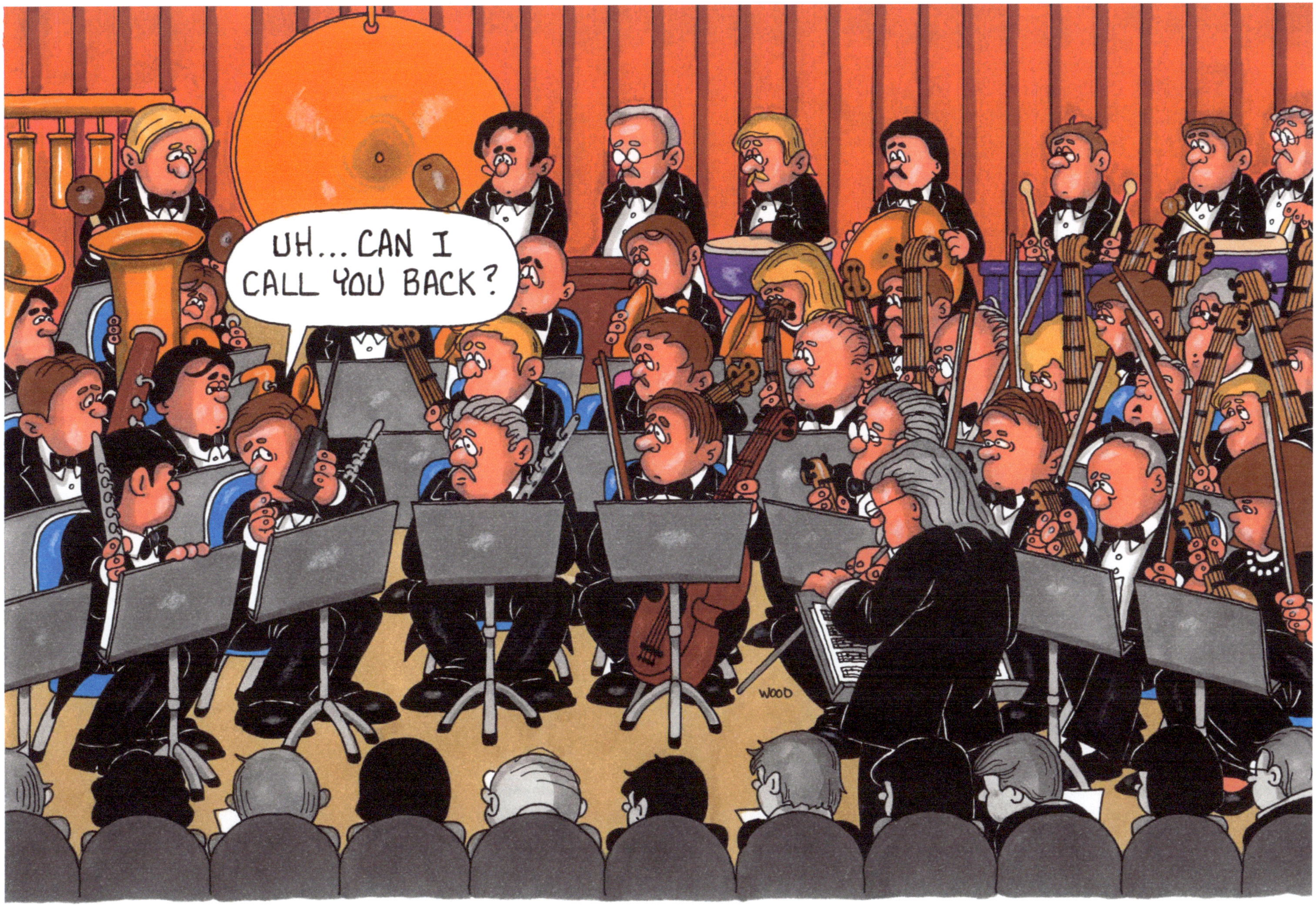
UH... CAN I CALL YOU BACK?
WOOD

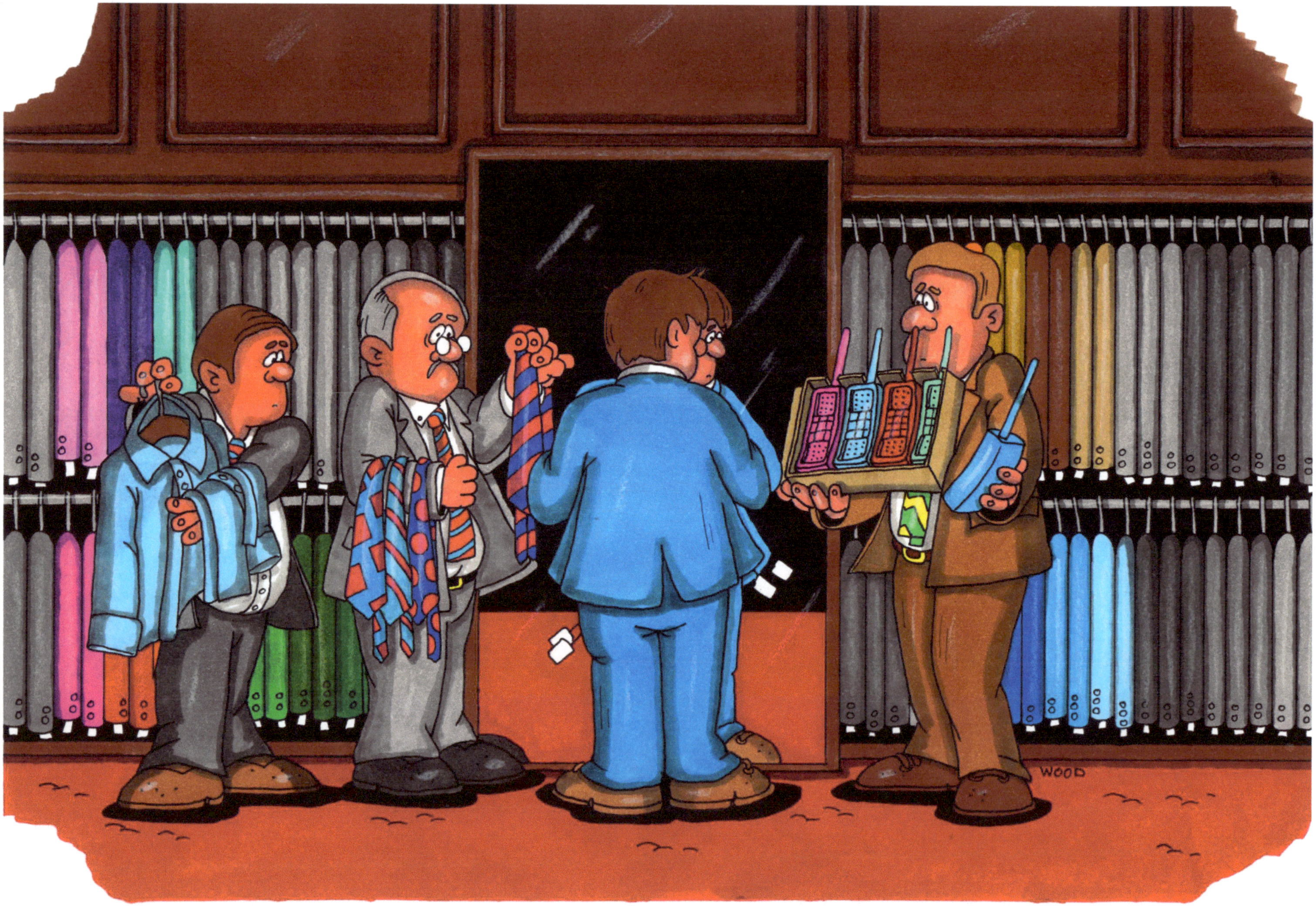
WOOD

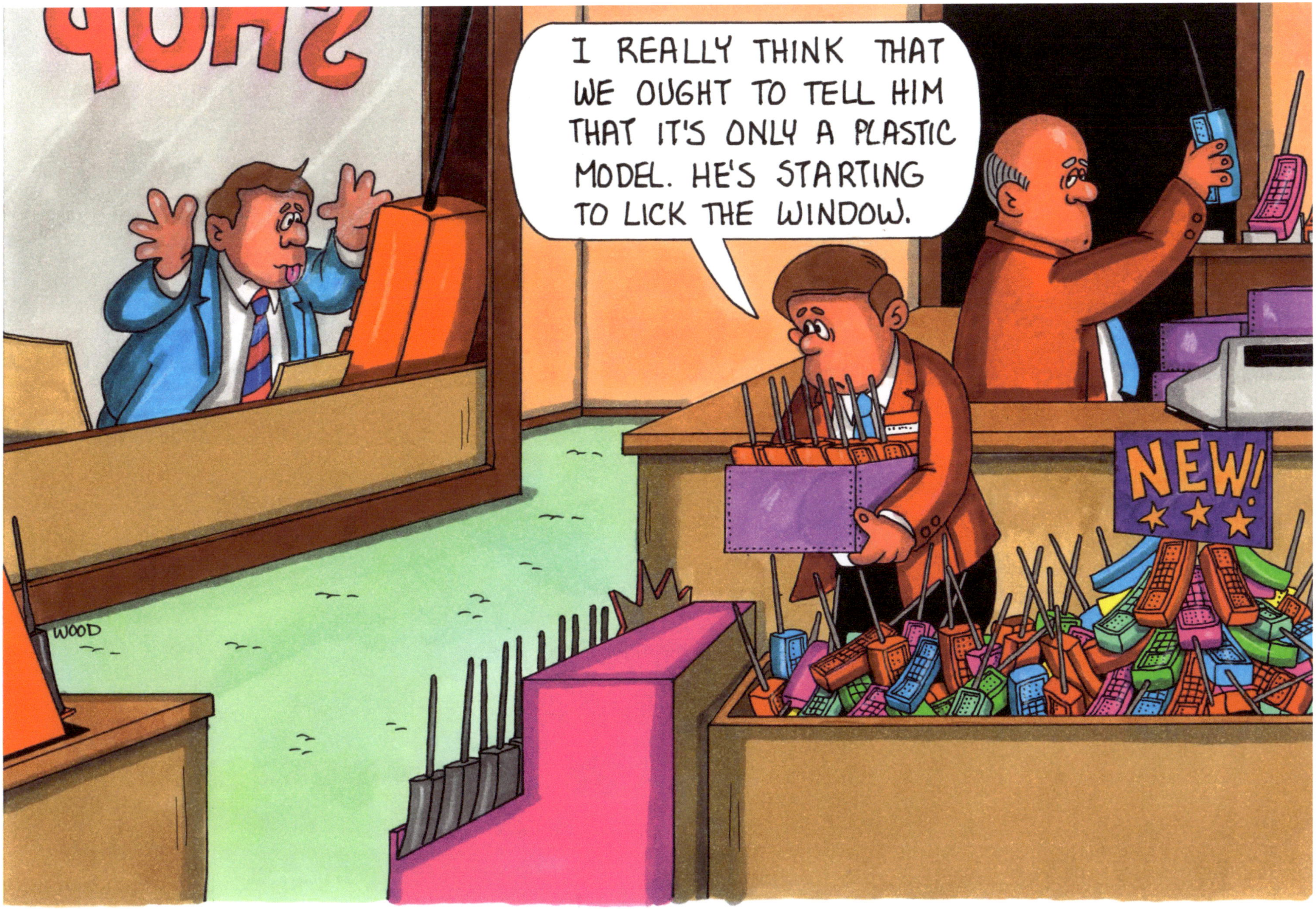
I REALLY THINK THAT WE OUGHT TO TELL HIM THAT IT'S ONLY A PLASTIC MODEL. HE'S STARTING TO LICK THE WINDOW.
NEW!
WOOD

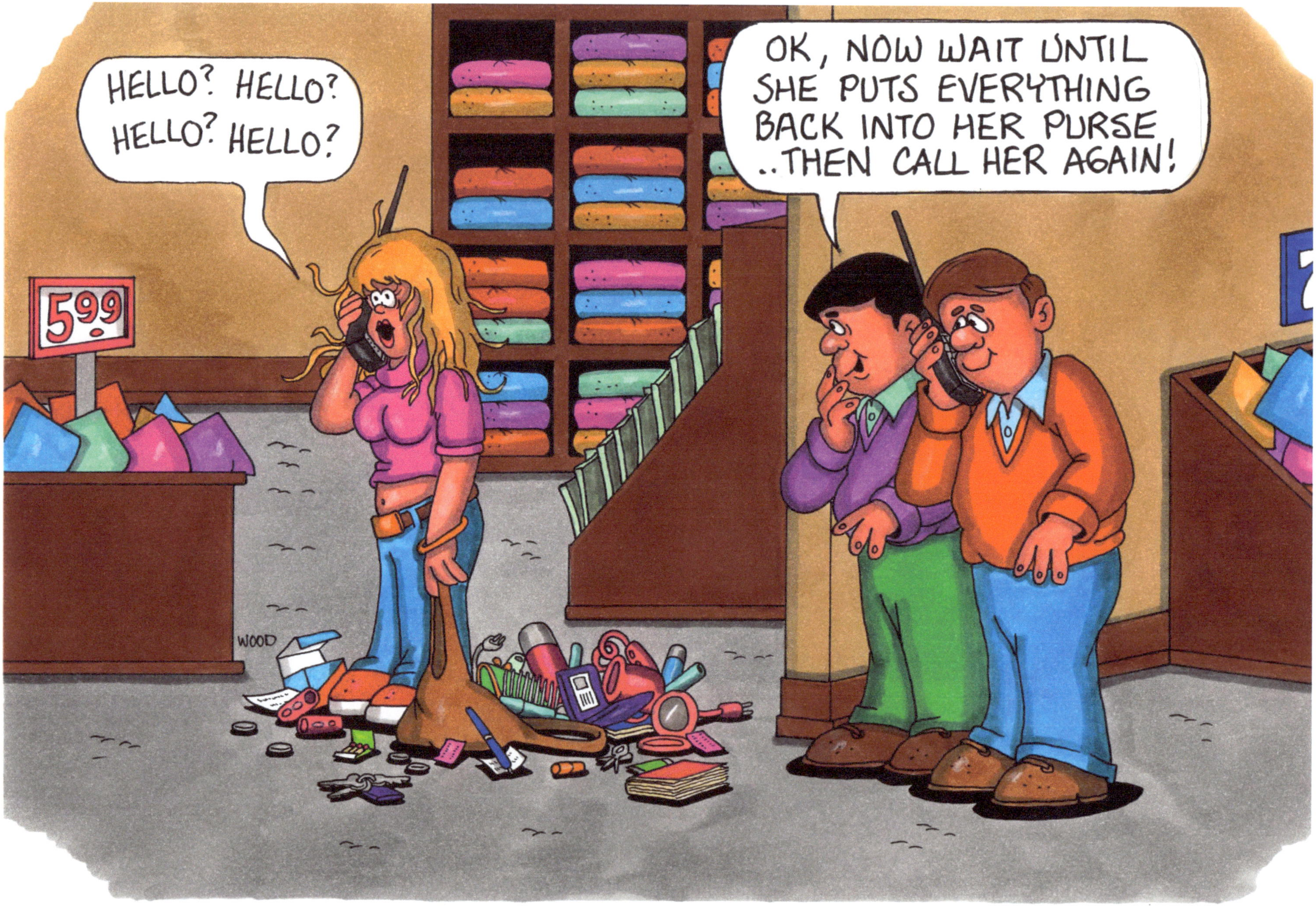
HELLO? HELLO?
HELLO? HELLO?
OK, NOW WAIT UNTIL SHE PUTS EVERYTHING BACK INTO HER PURSE ..THEN CALL HER AGAIN!
5.99
WOOD

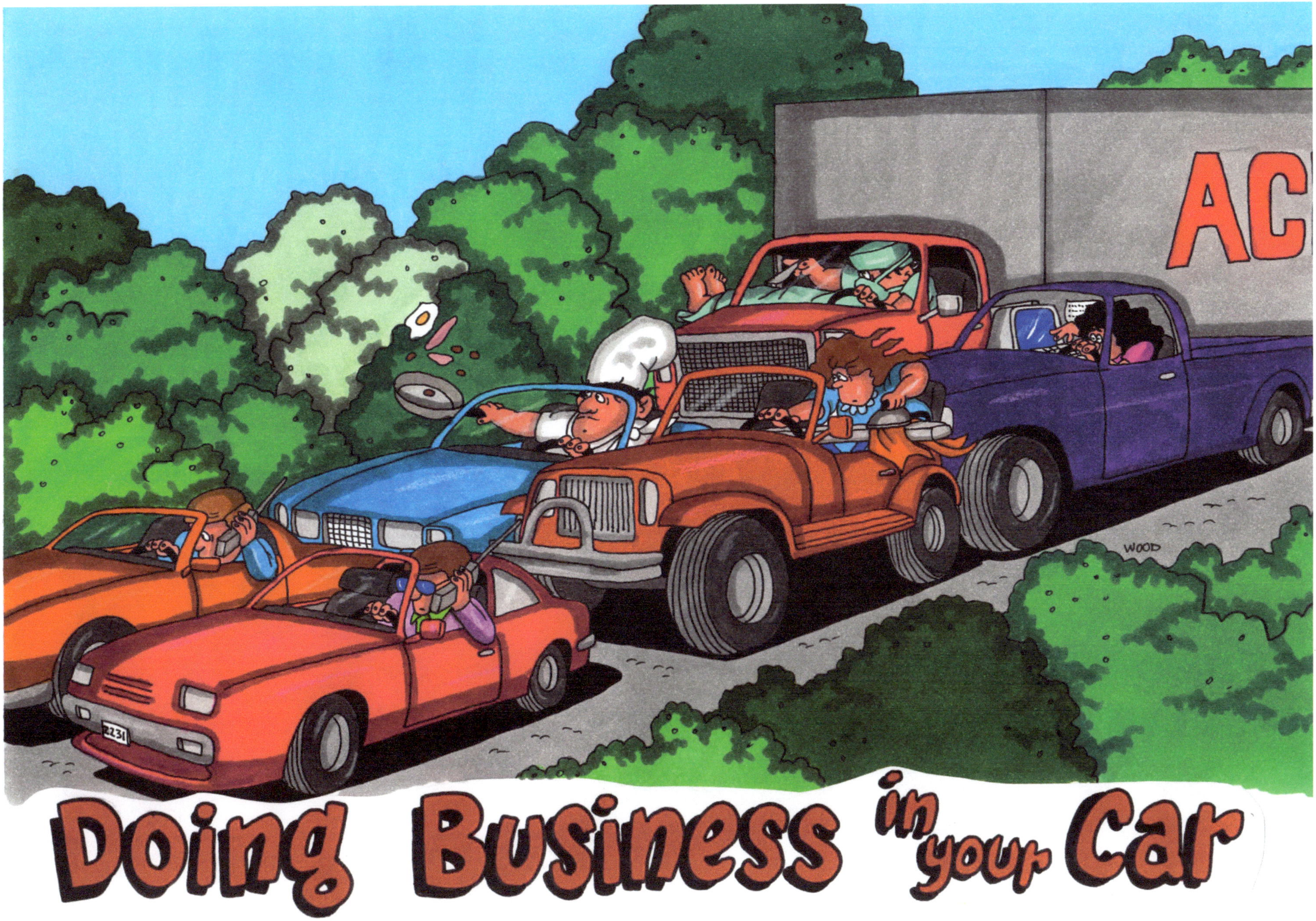
AC
WOOD

Doing Business in your Car

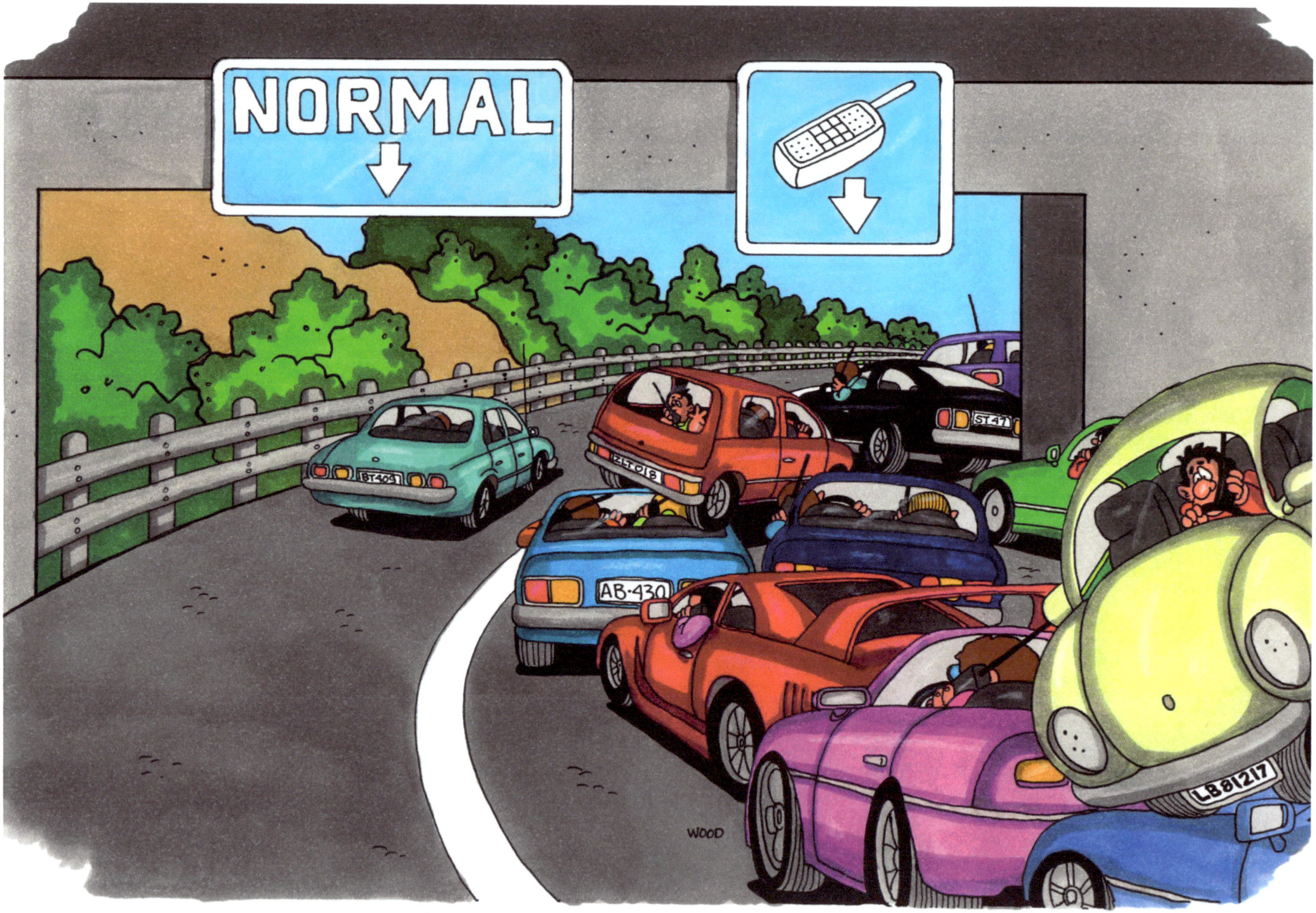
NORMAL
BT-409
AB-430
ST 471
LB81217
WOOD

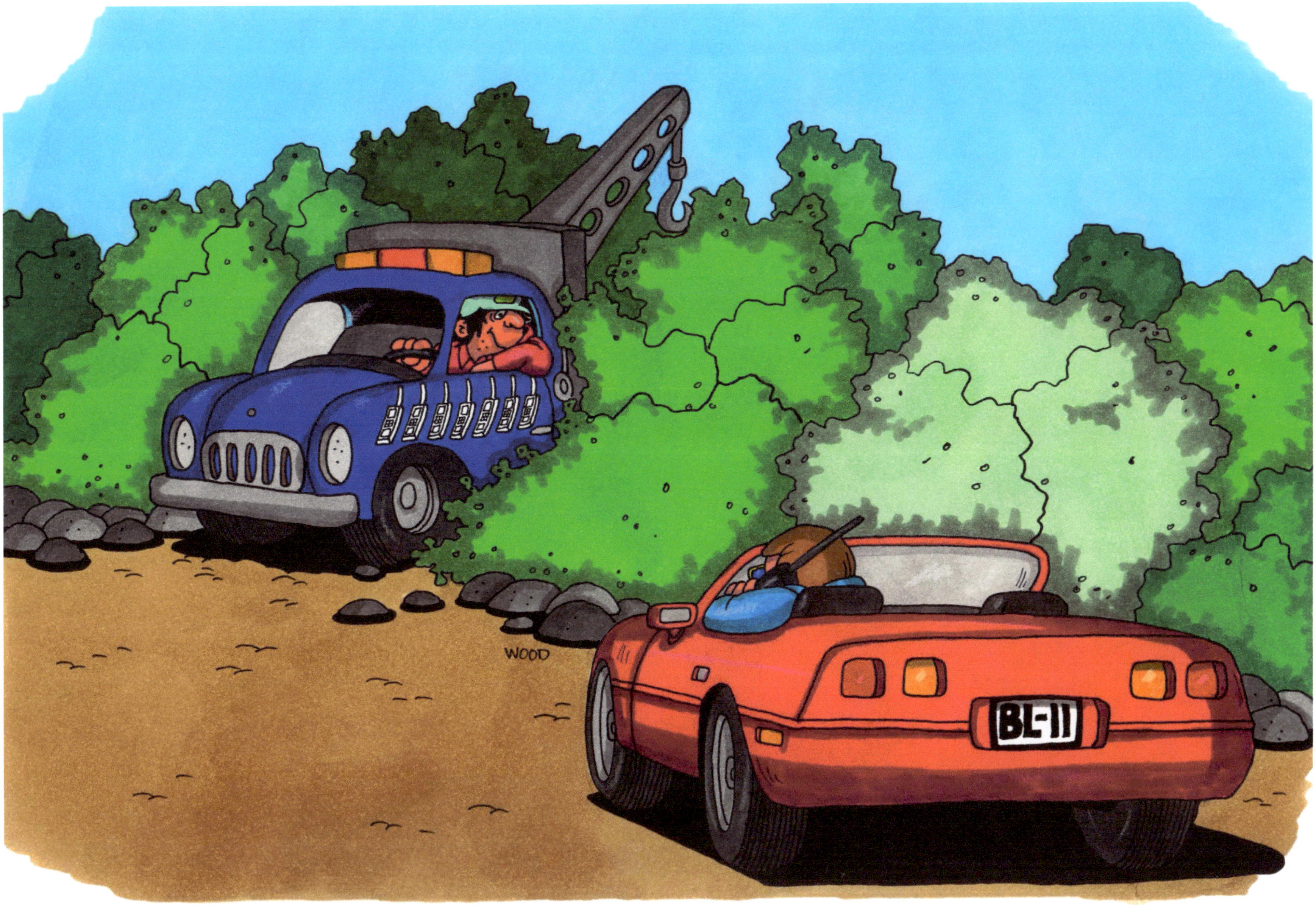
WOOD
BL-11

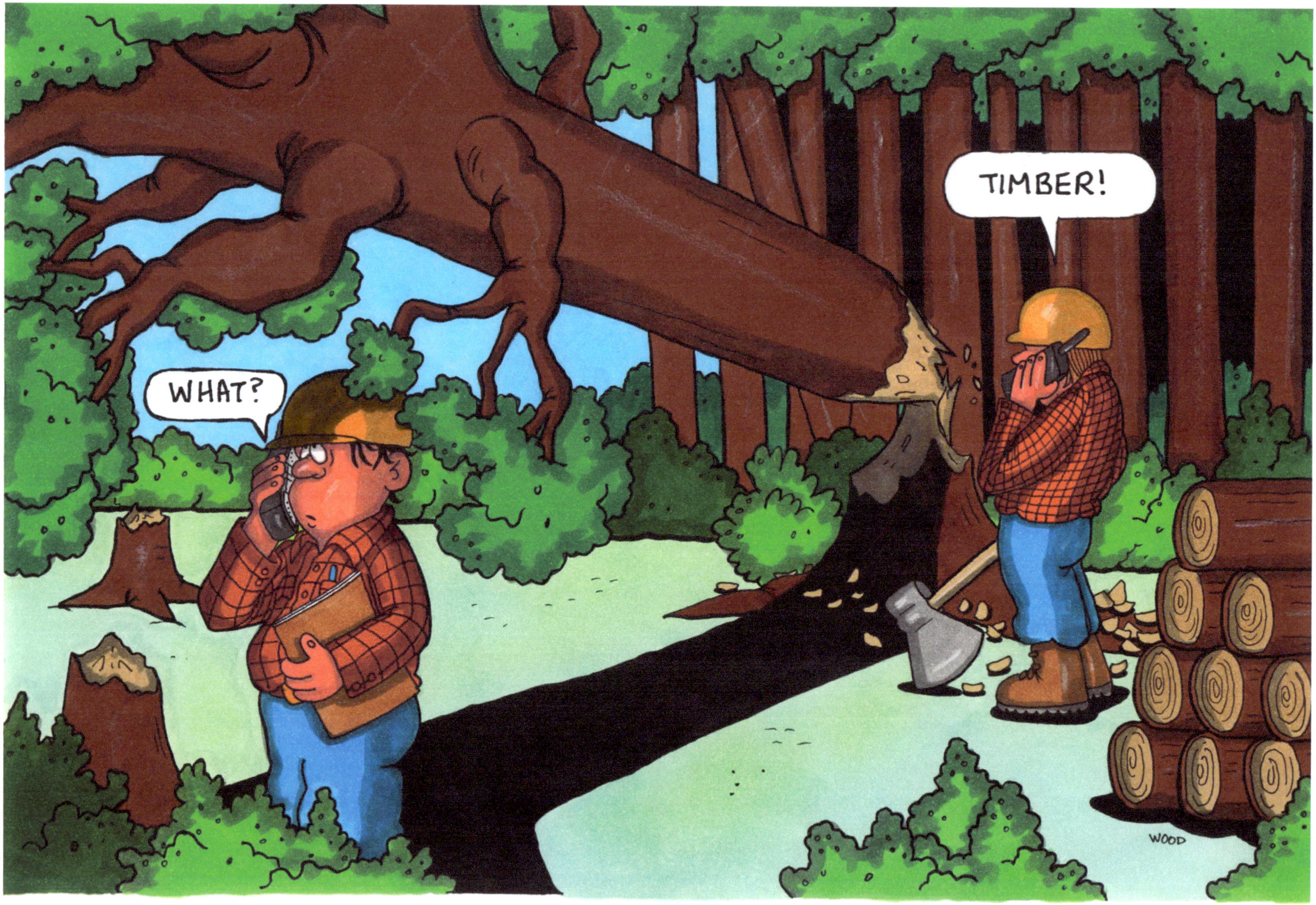
TIMBER!
WHAT?
WOOD

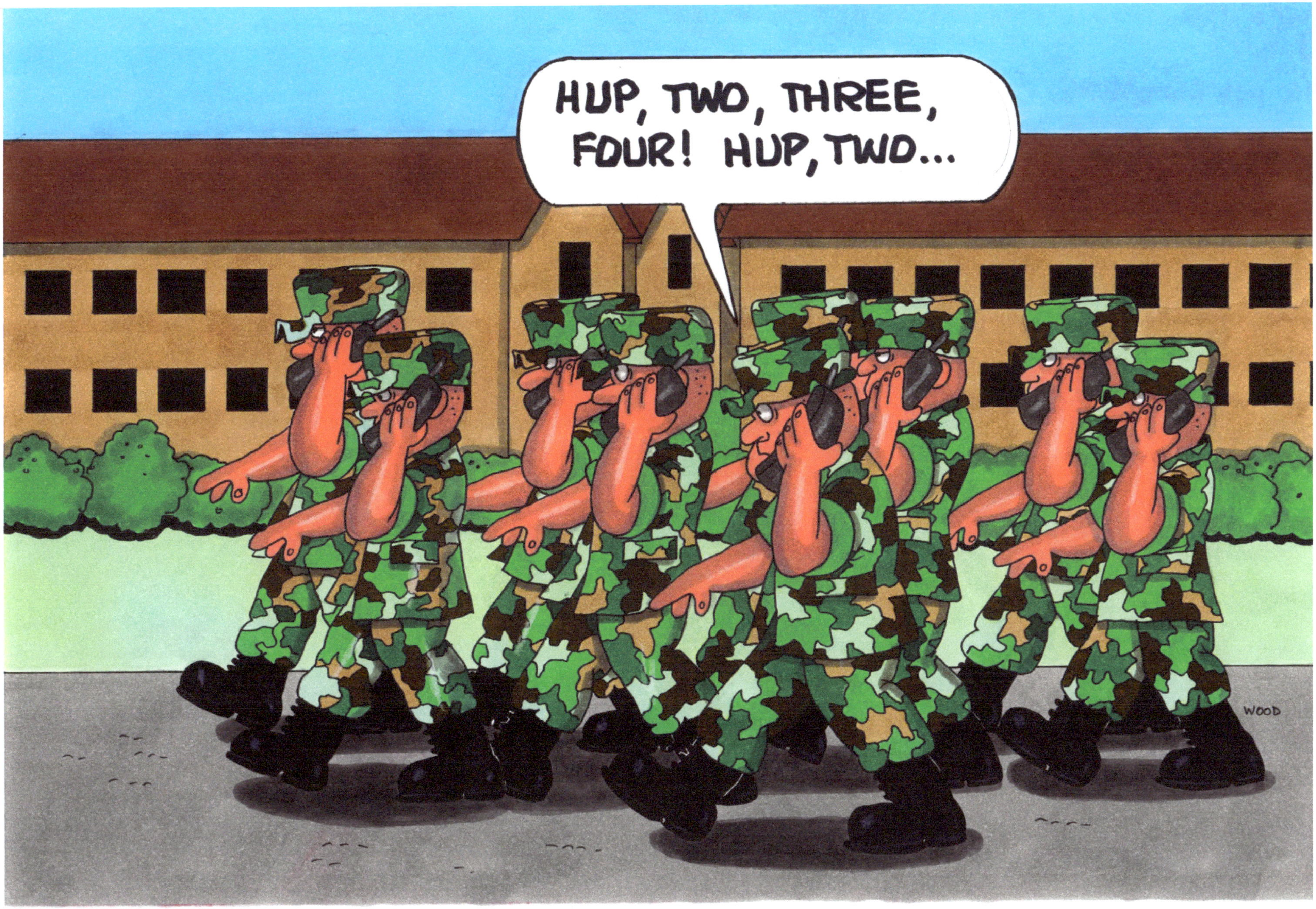
HUP, TWO, THREE, FOUR! HUP, TWO...
WOOD

...Or Play

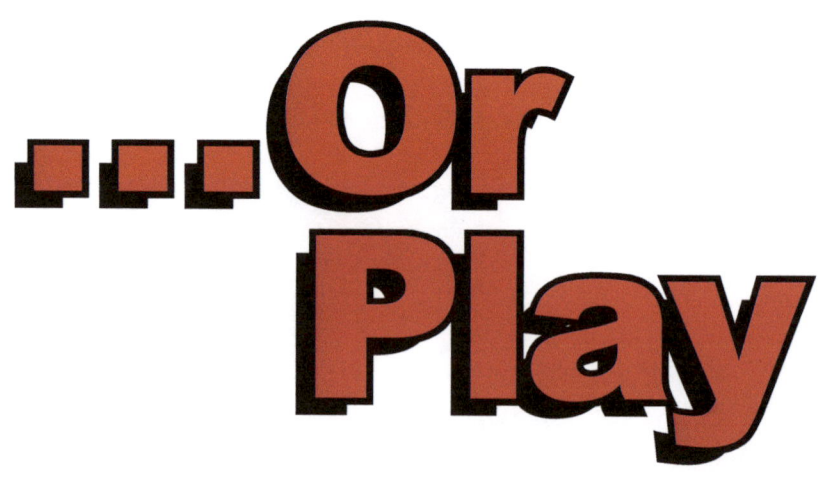

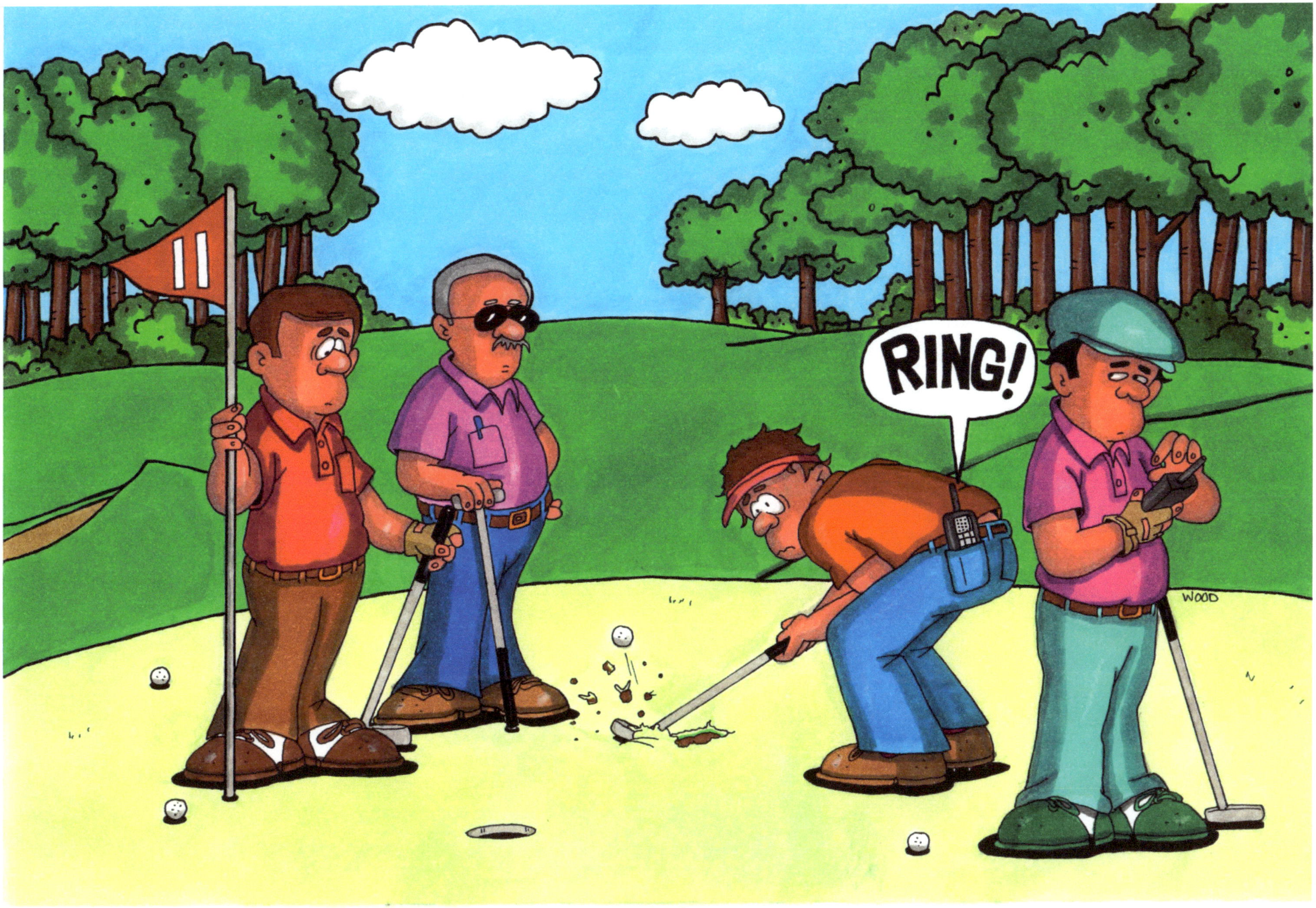
RING!
WOOD

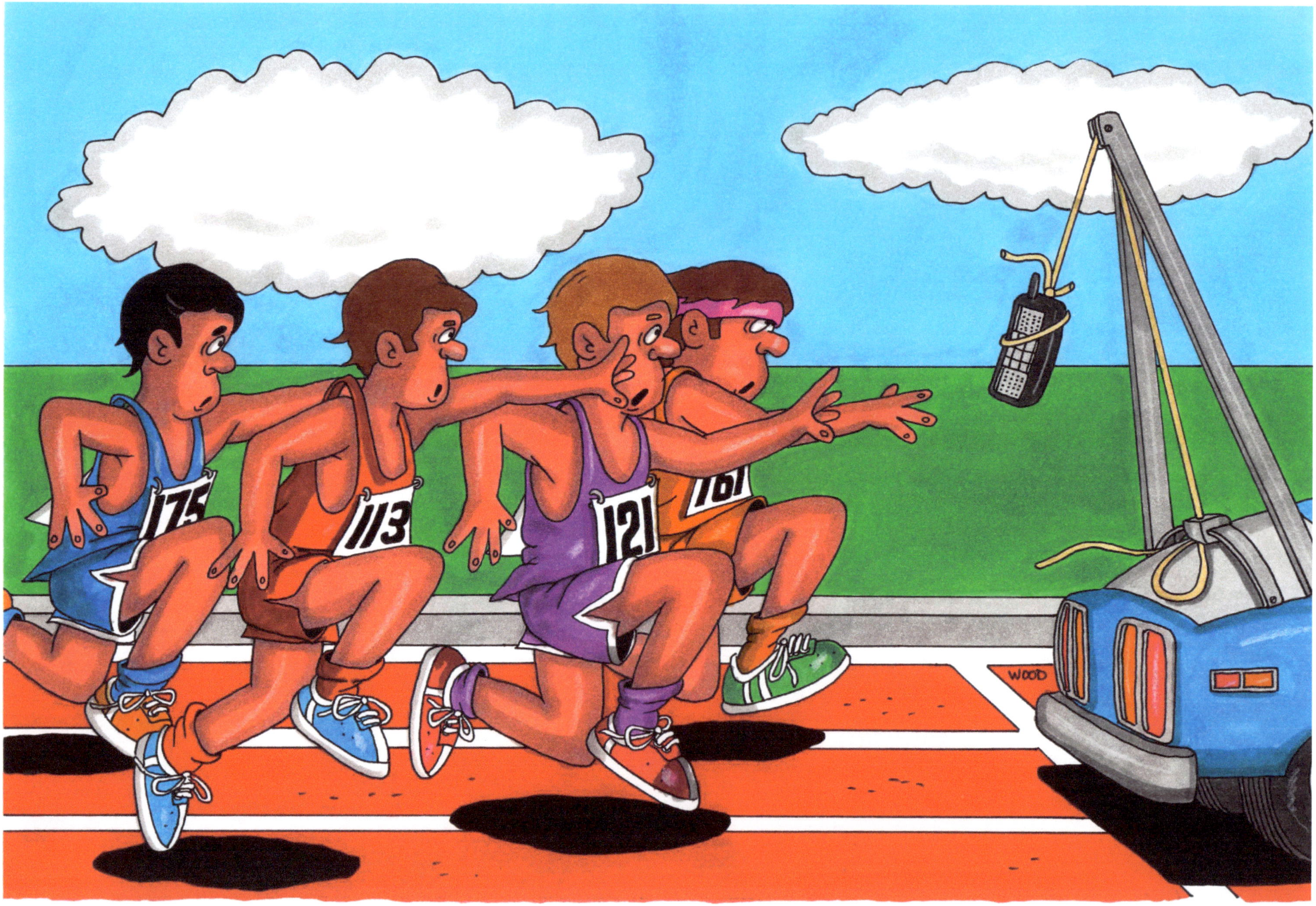
175
113
121
161
WOOD

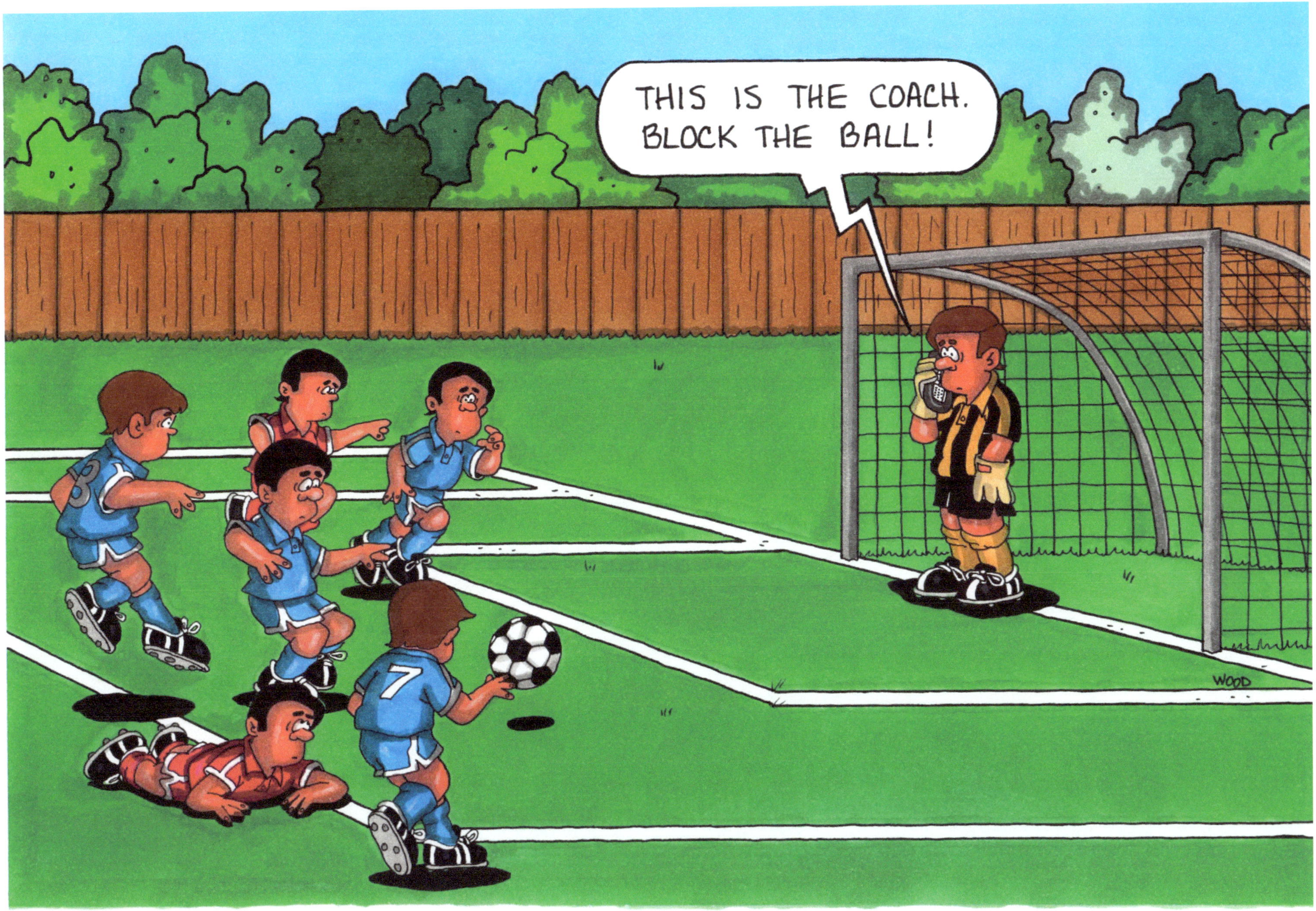
THIS IS THE COACH. BLOCK THE BALL!
WOOD

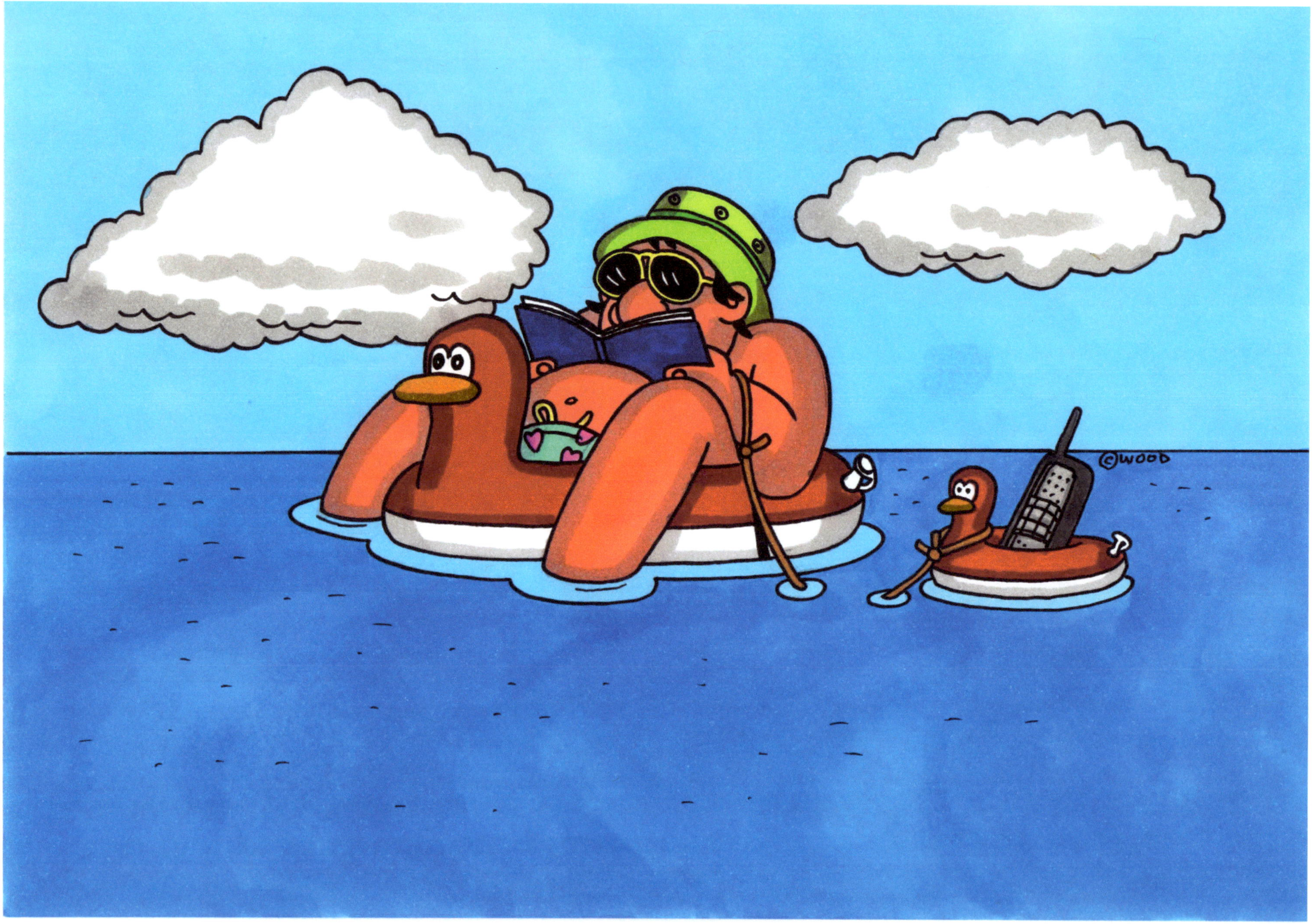
©WOOD

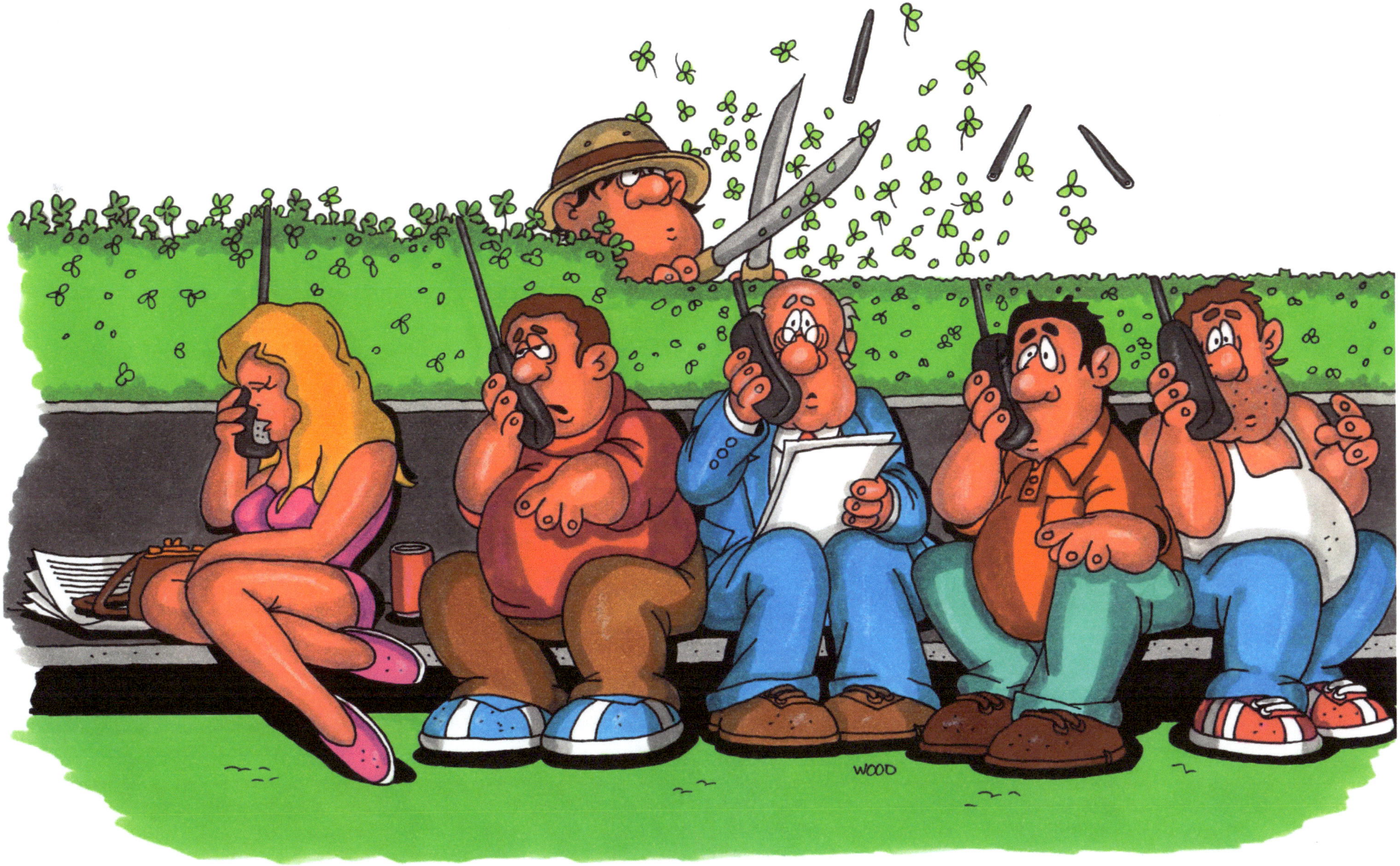
WOOD

Life's Little Moments

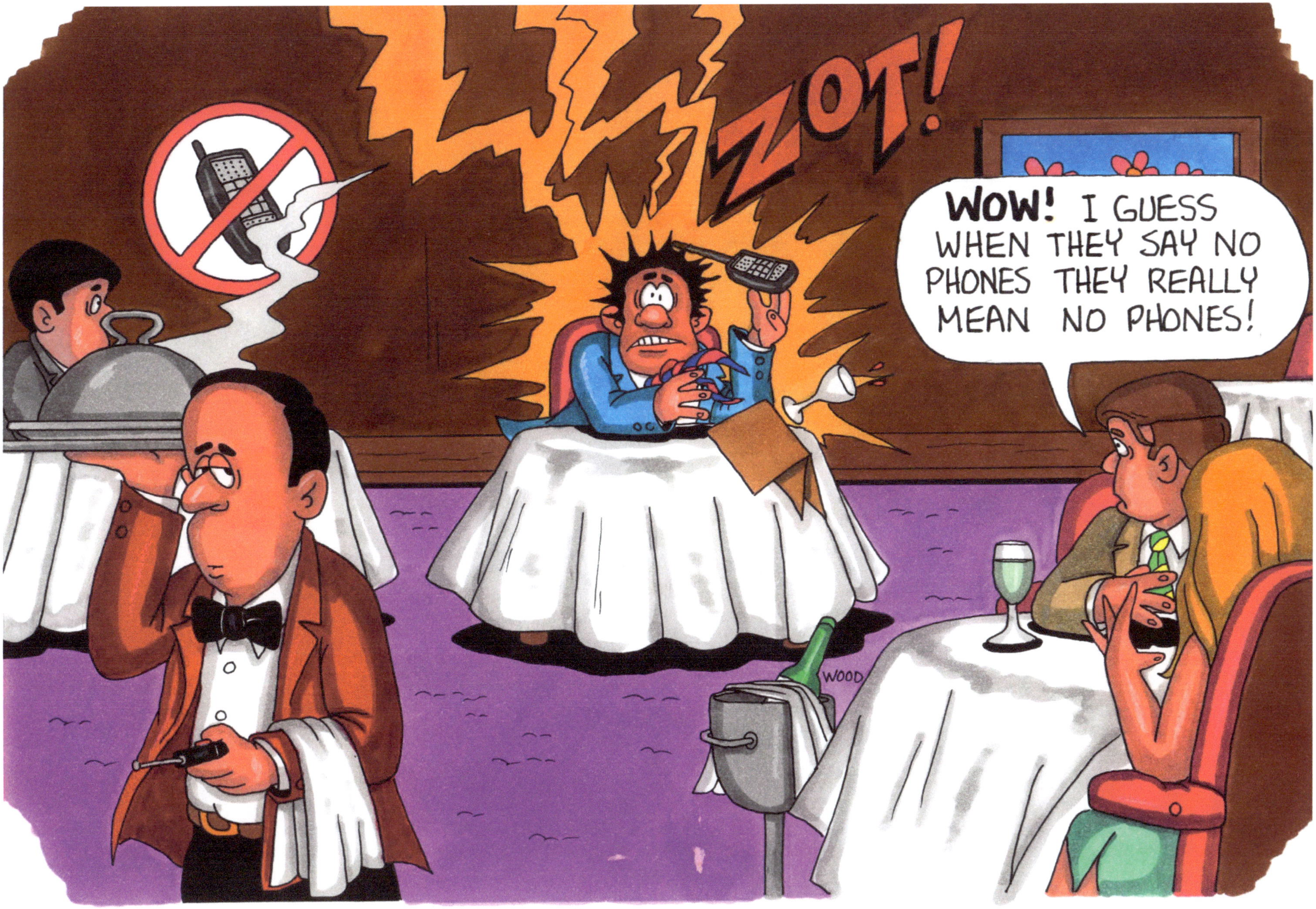
ZOT!
WOW! I GUESS WHEN THEY SAY NO PHONES THEY REALLY MEAN NO PHONES!
WOOD

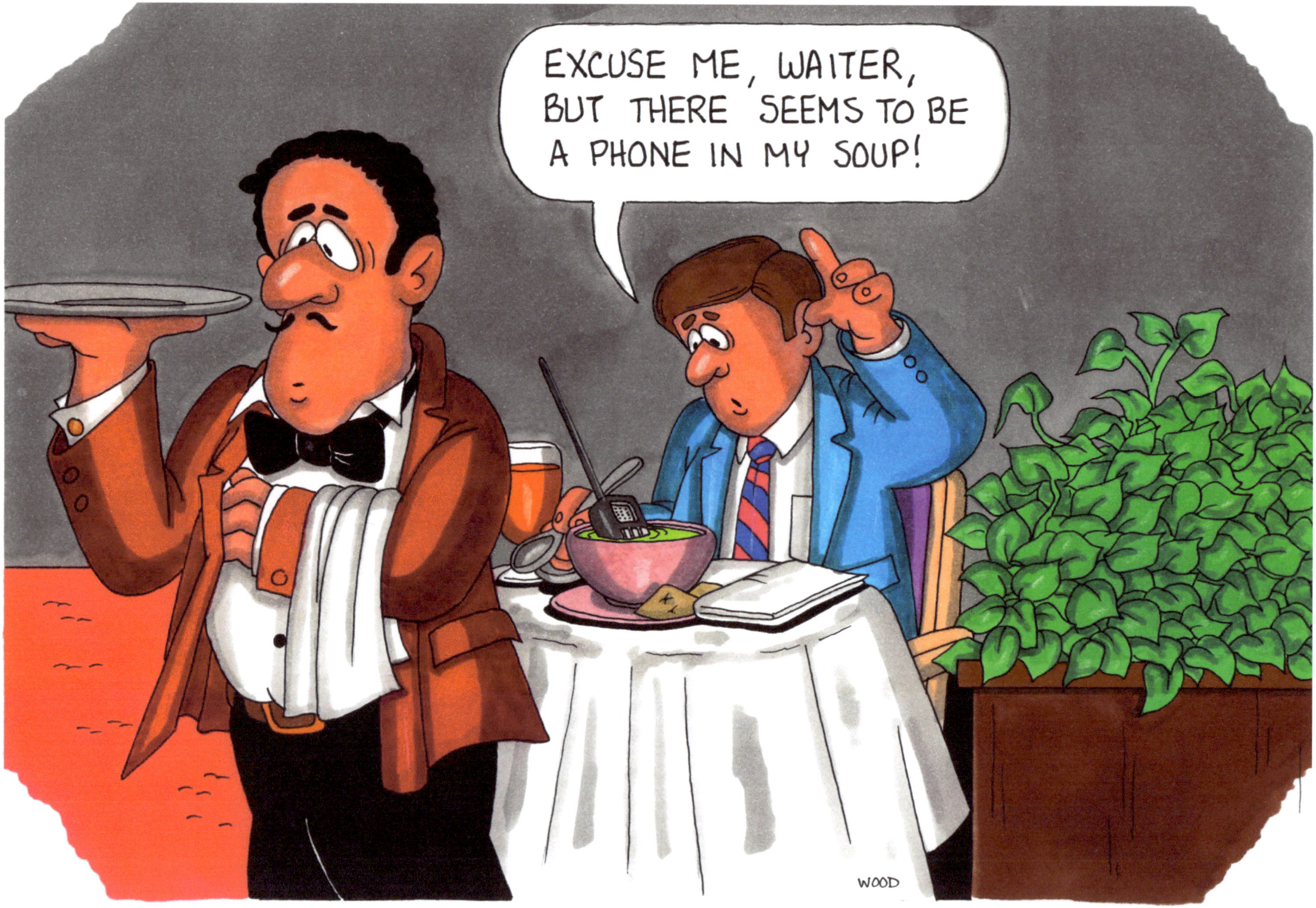
EXCUSE ME, WAITER, BUT THERE SEEMS TO BE A PHONE IN MY SOUP!
WOOD

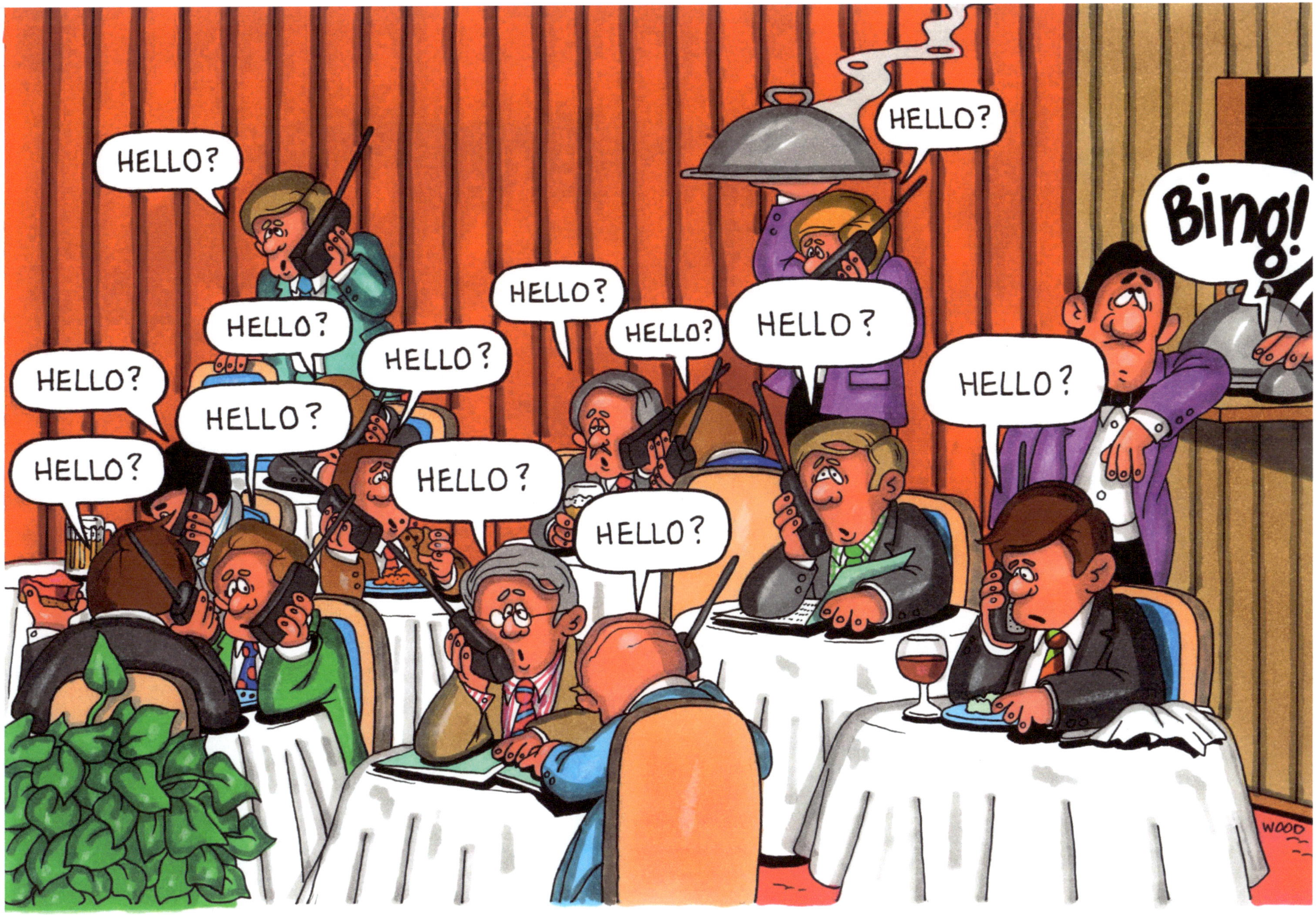
HELLO?
HELLO?
HELLO?
HELLO?
HELLO?
HELLO?
HELLO?
HELLO?
HELLO?
HELLO?
HELLO?
HELLO?
HELLO?
Bing!
WOOD

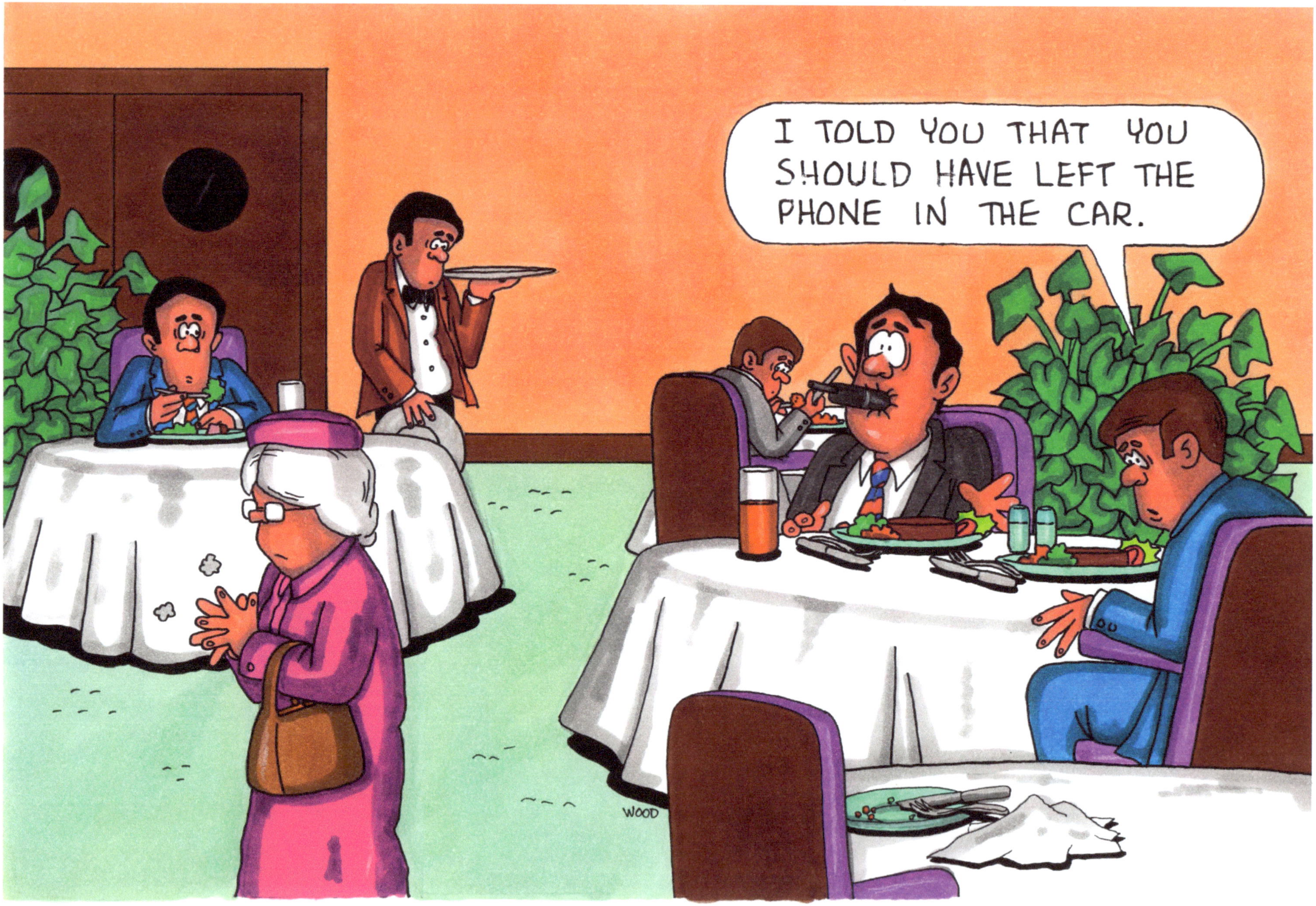
I TOLD YOU THAT YOU SHOULD HAVE LEFT THE PHONE IN THE CAR.
WOOD

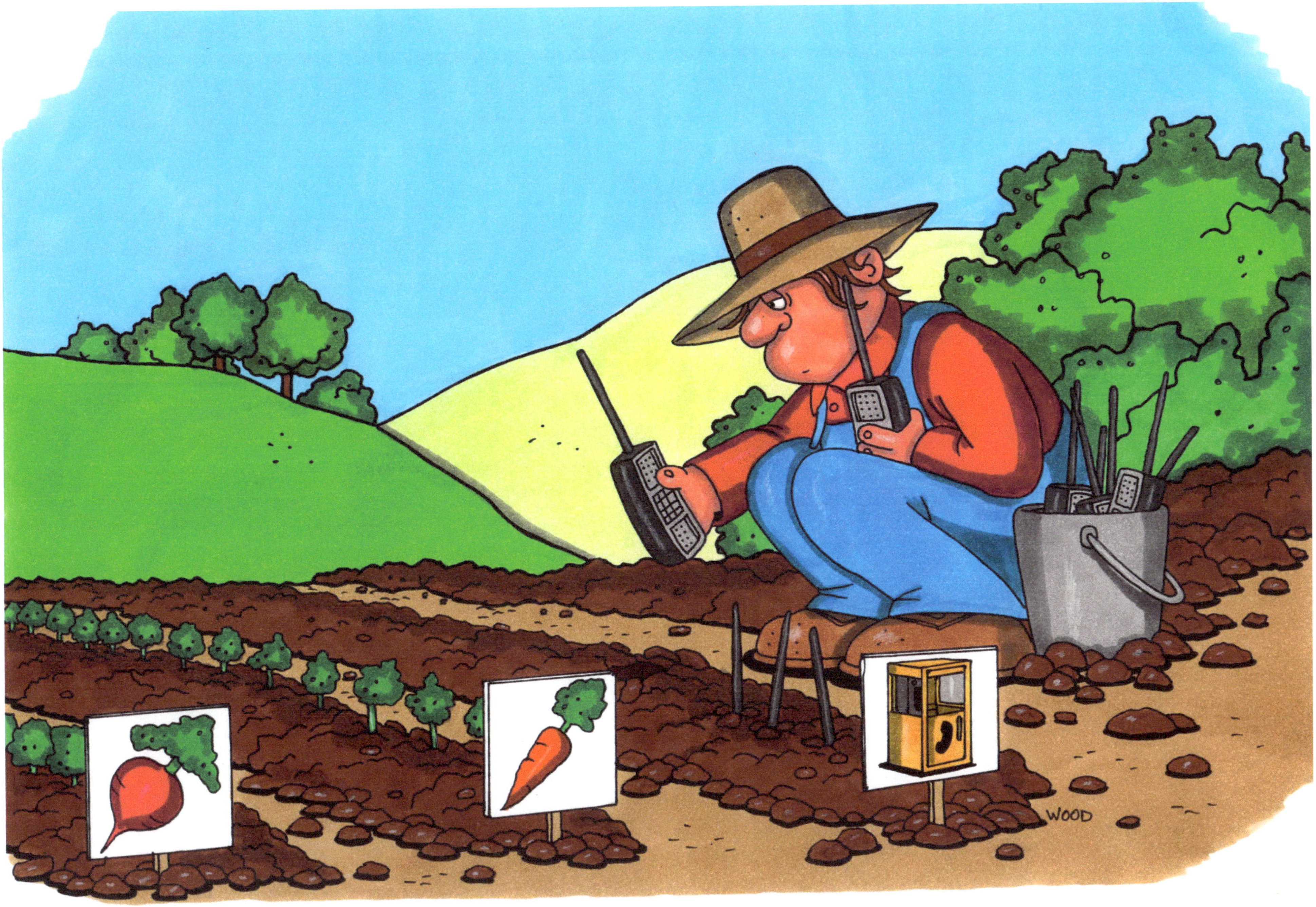
WOOD

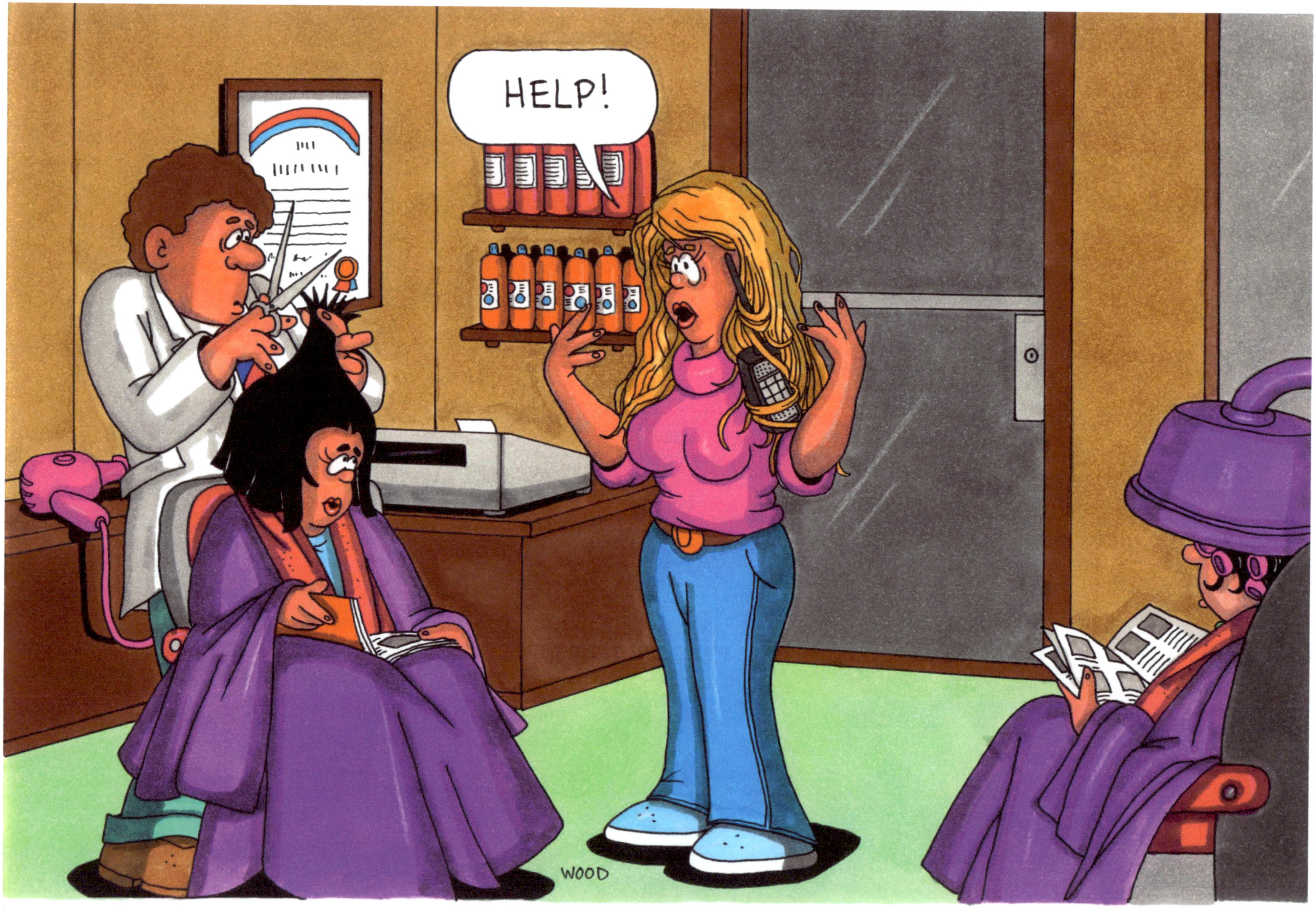
HELP!
WOOD

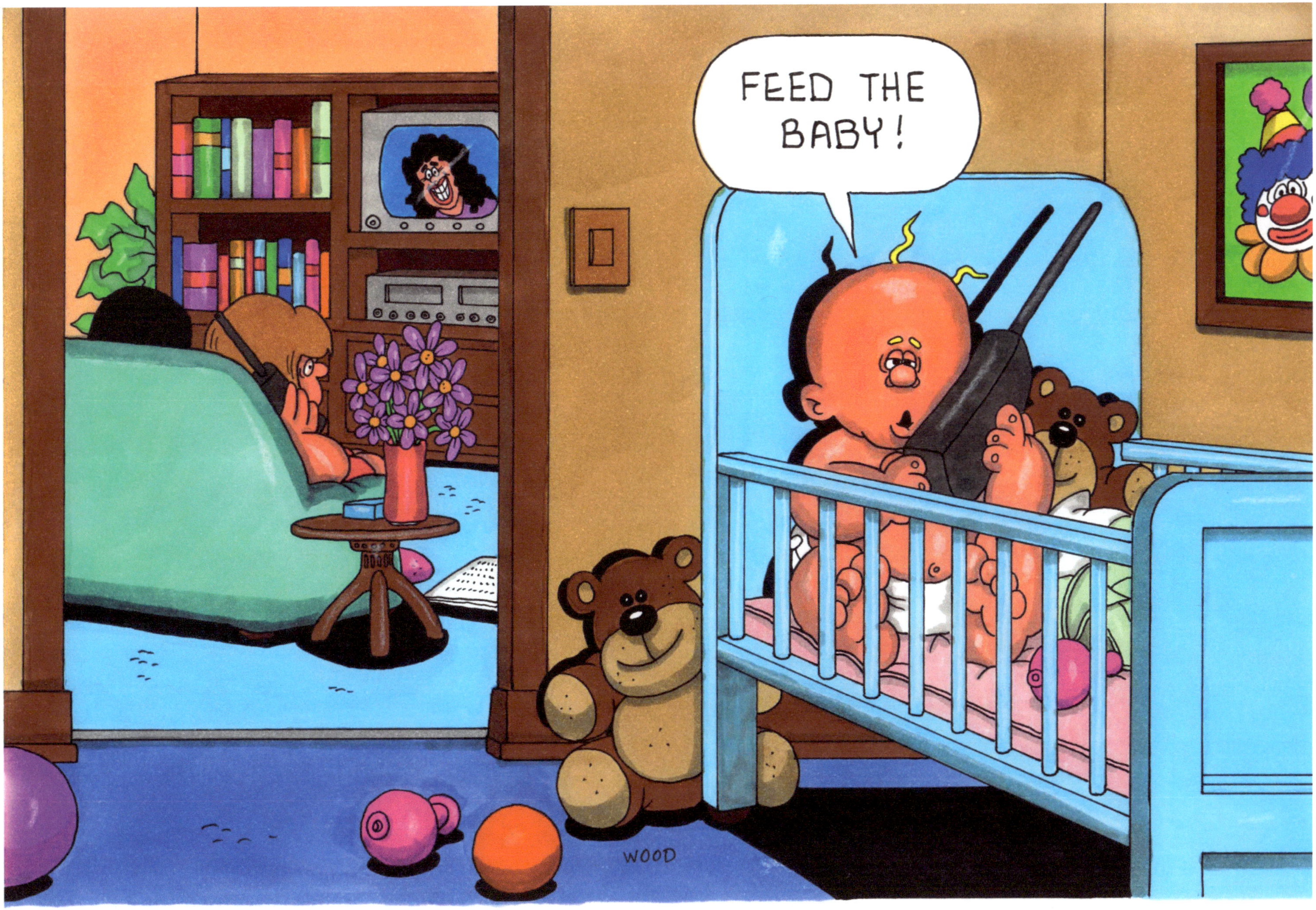
FEED THE BABY!
WOOD

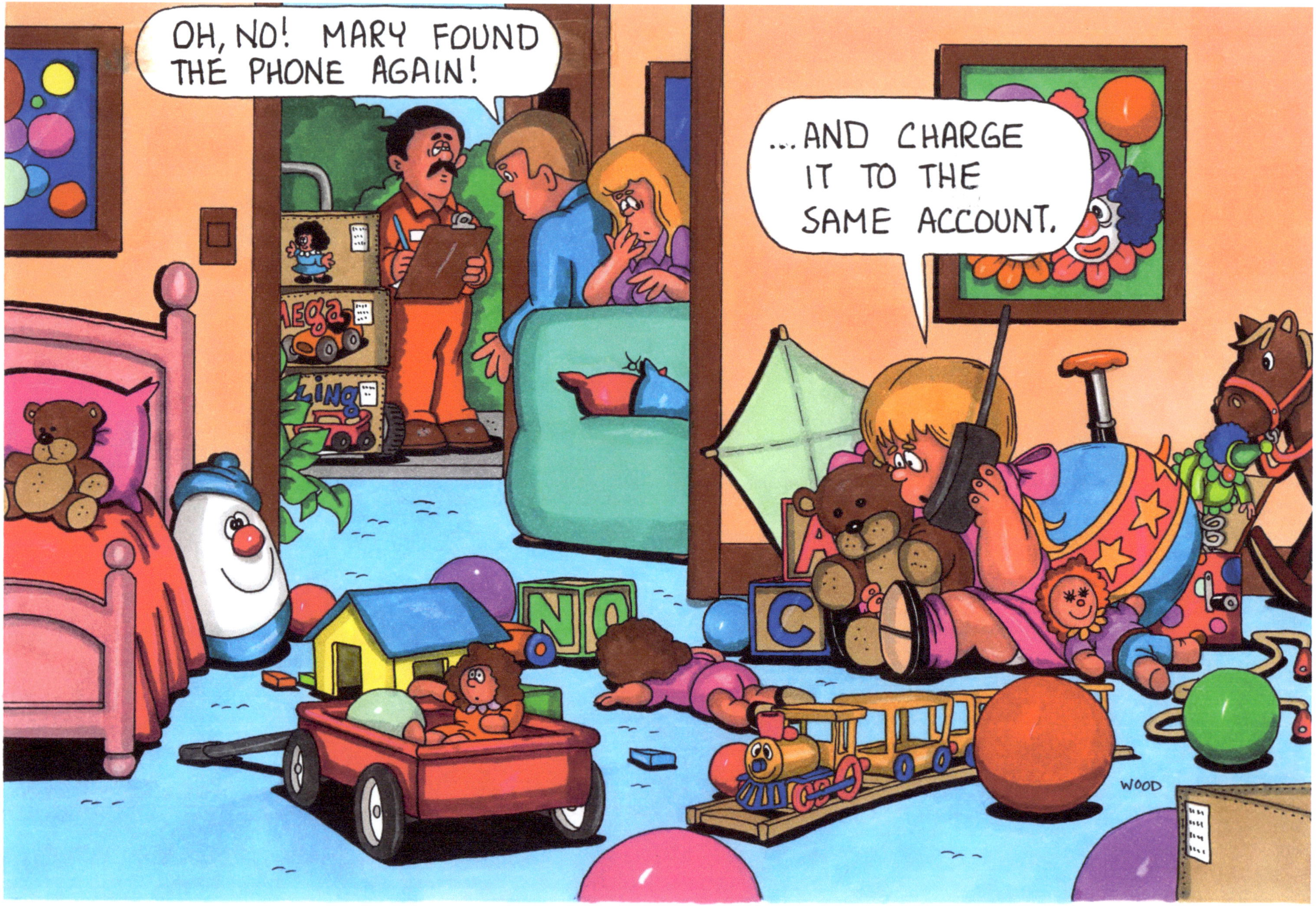
OH, NO! MARY FOUND THE PHONE AGAIN!
...AND CHARGE IT TO THE SAME ACCOUNT.
WOOD

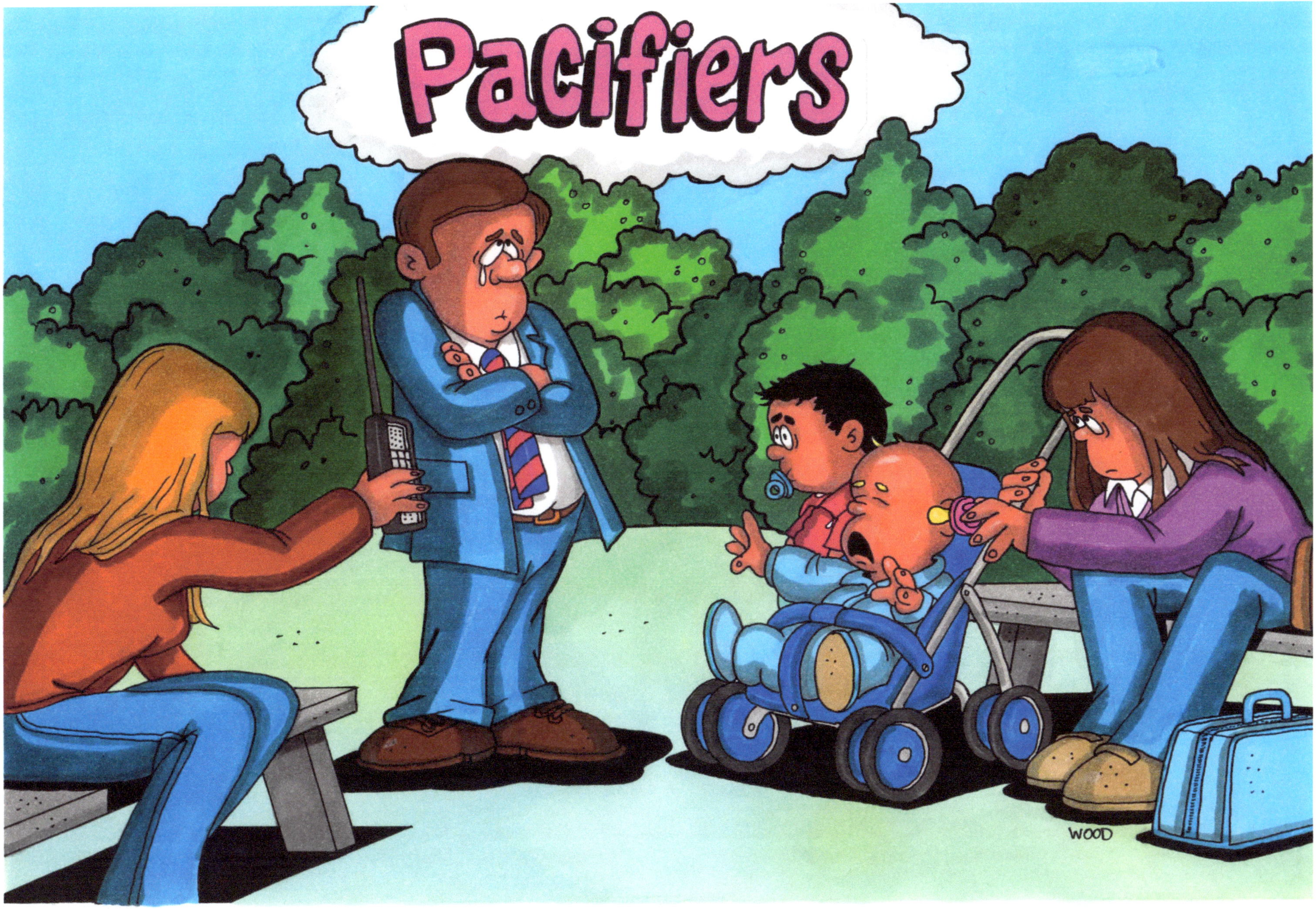
Pacifiers
WOOD

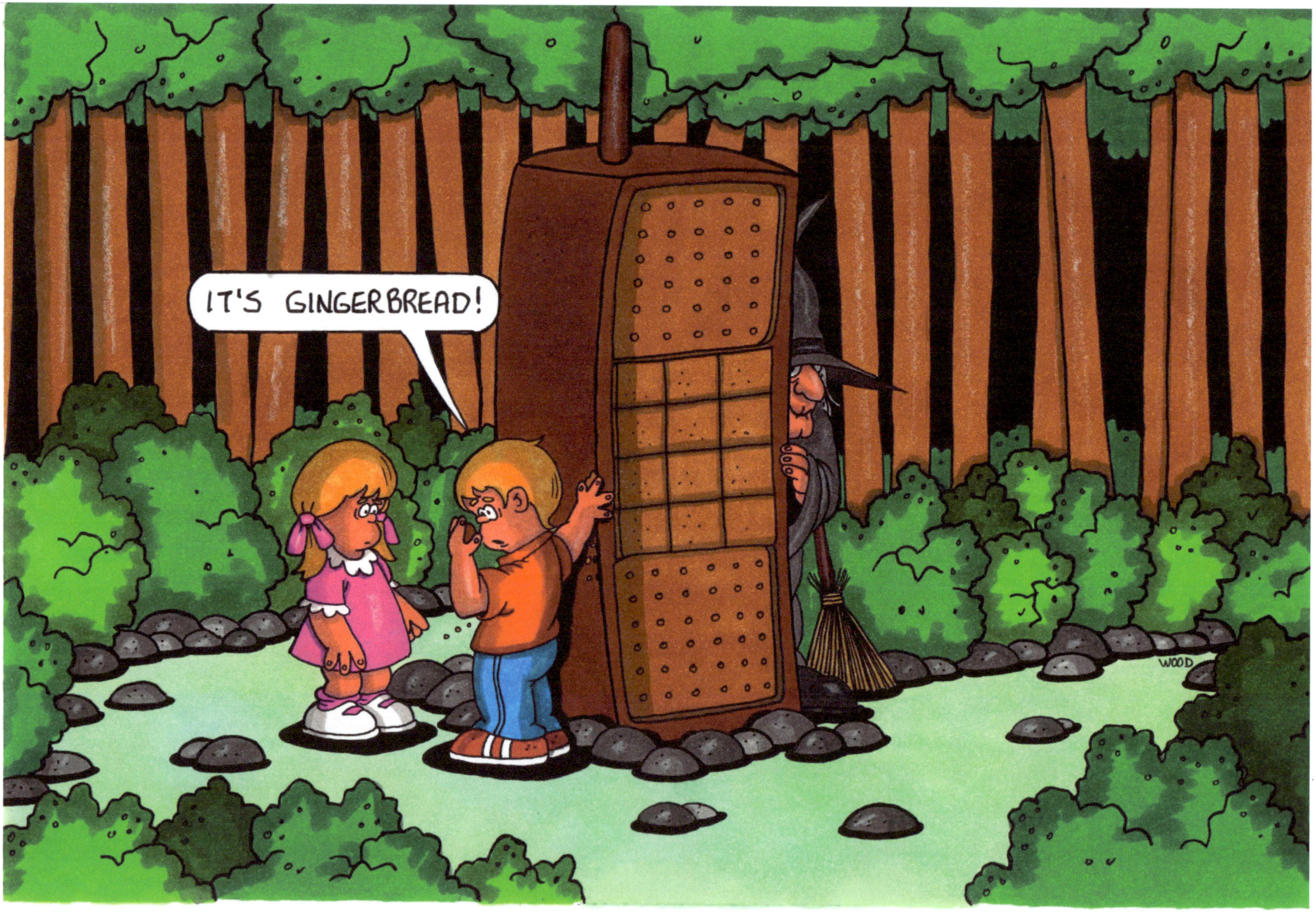
IT'S GINGERBREAD!
WOOD

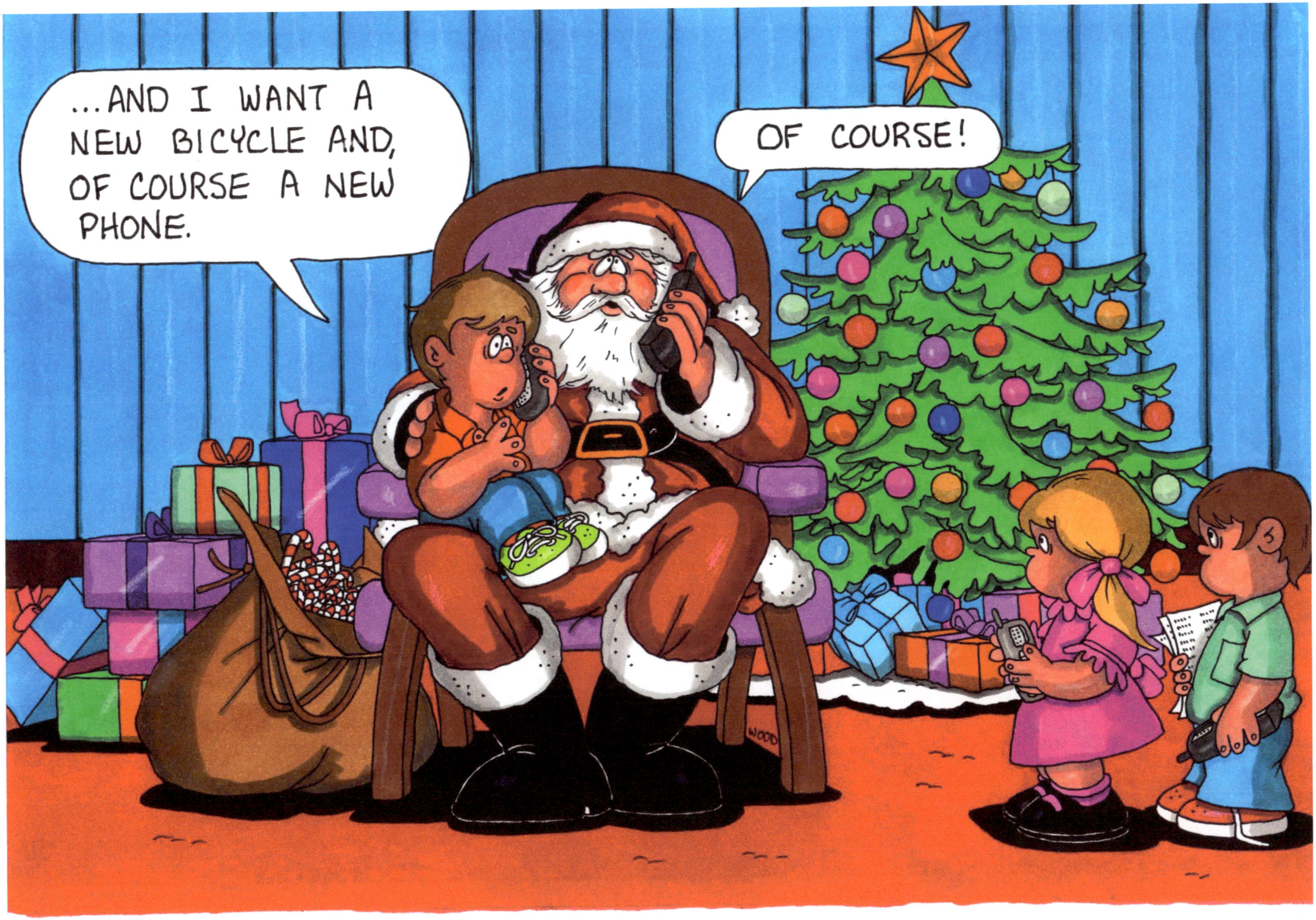
...AND I WANT A NEW BICYCLE AND, OF COURSE A NEW PHONE.
OF COURSE!
WOOD

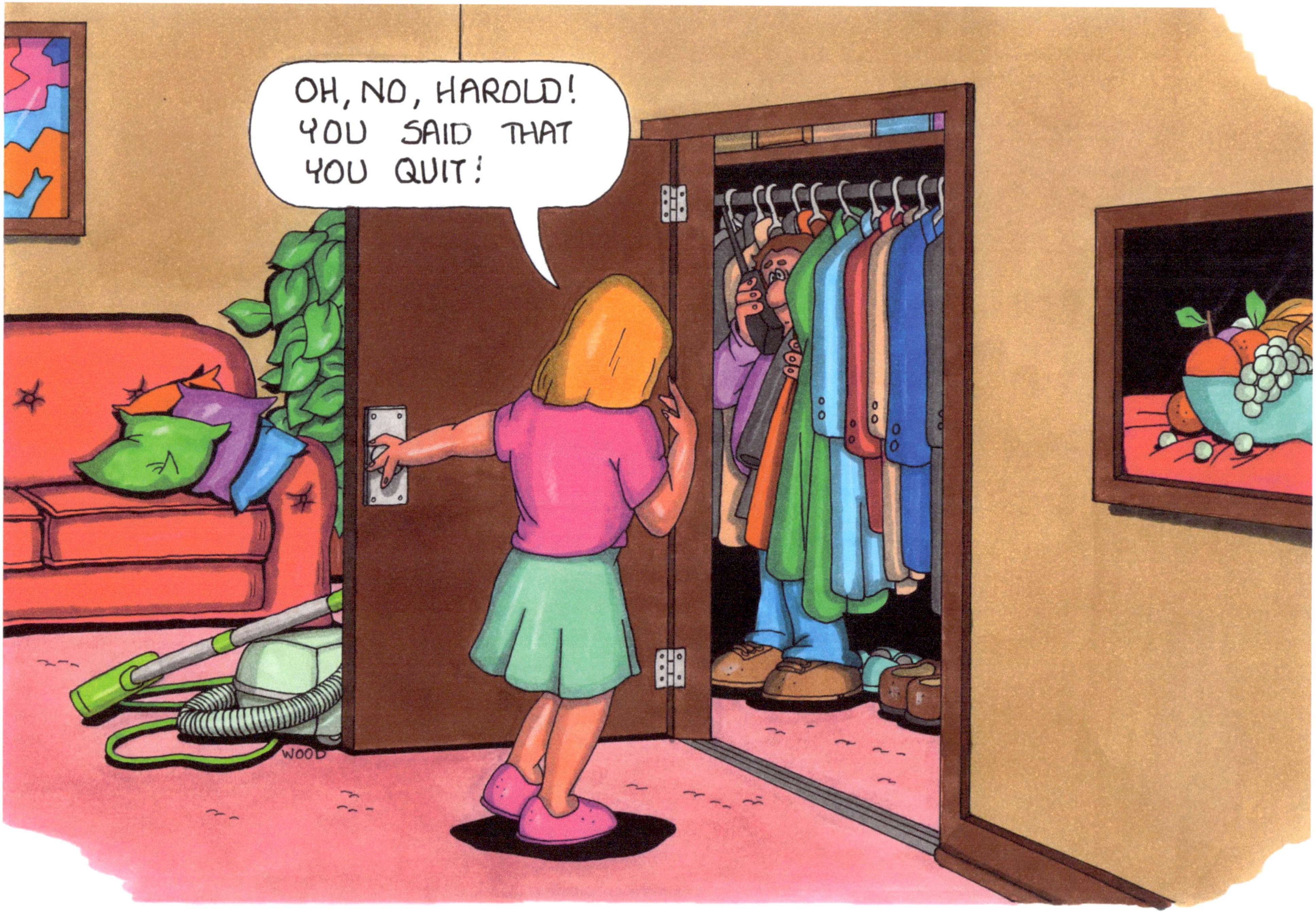
OH, NO, HAROLD! YOU SAID THAT YOU QUIT!
WOOD

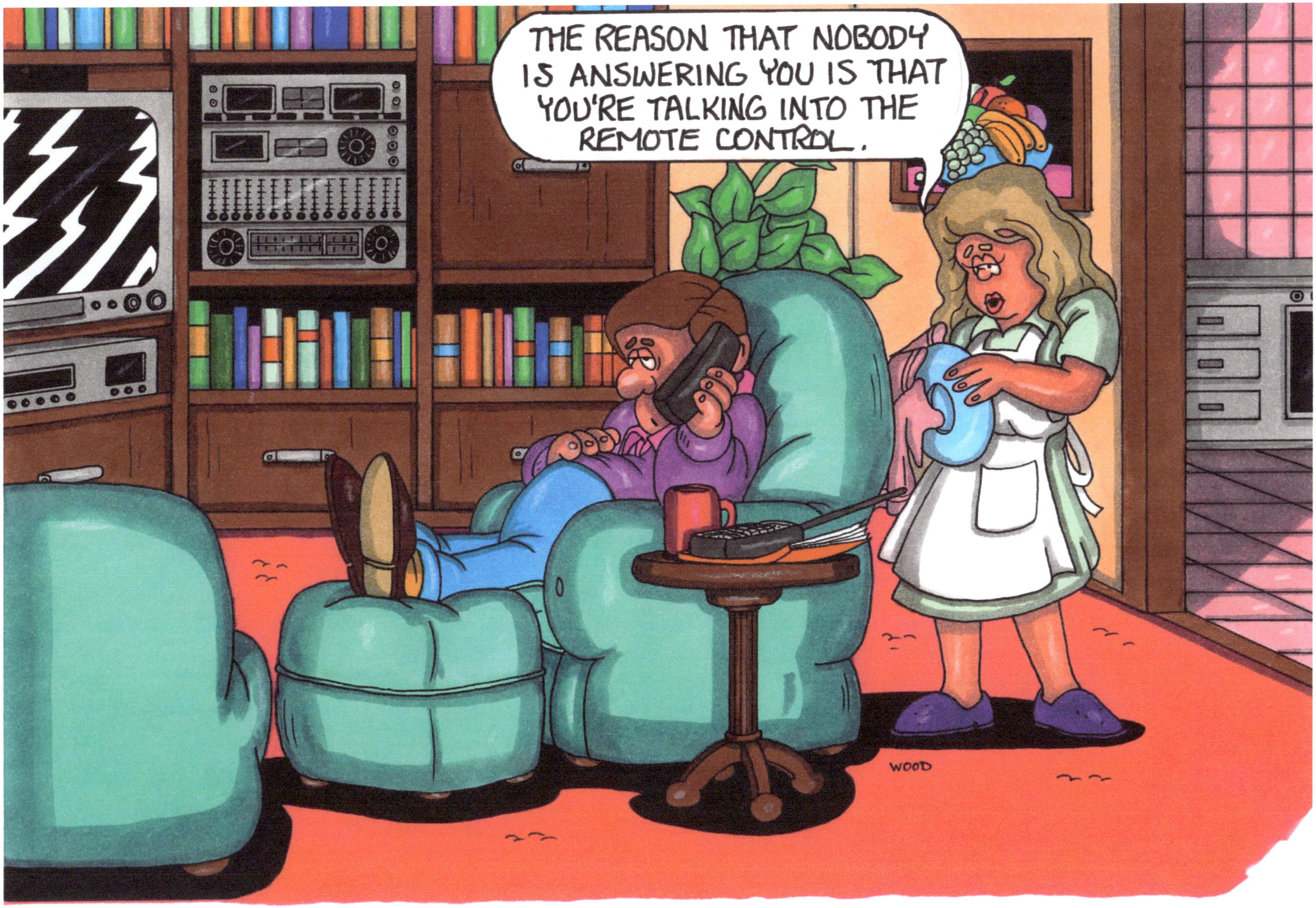
THE REASON THAT NOBODY IS ANSWERING YOU IS THAT YOU'RE TALKING INTO THE REMOTE CONTROL.
WOOD

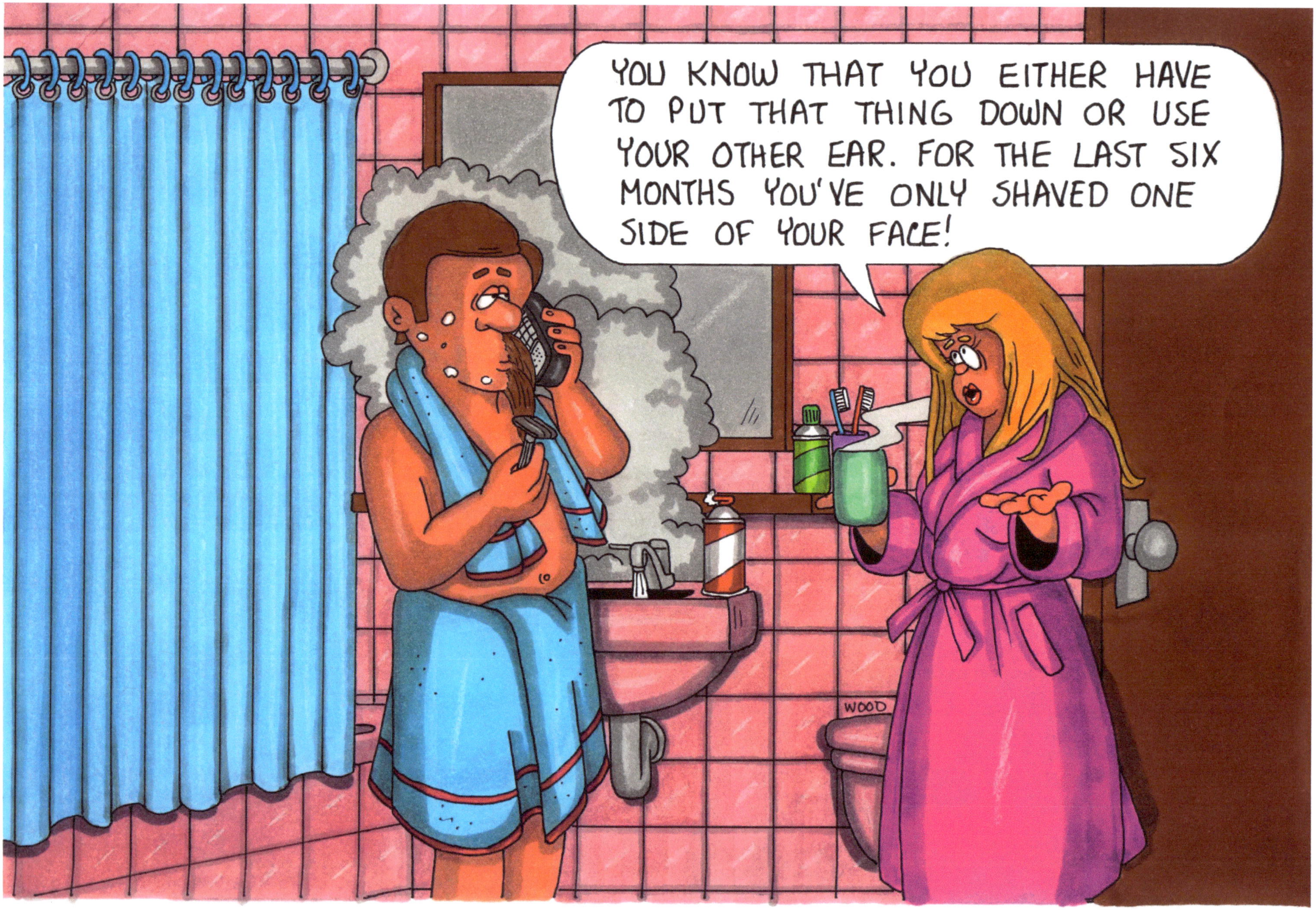
YOU KNOW THAT YOU EITHER HAVE TO PUT THAT THING DOWN OR USE YOUR OTHER EAR. FOR THE LAST SIX MONTHS YOU'VE ONLY SHAVED ONE SIDE OF YOUR FACE!
WOOD

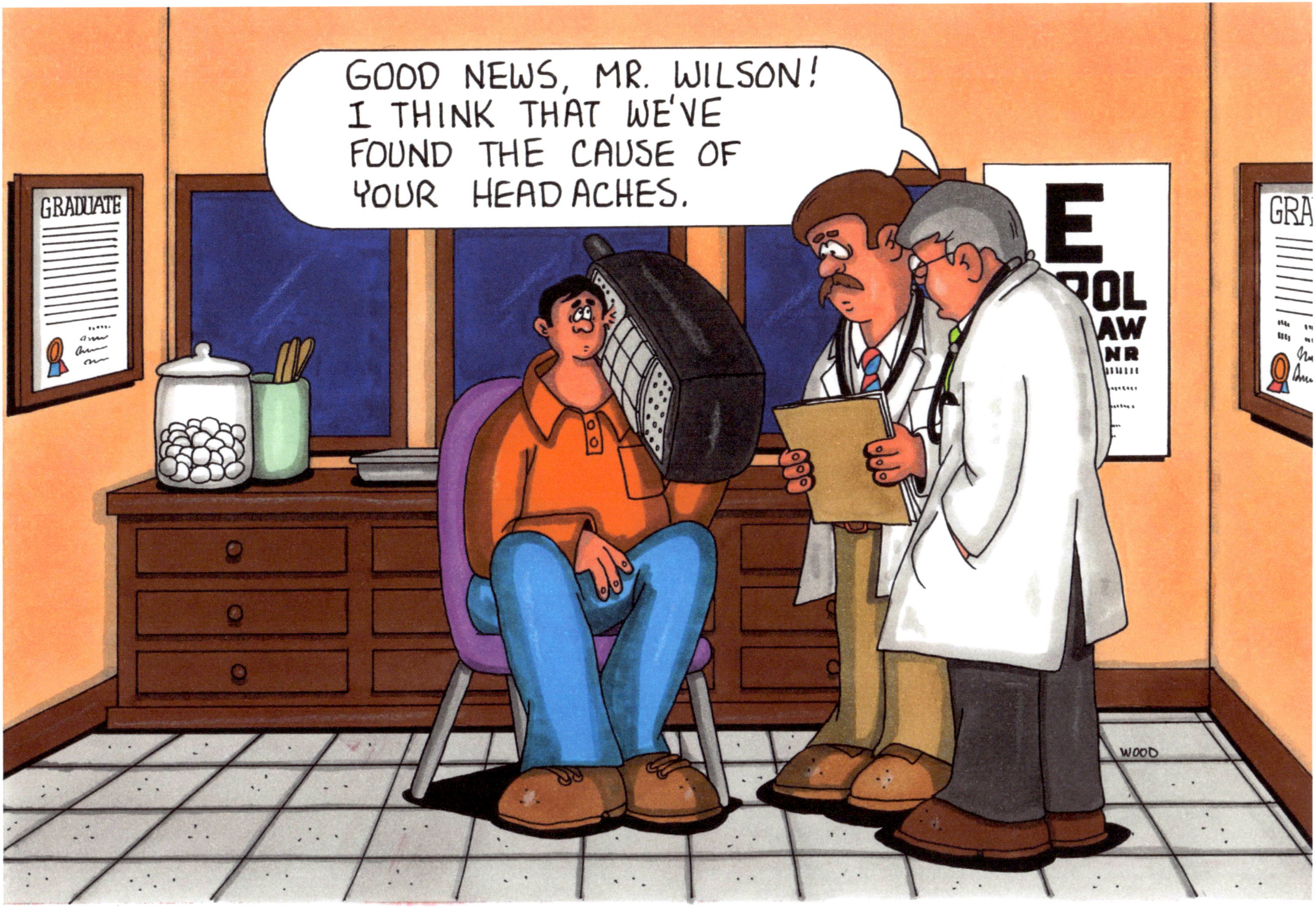
GOOD NEWS, MR. WILSON! I THINK THAT WE'VE FOUND THE CAUSE OF YOUR HEADACHES.
GRADUATE
E
WOOD

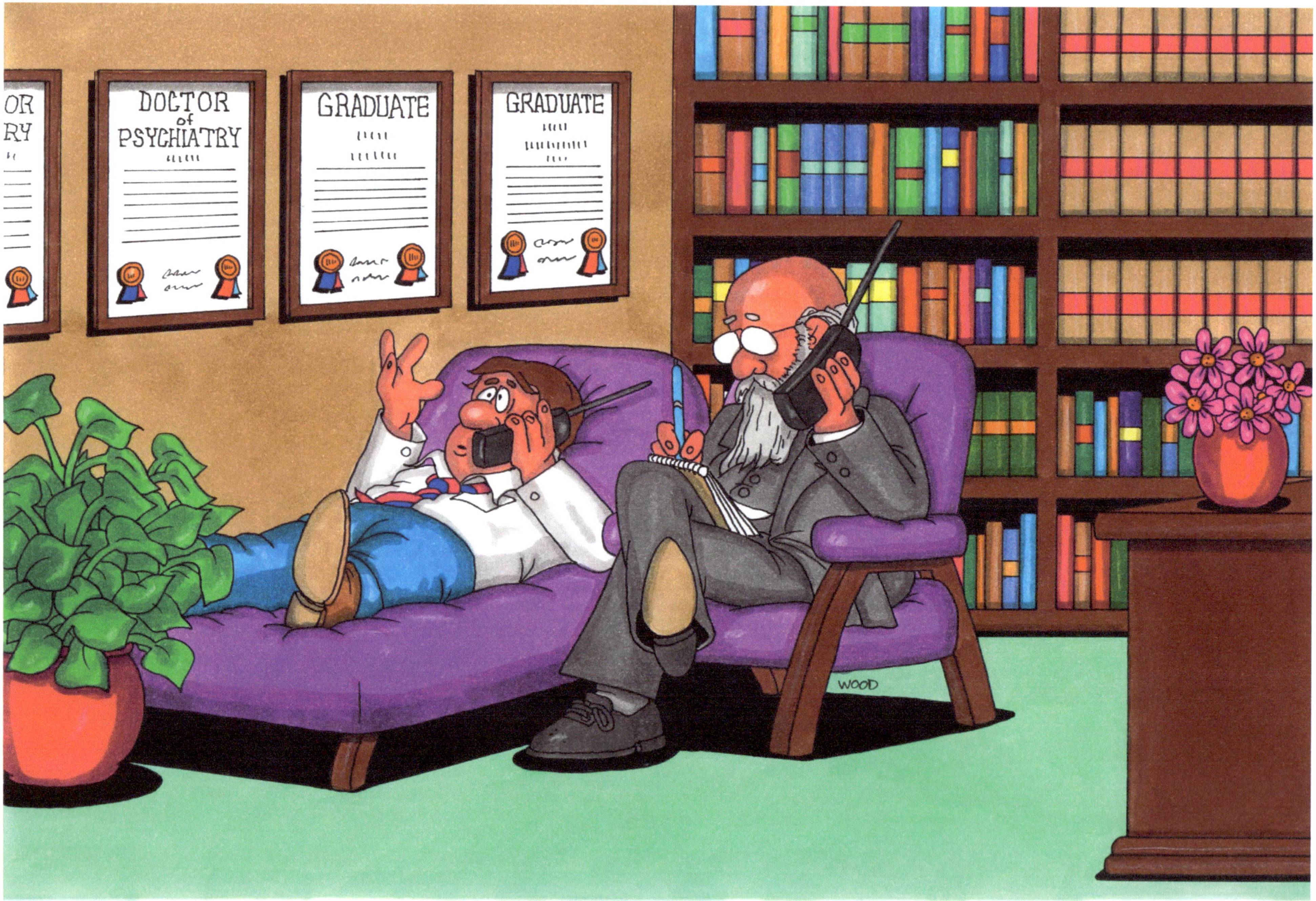

OR
RY
DOCTOR
of
PSYCHIATRY
GRADUATE
GRADUATE
WOOD

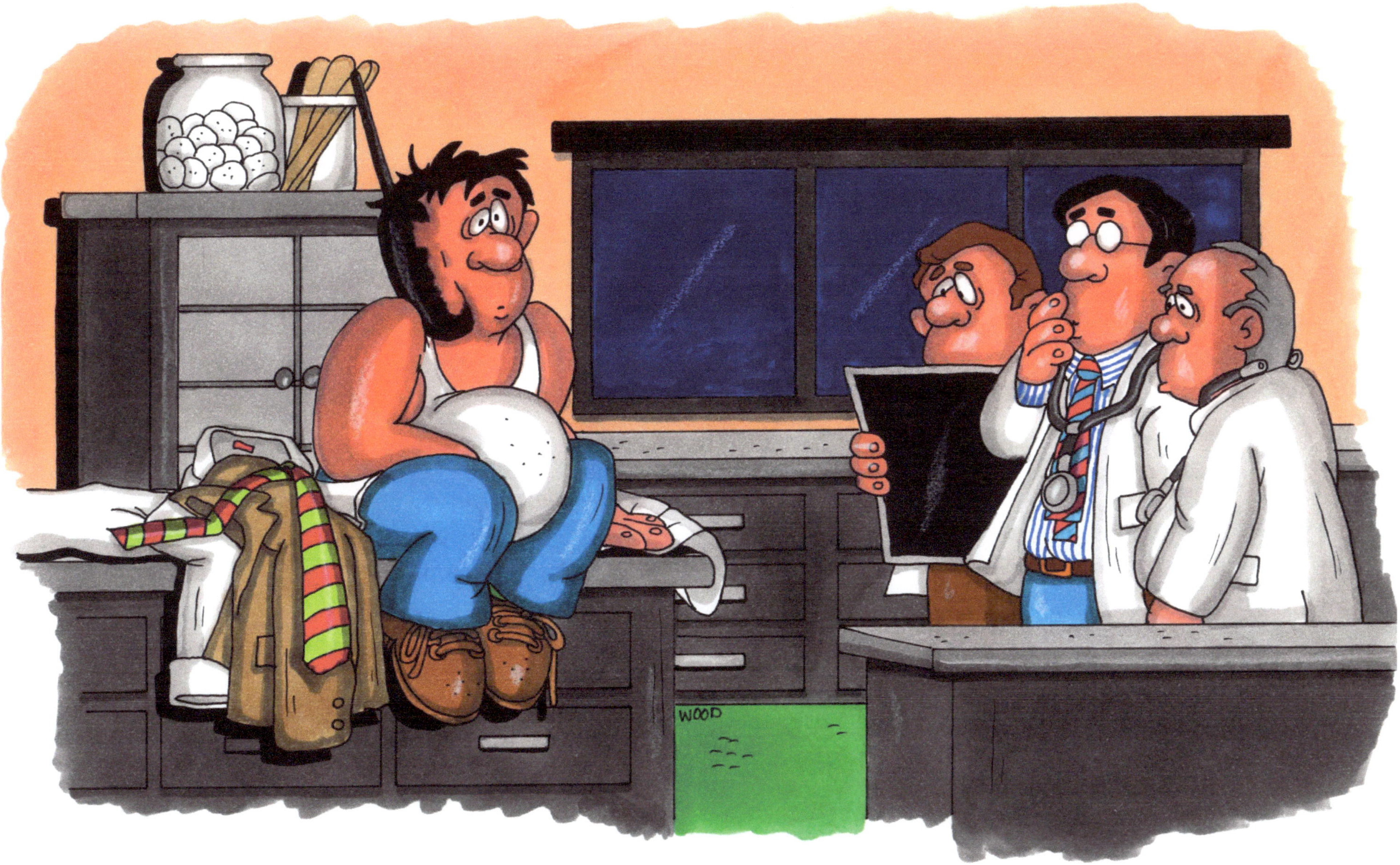
WOOD

The Cell Phone

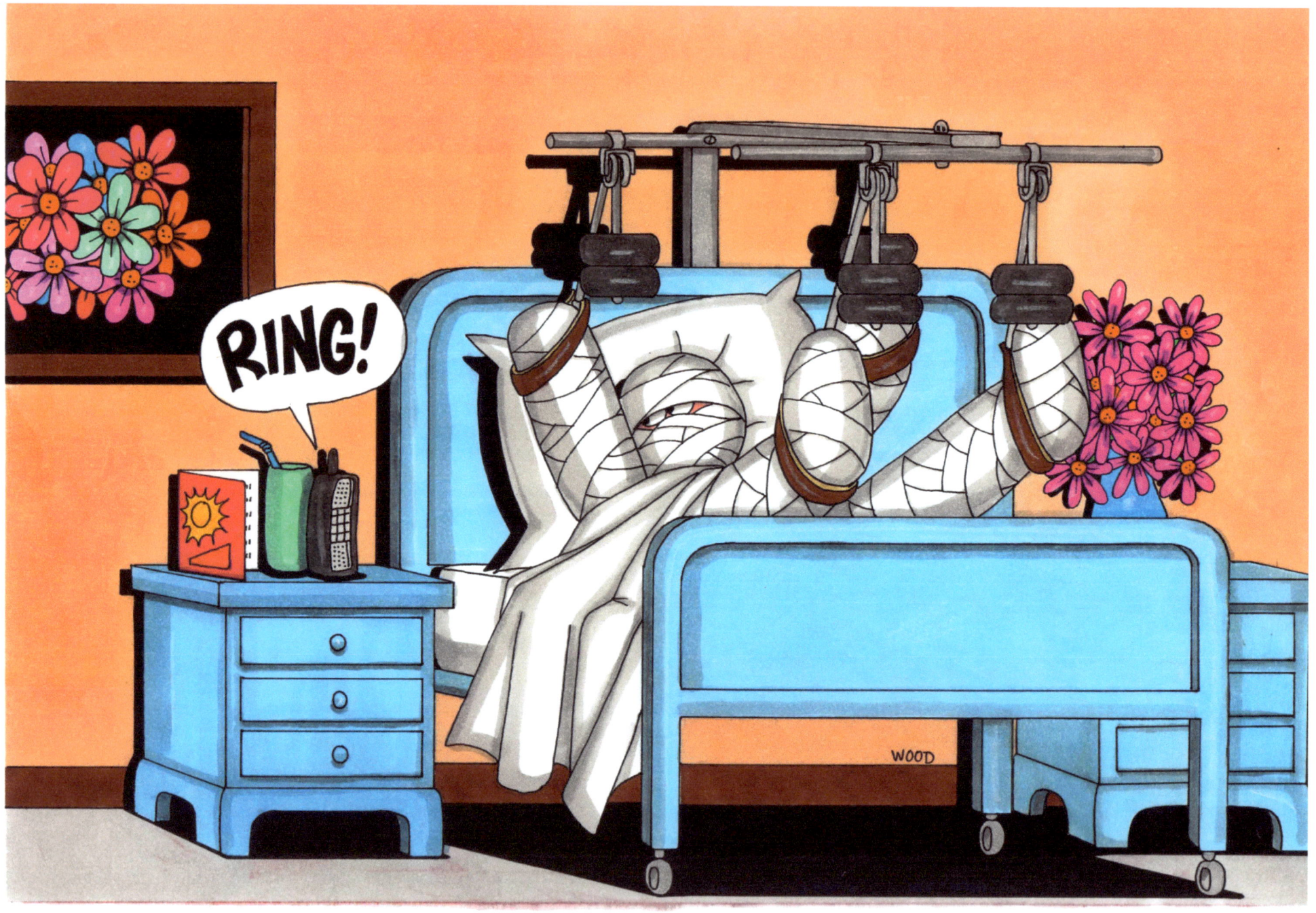

72

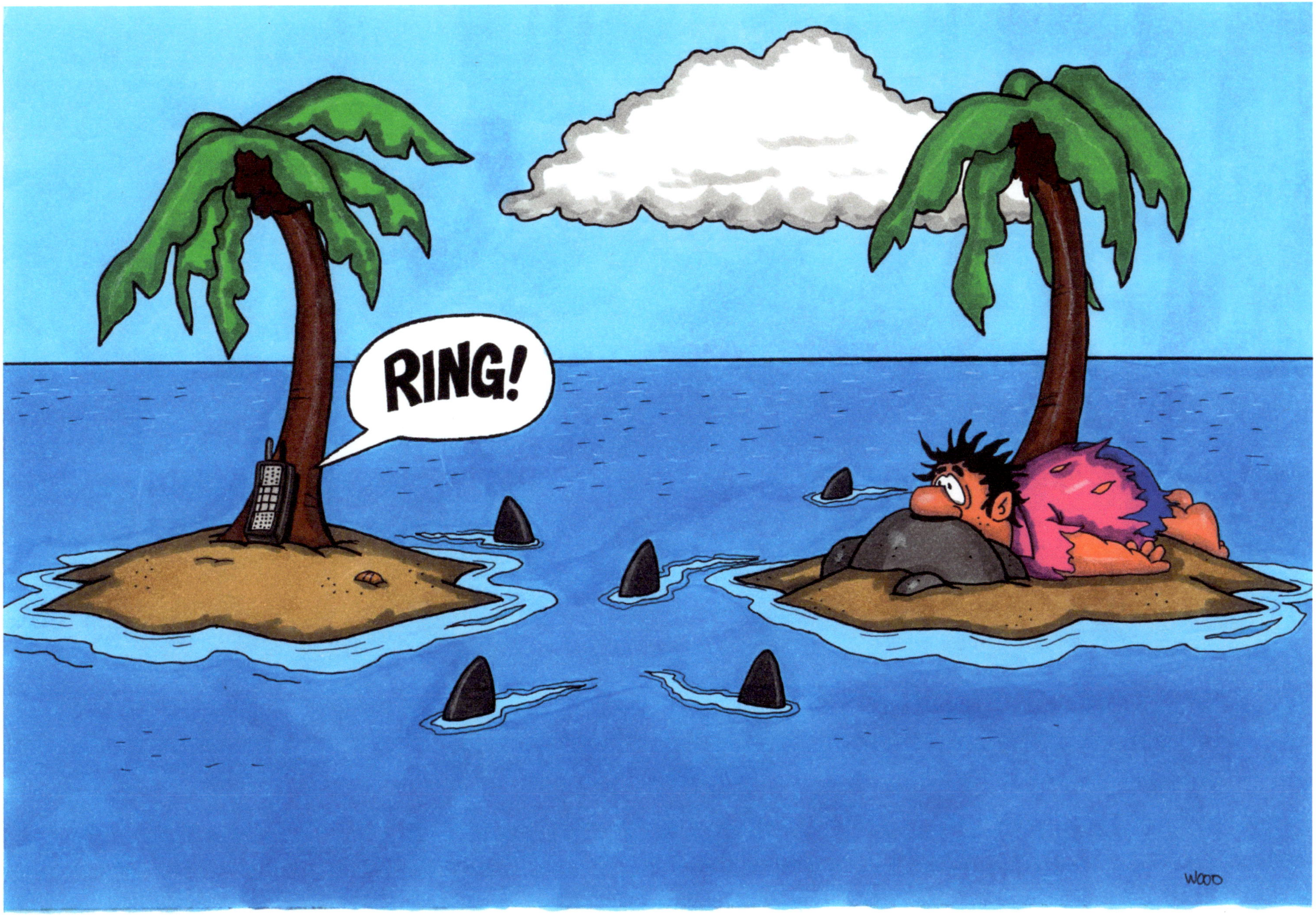
RING!
WOOD

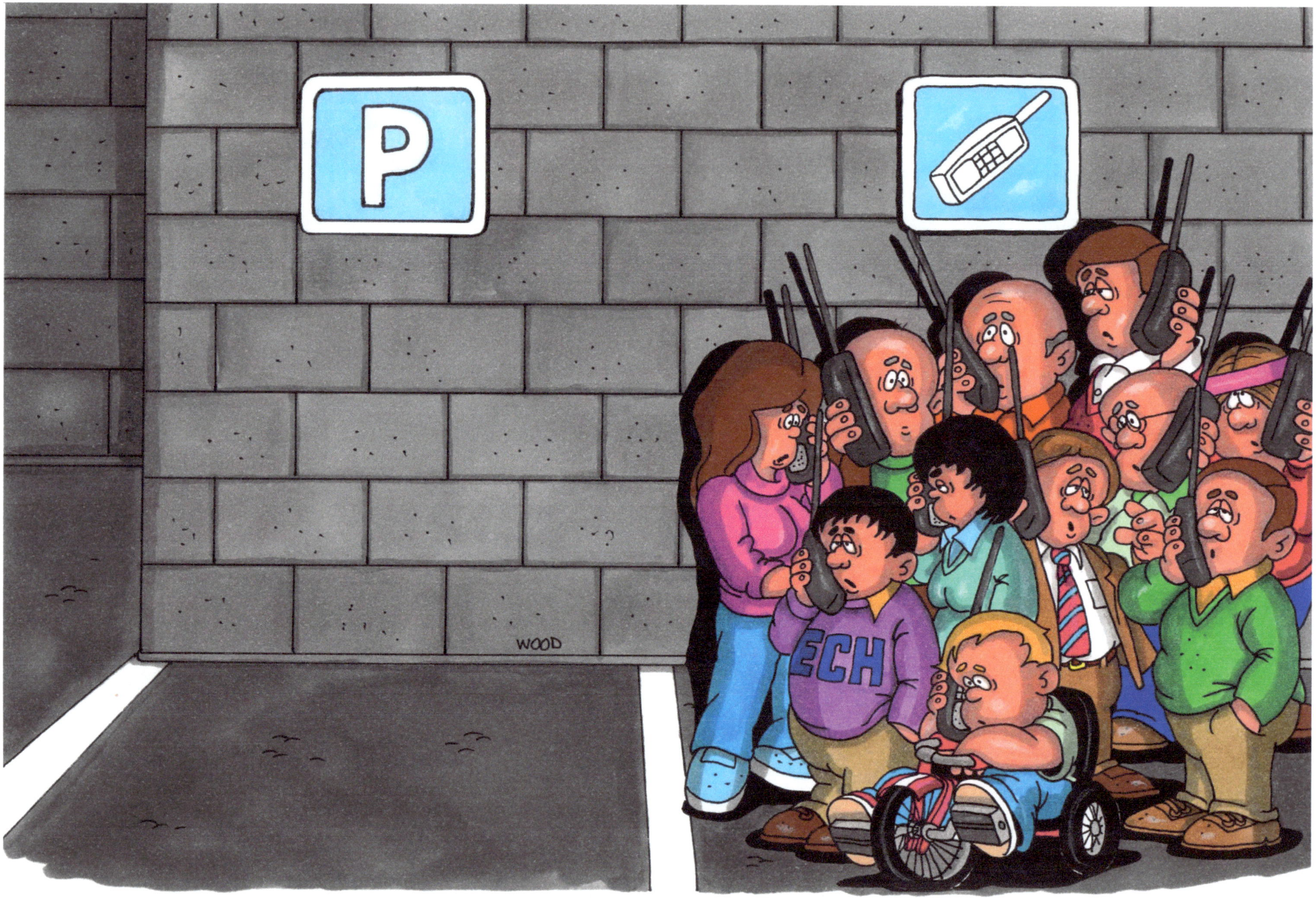
P
ECH
WOOD

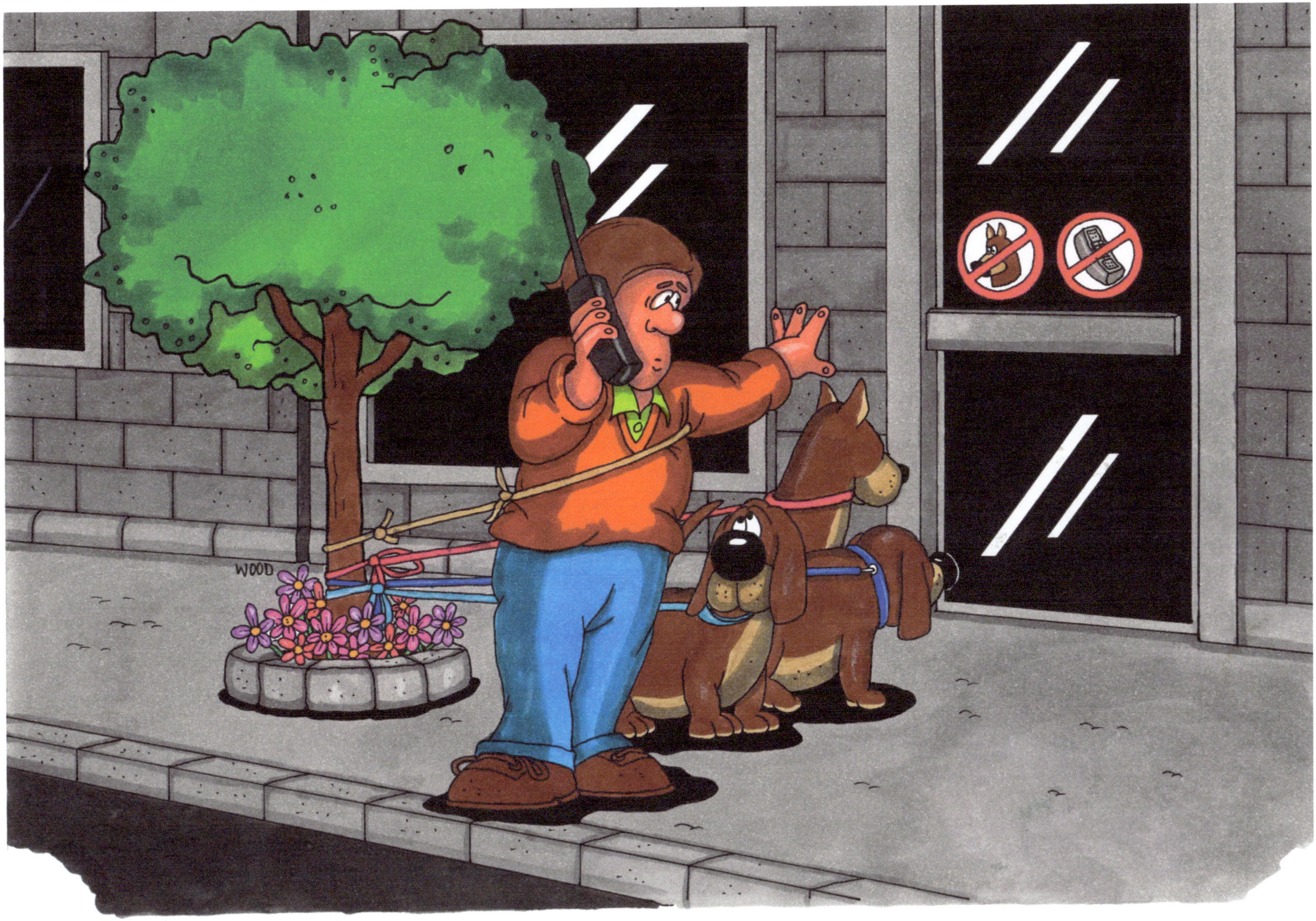
WOOD

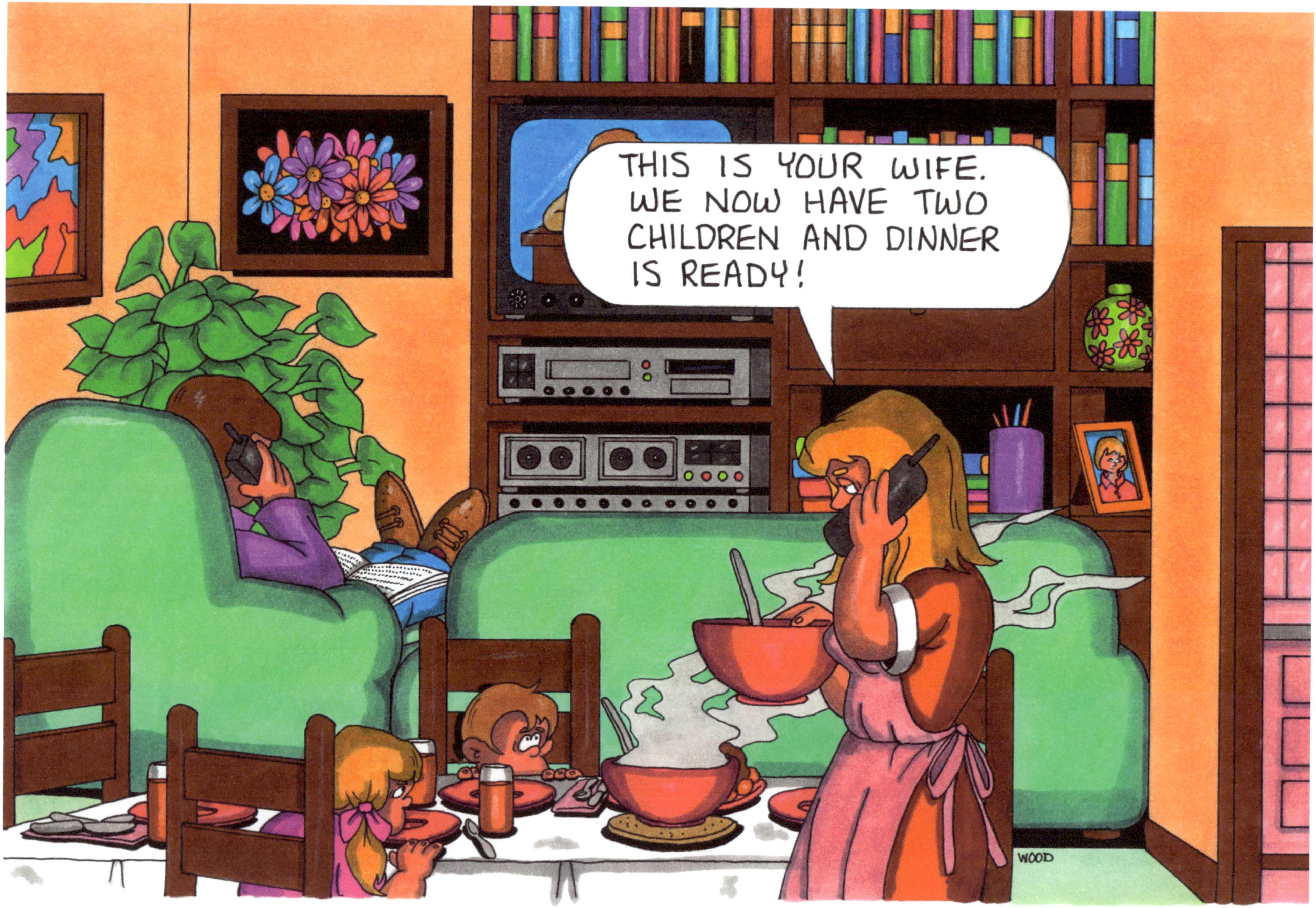
THIS IS YOUR WIFE. WE NOW HAVE TWO CHILDREN AND DINNER IS READY!
WOOD

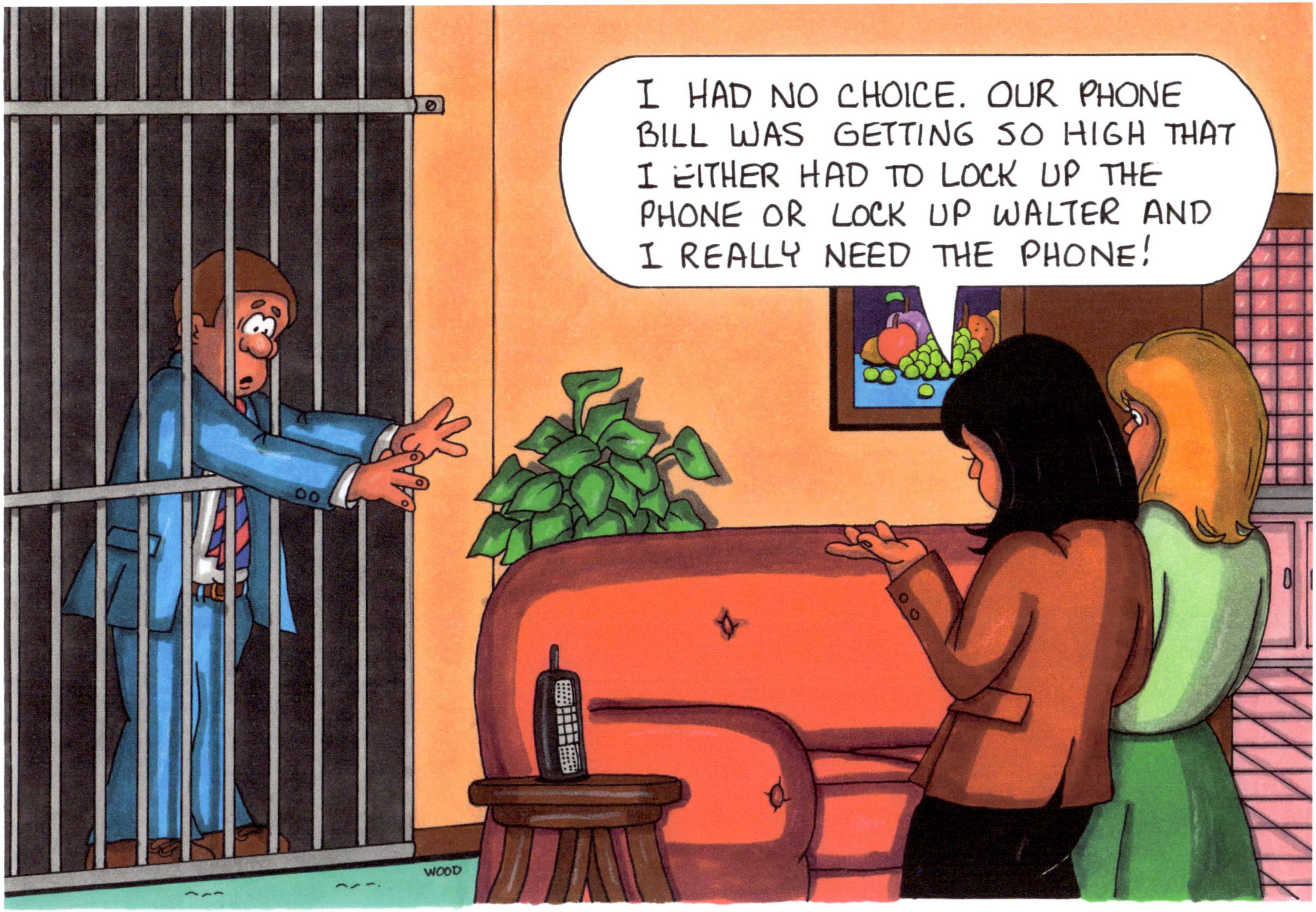
I HAD NO CHOICE. OUR PHONE BILL WAS GETTING SO HIGH THAT I EITHER HAD TO LOCK UP THE PHONE OR LOCK UP WALTER AND I REALLY NEED THE PHONE!
WOOD

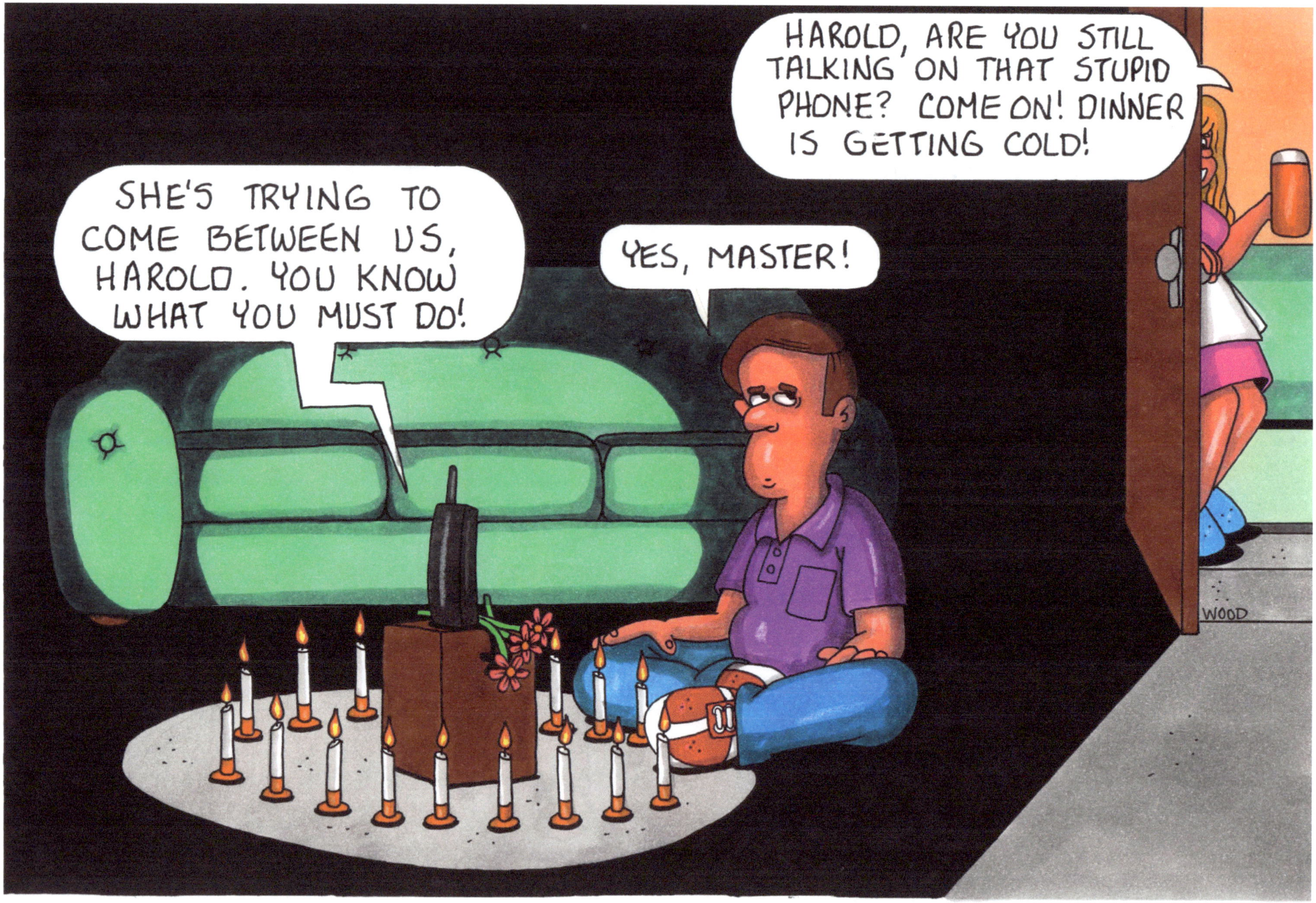
HAROLD, ARE YOU STILL TALKING ON THAT STUPID PHONE? COME ON! DINNER IS GETTING COLD!
SHE'S TRYING TO COME BETWEEN US, HAROLD. YOU KNOW WHAT YOU MUST DO!
YES, MASTER!
WOOD

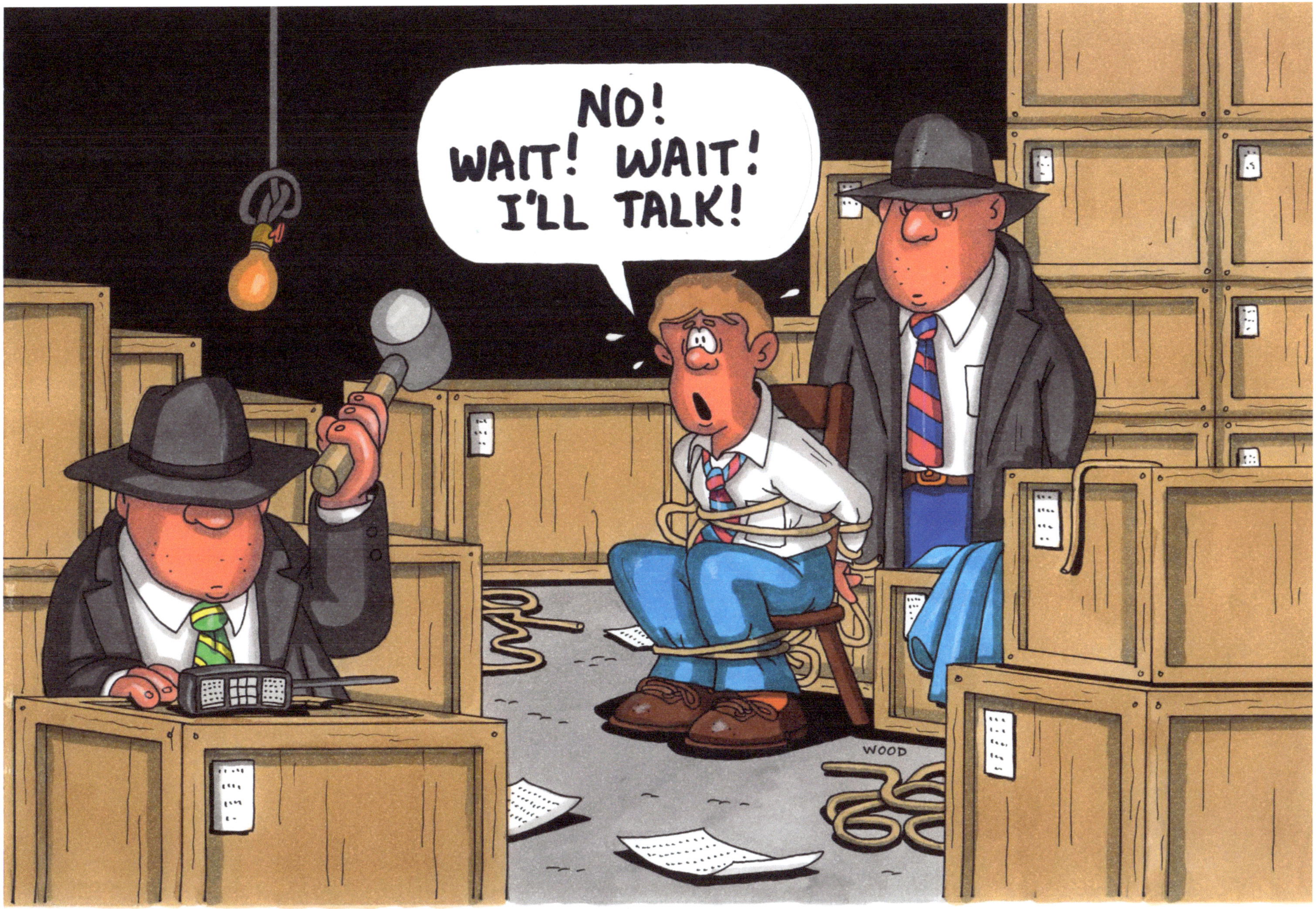
NO!
WAIT! WAIT!
I'LL TALK!
WOOD

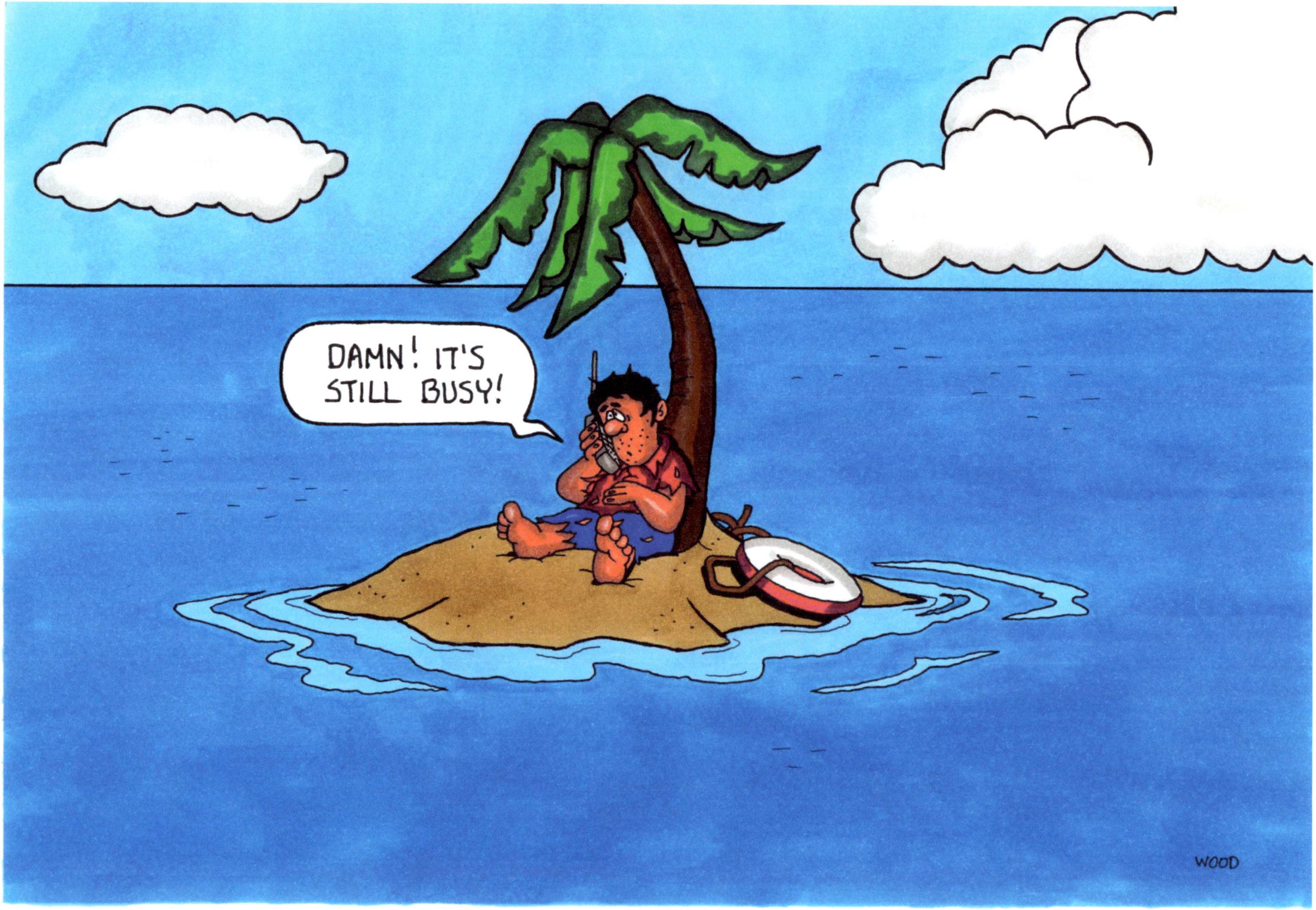
DAMN! IT'S STILL BUSY!
WOOD

Scott Wood

The Animal Kingdom

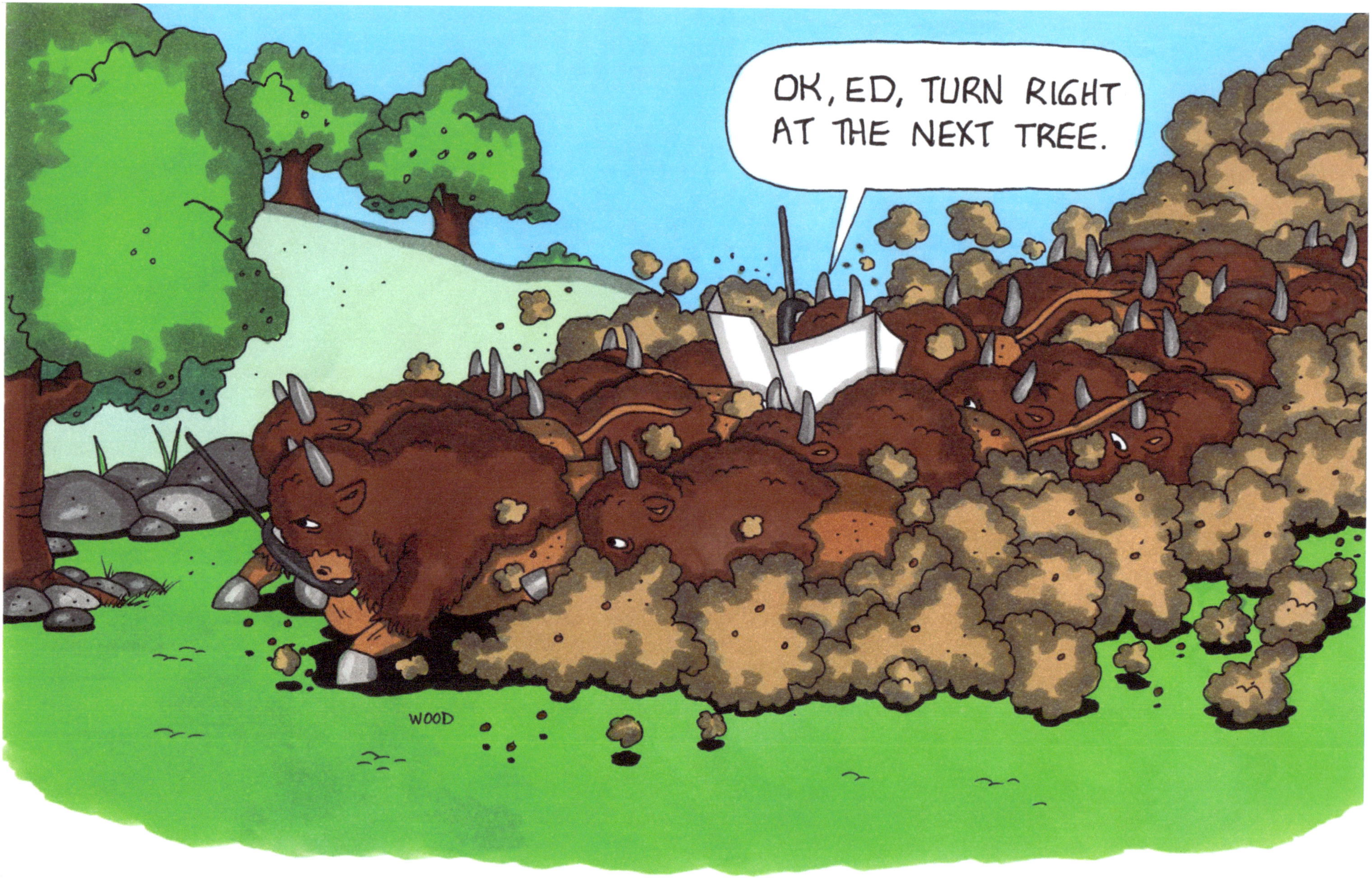
OK, ED, TURN RIGHT AT THE NEXT TREE.
WOOD

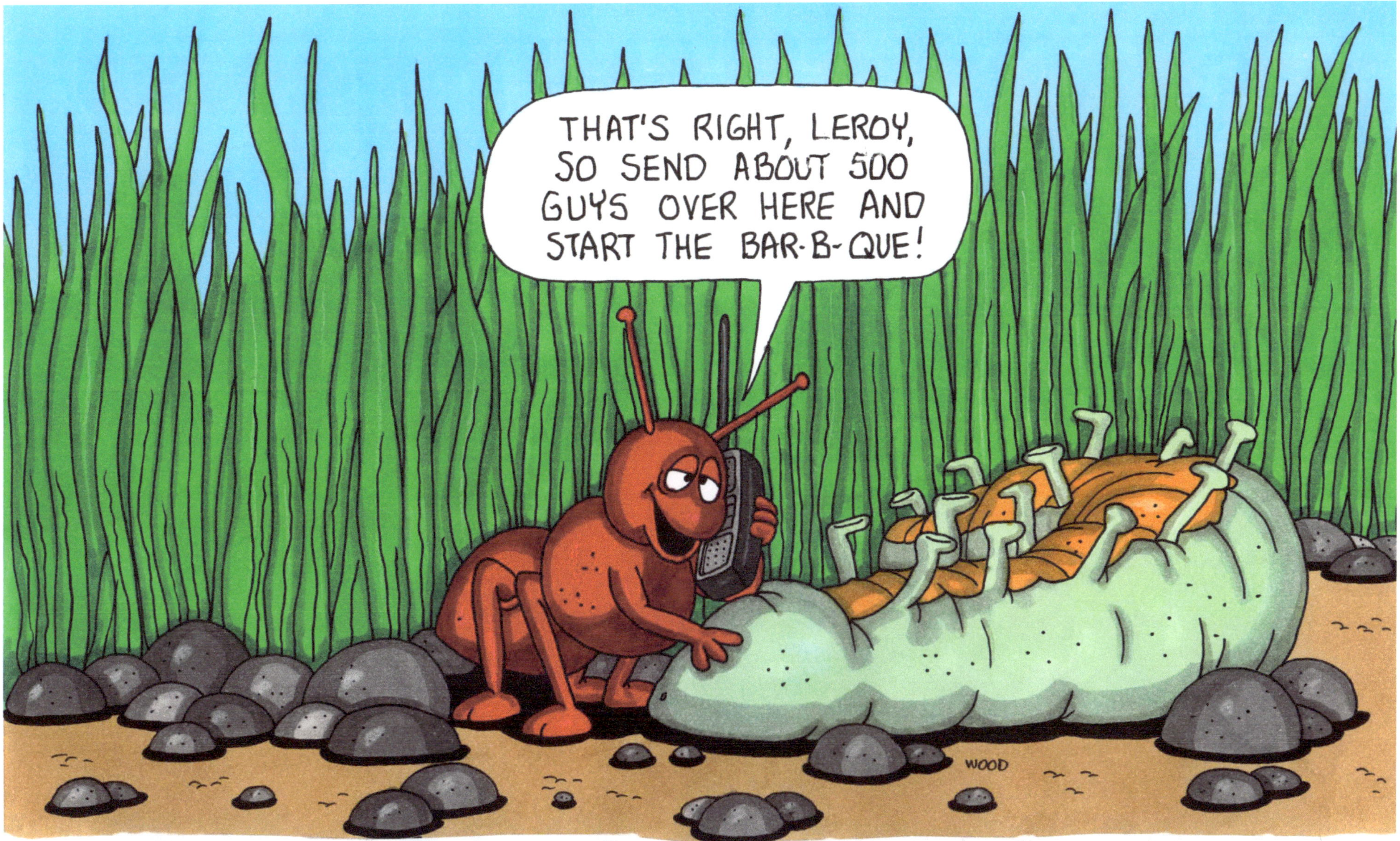
THAT'S RIGHT, LEROY, SO SEND ABOUT 500 GUYS OVER HERE AND START THE BAR-B-QUE!
WOOD

HOW ANTS COMMUNICATE

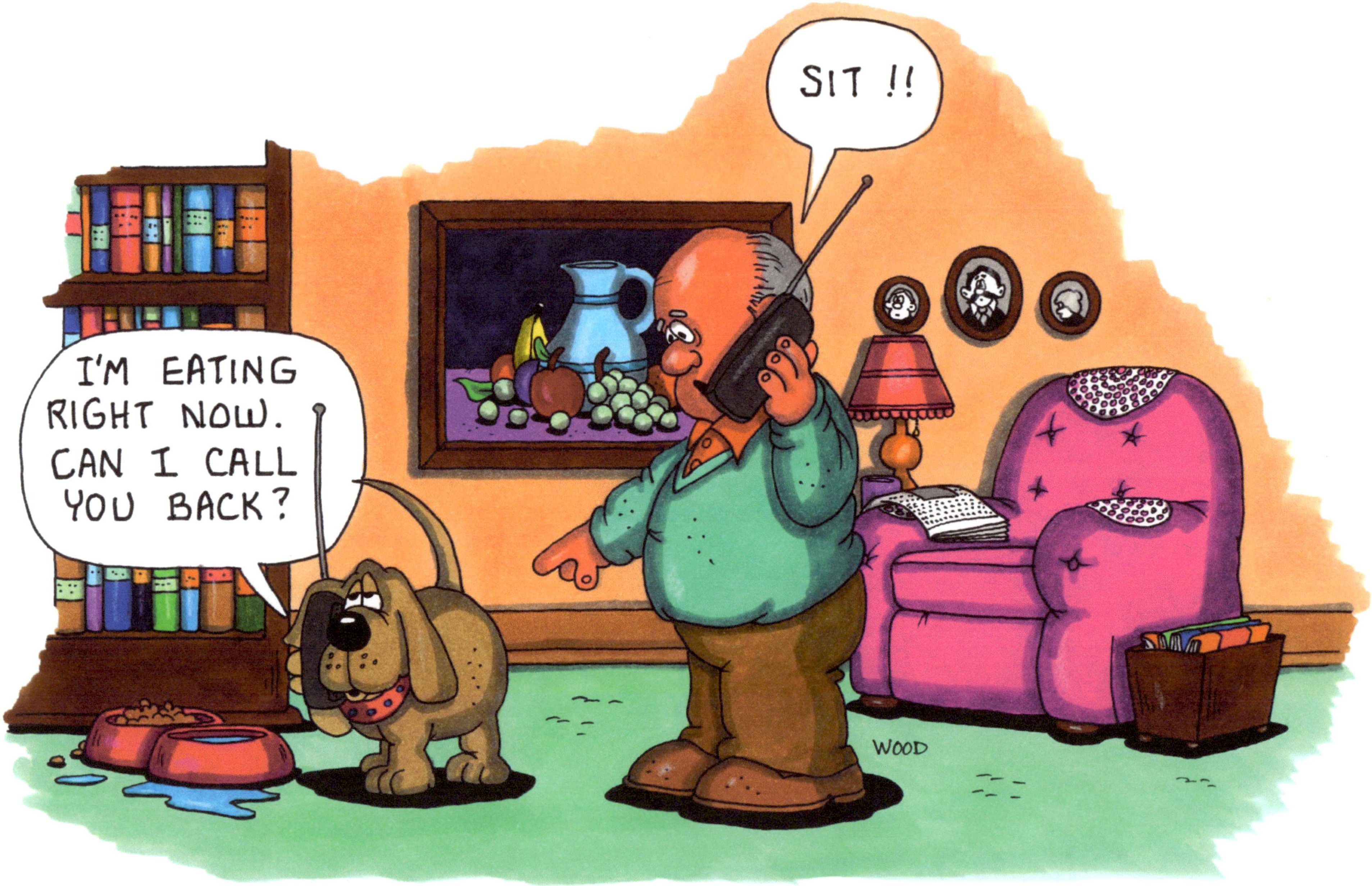
SIT !!
I'M EATING RIGHT NOW. CAN I CALL YOU BACK?
WOOD

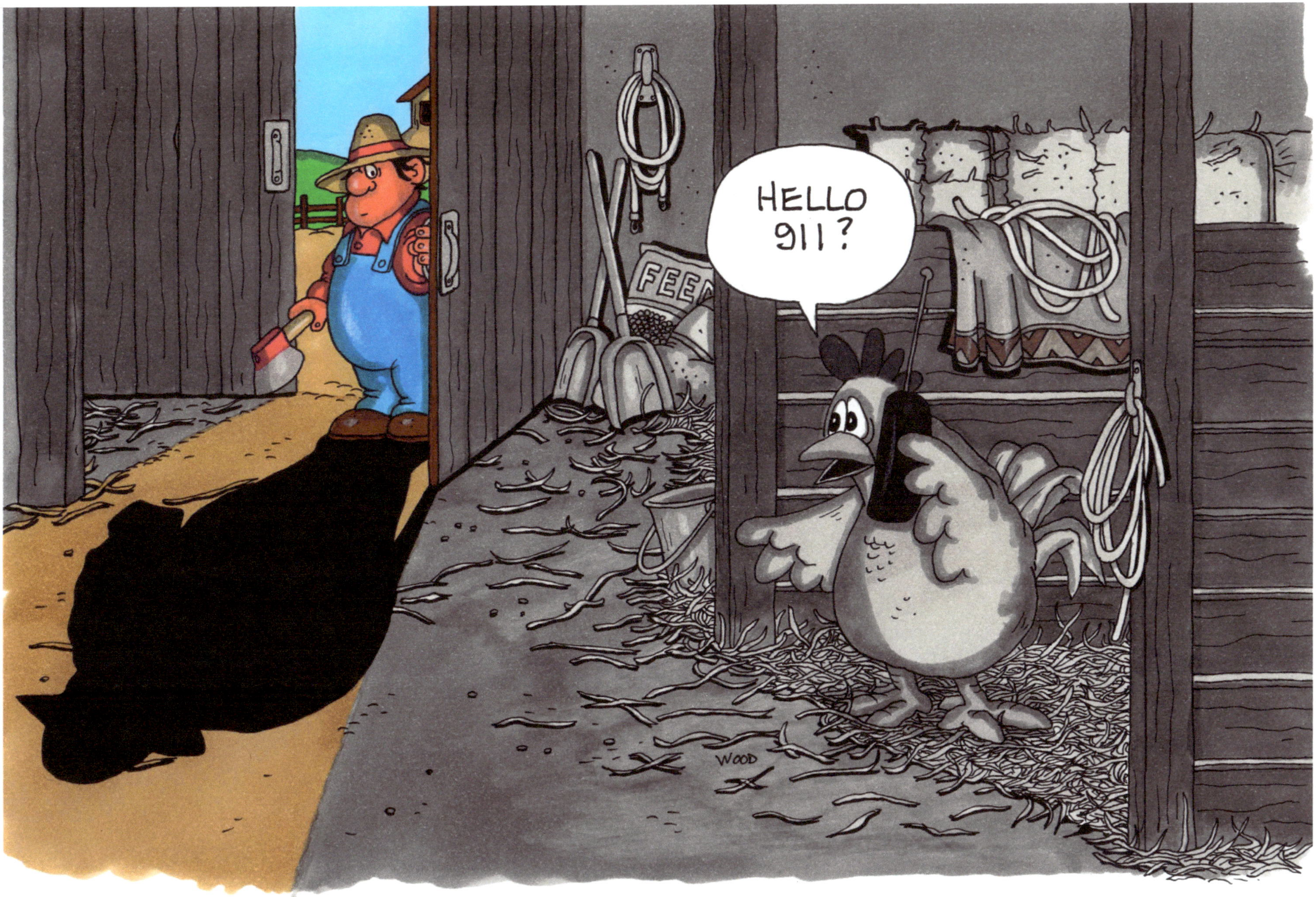
HELLO
911?
FEED
WOOD

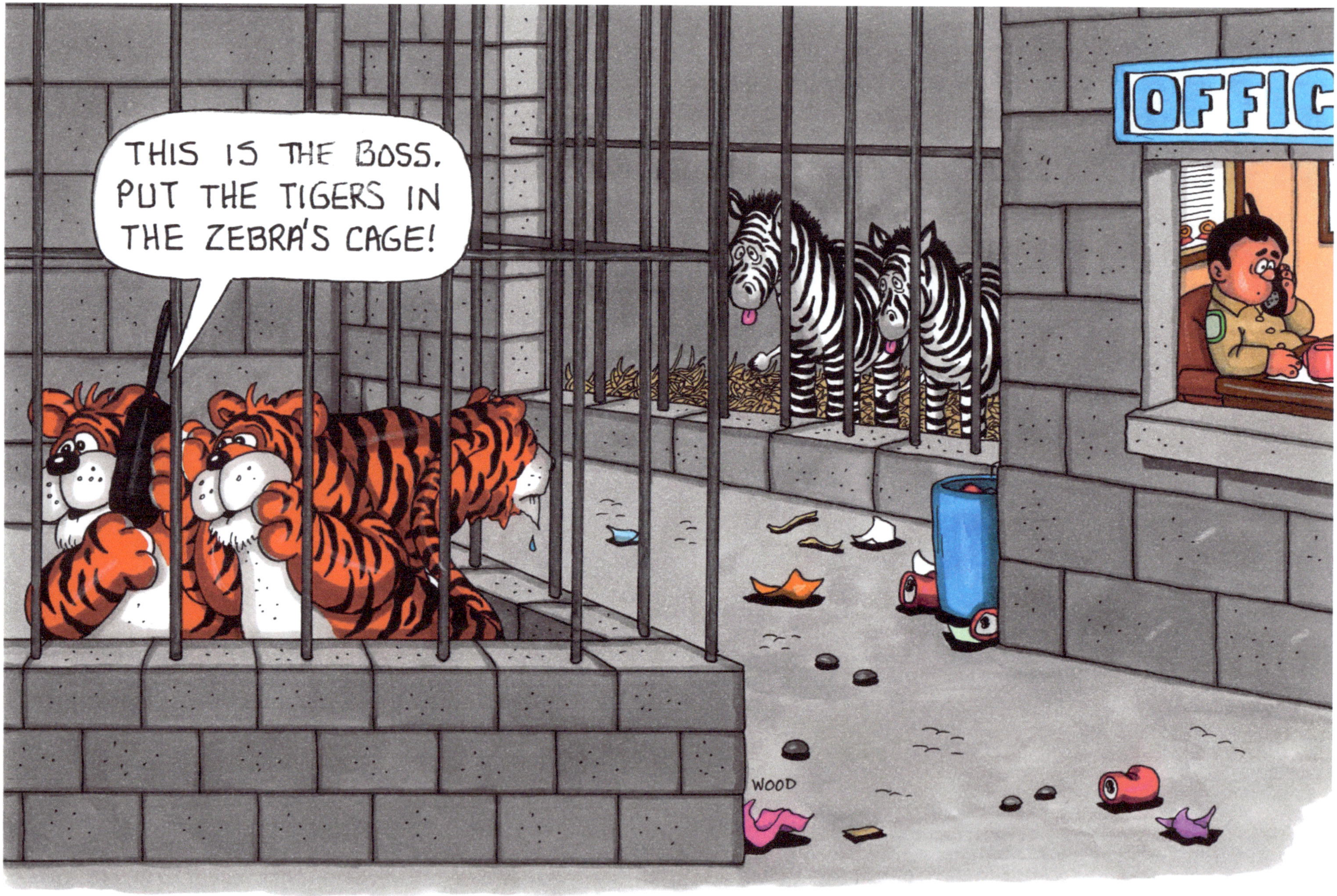
OFFIC
THIS IS THE BOSS. PUT THE TIGERS IN THE ZEBRA'S CAGE!
WOOD

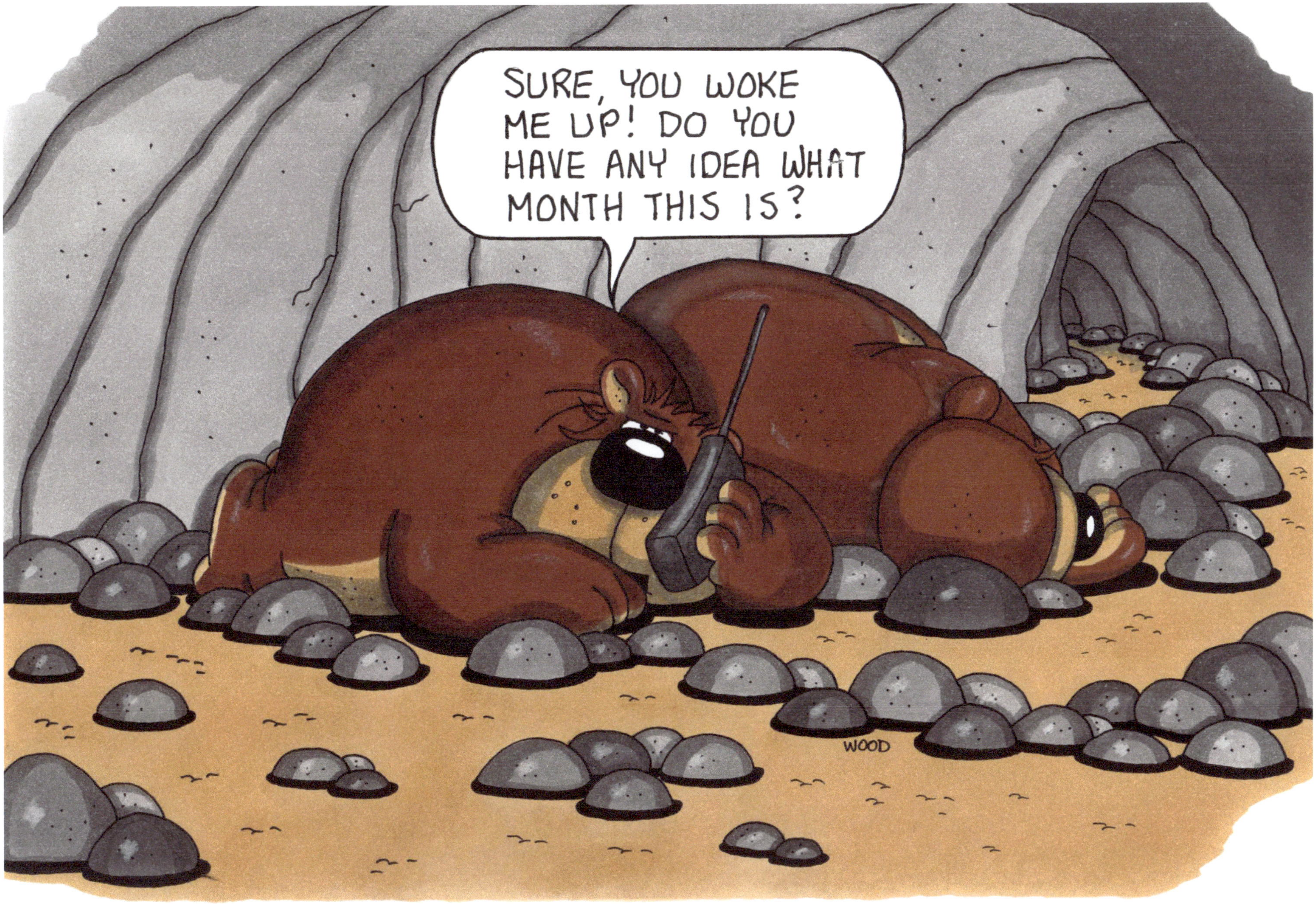
SURE, YOU WOKE ME UP! DO YOU HAVE ANY IDEA WHAT MONTH THIS IS?
WOOD

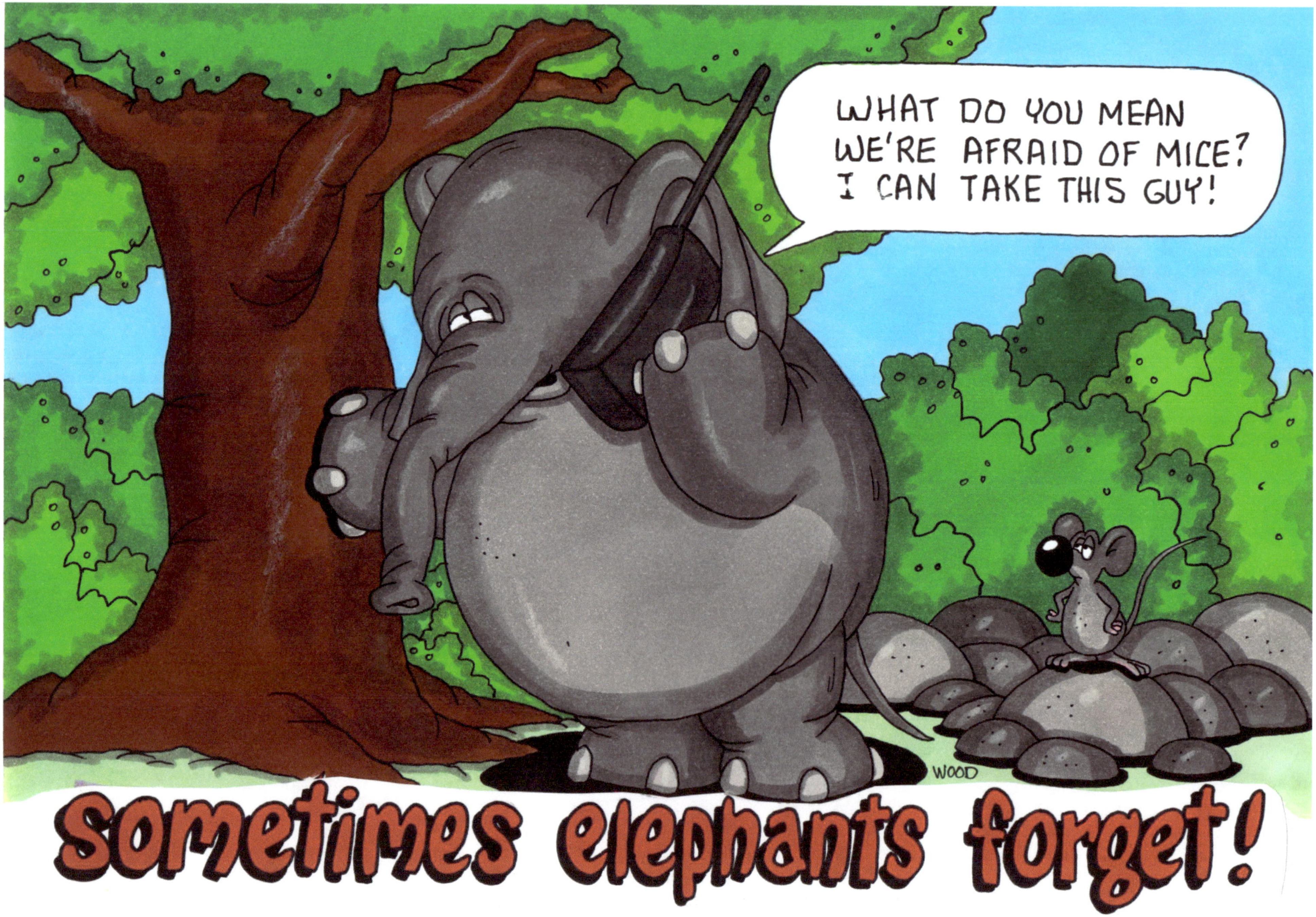
WHAT DO YOU MEAN WE'RE AFRAID OF MICE? I CAN TAKE THIS GUY!
WOOD
sometimes elephants forget!

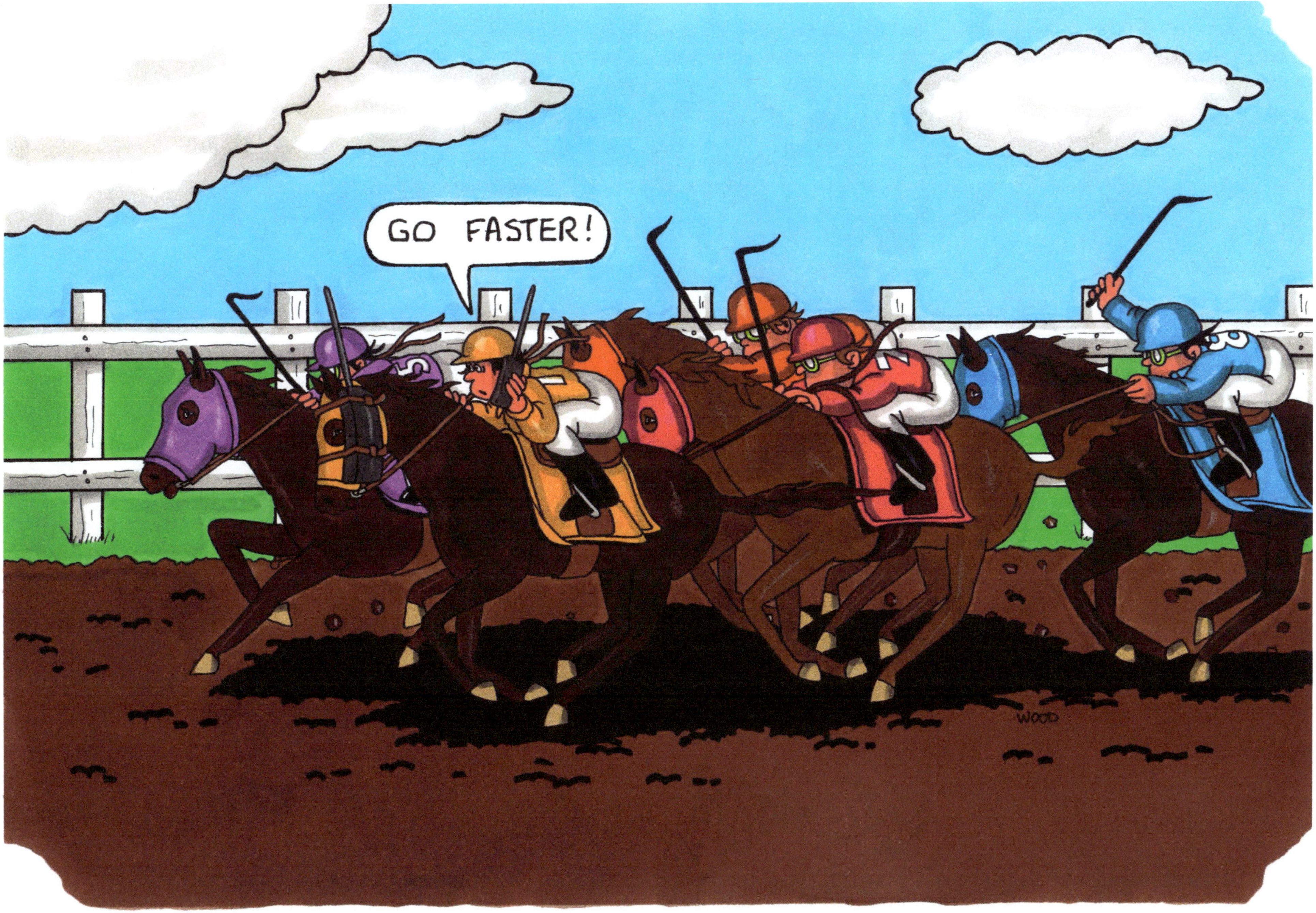
GO FASTER!
WOOD

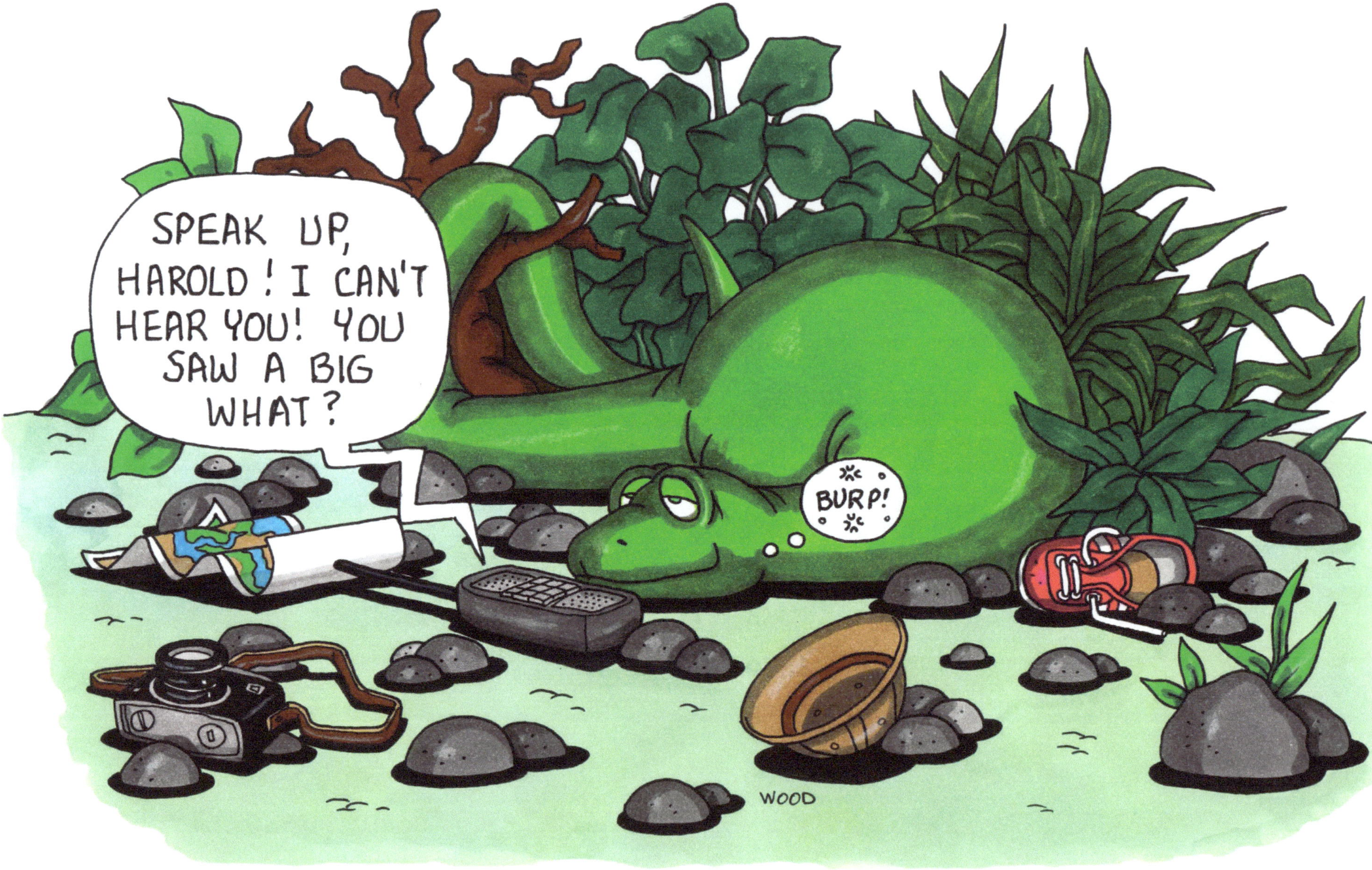
SPEAK UP, HAROLD! I CAN'T HEAR YOU! YOU SAW A BIG WHAT?
BURP!
WOOD

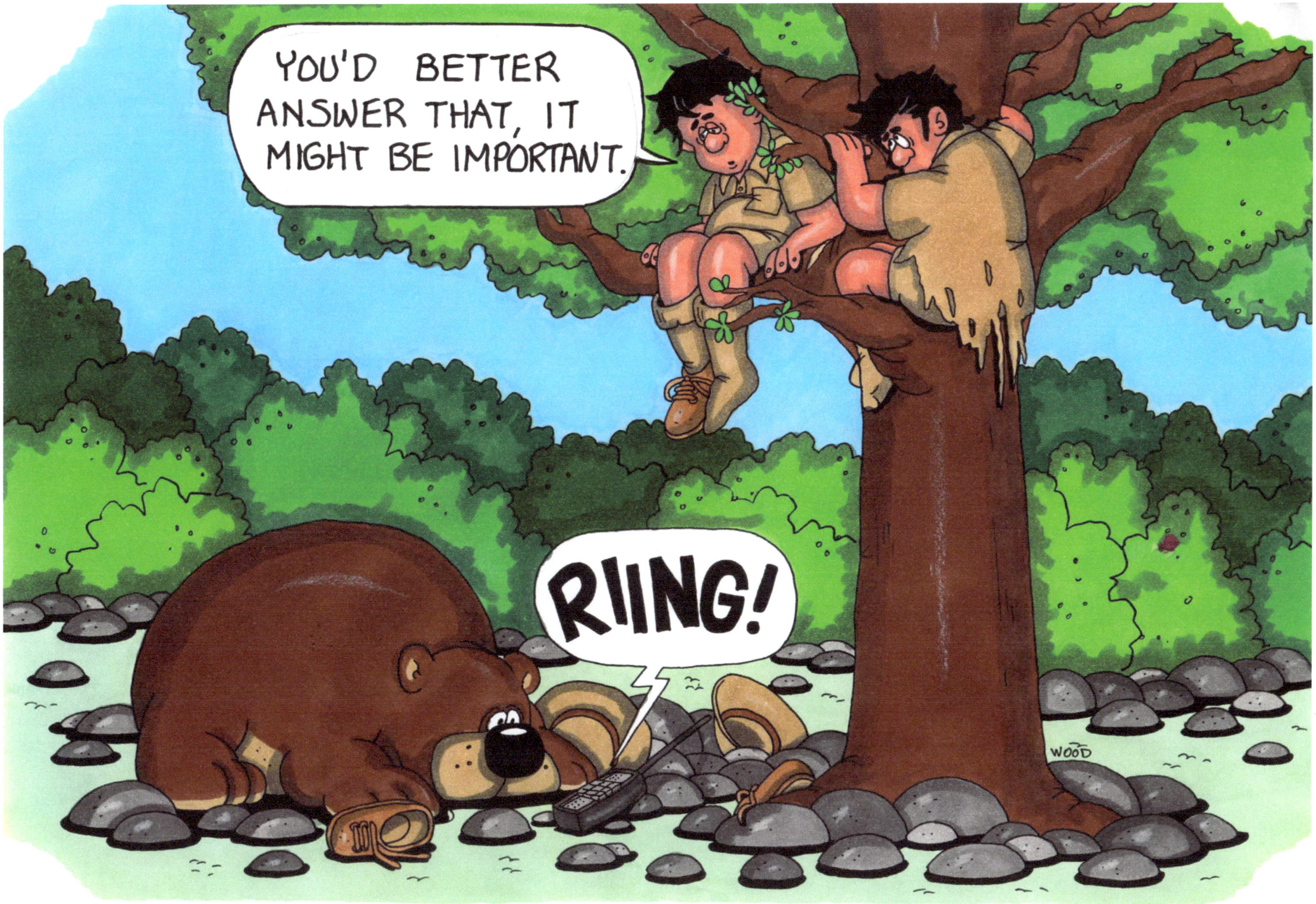
YOU'D BETTER ANSWER THAT, IT MIGHT BE IMPORTANT.
RIING!
WOOD

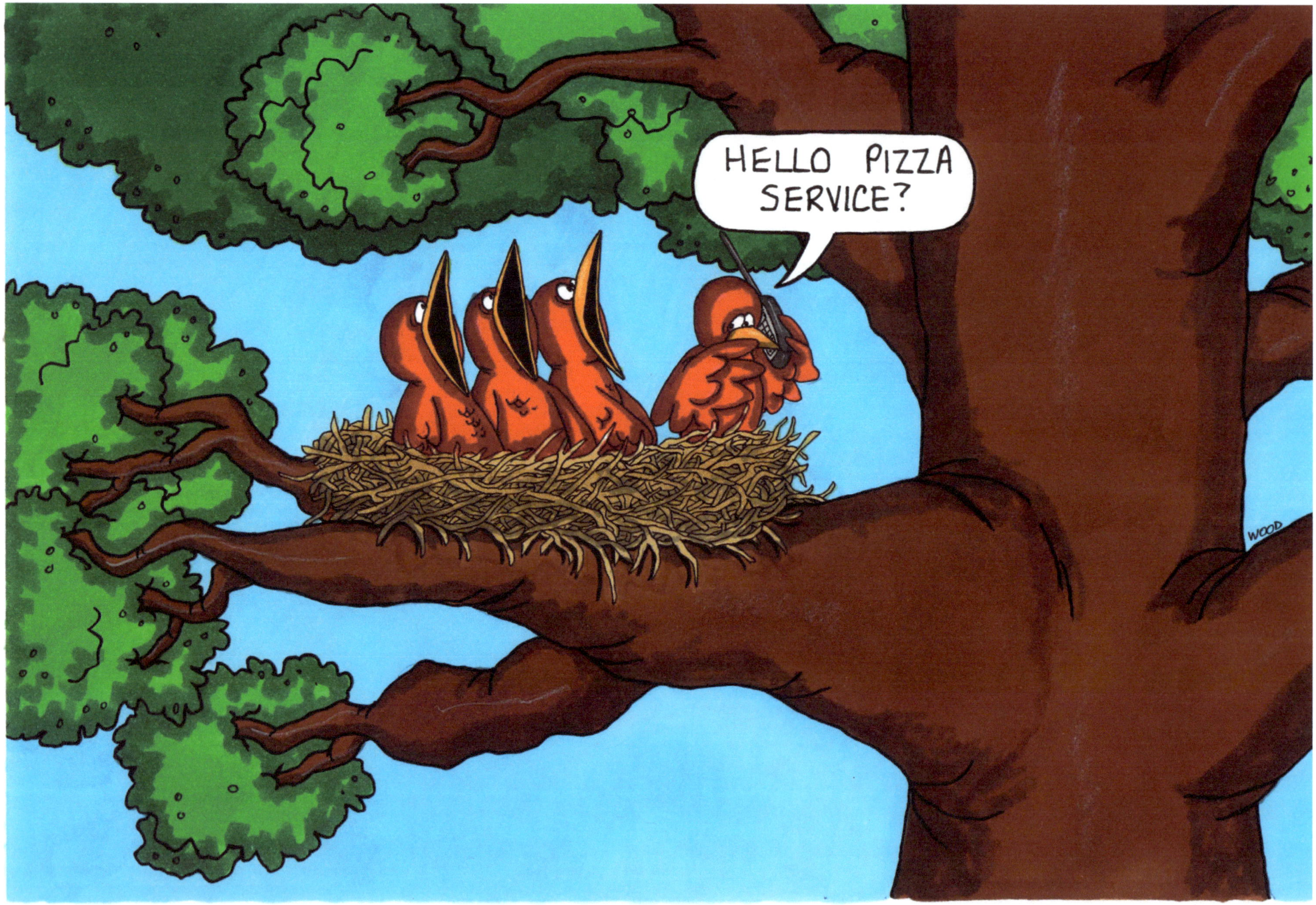
HELLO PIZZA SERVICE?
WOOD

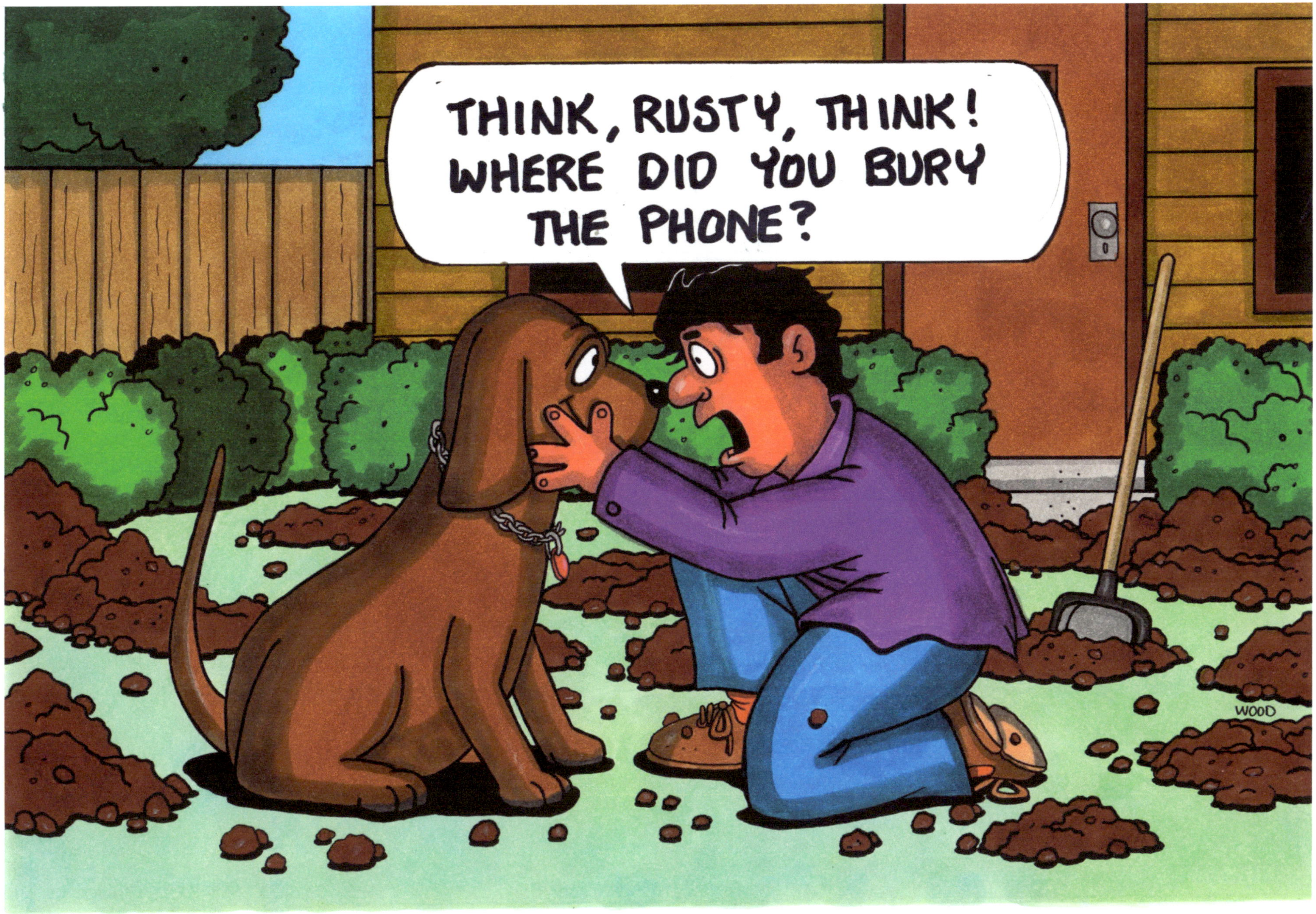
THINK, RUSTY, THINK! WHERE DID YOU BURY THE PHONE?
WOOD

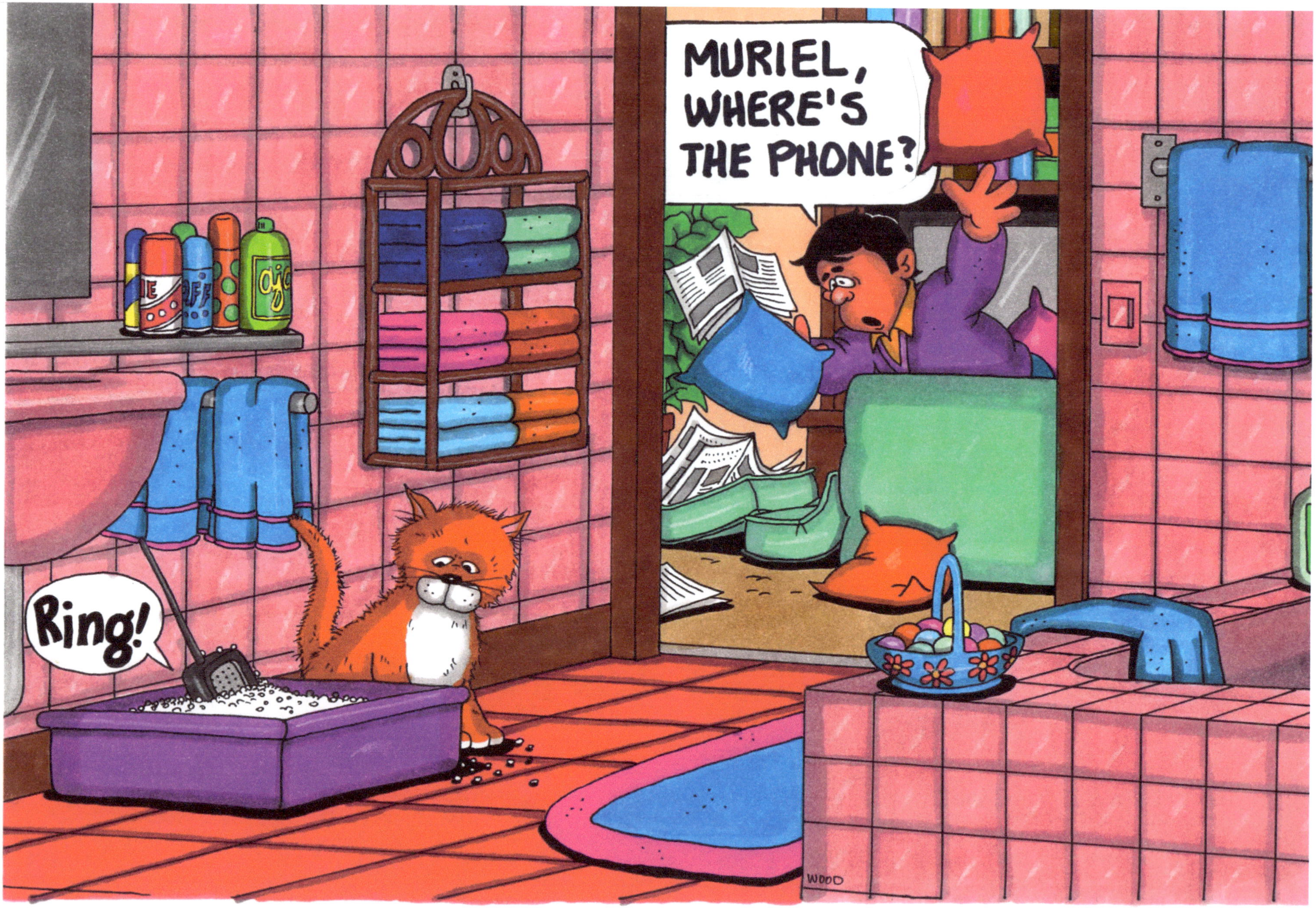
MURIEL, WHERE'S THE PHONE?
Ring!
WOOD

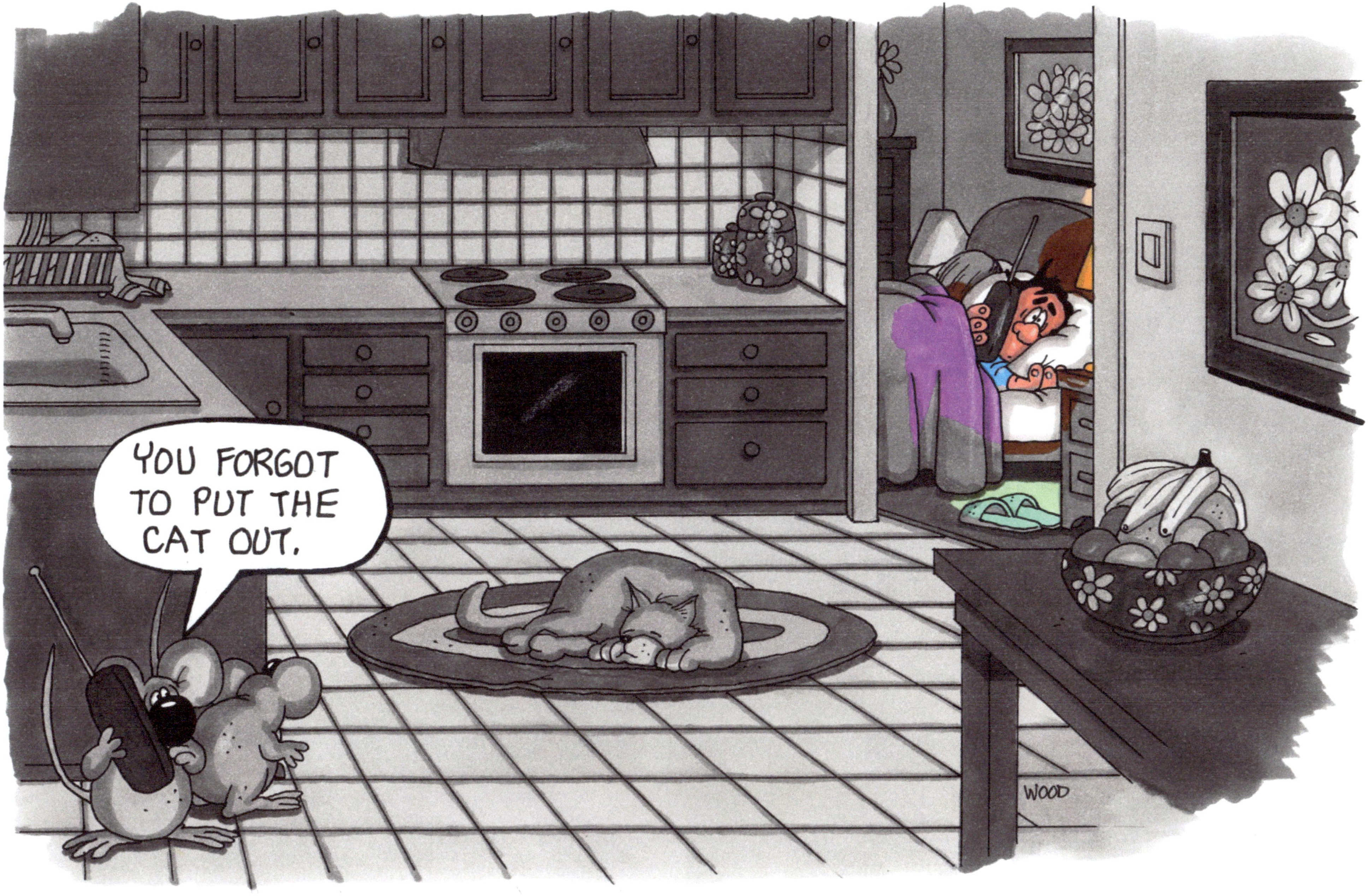
YOU FORGOT TO PUT THE CAT OUT.
WOOD

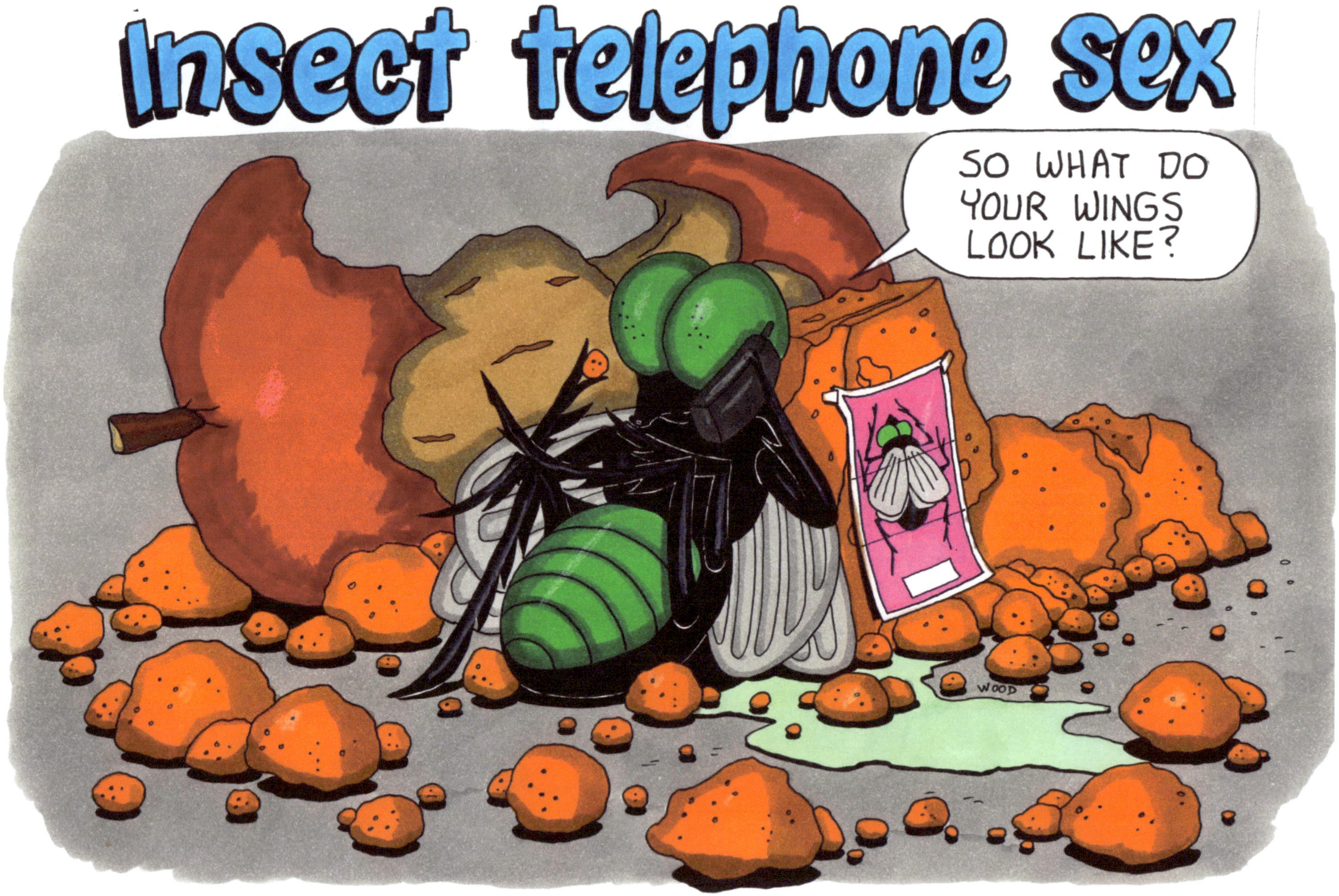
Insect telephone sex
SO WHAT DO YOUR WINGS LOOK LIKE?
WOOD

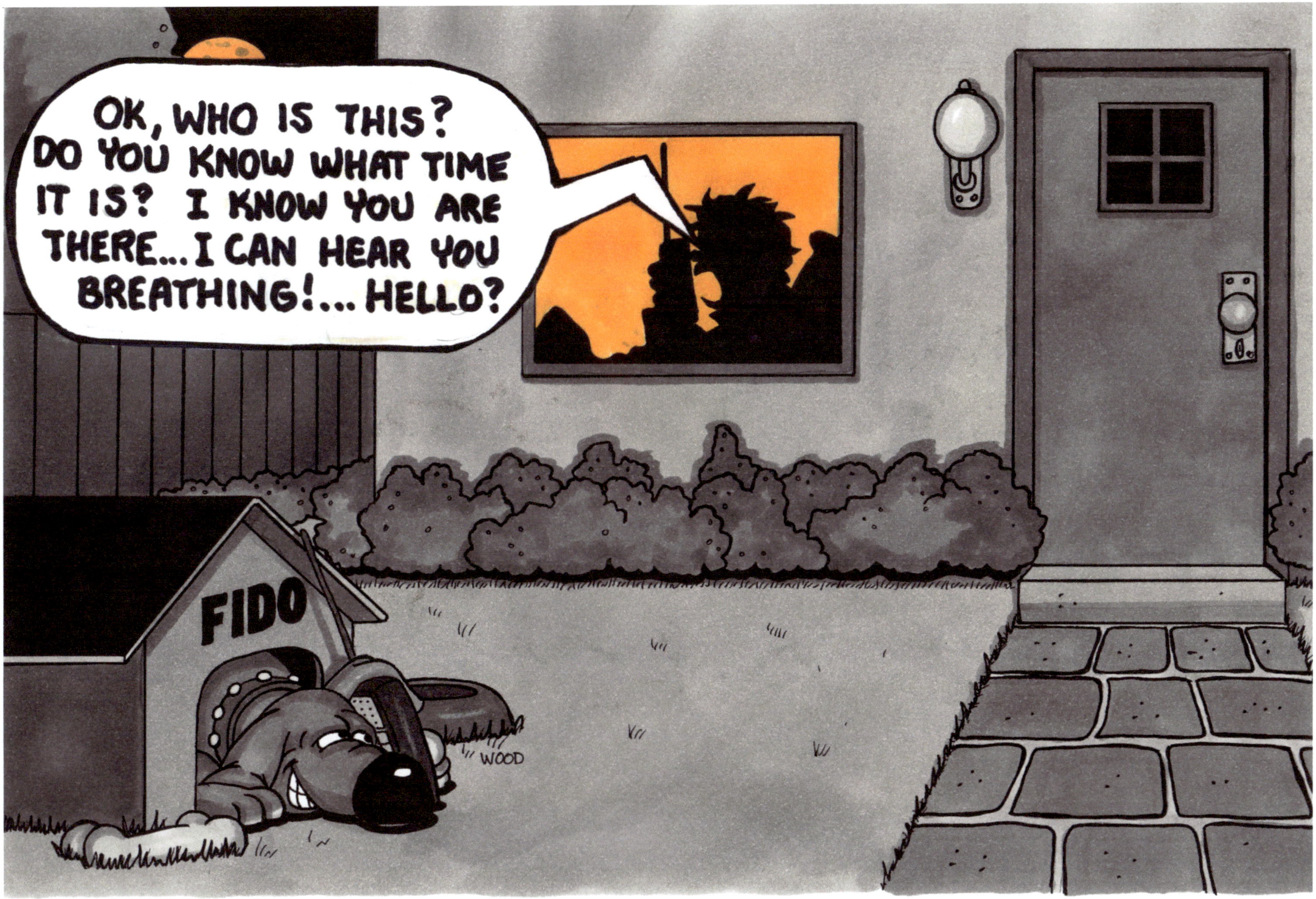
OK, WHO IS THIS? DO YOU KNOW WHAT TIME IT IS? I KNOW YOU ARE THERE...I CAN HEAR YOU BREATHING!... HELLO?
FIDO
WOOD

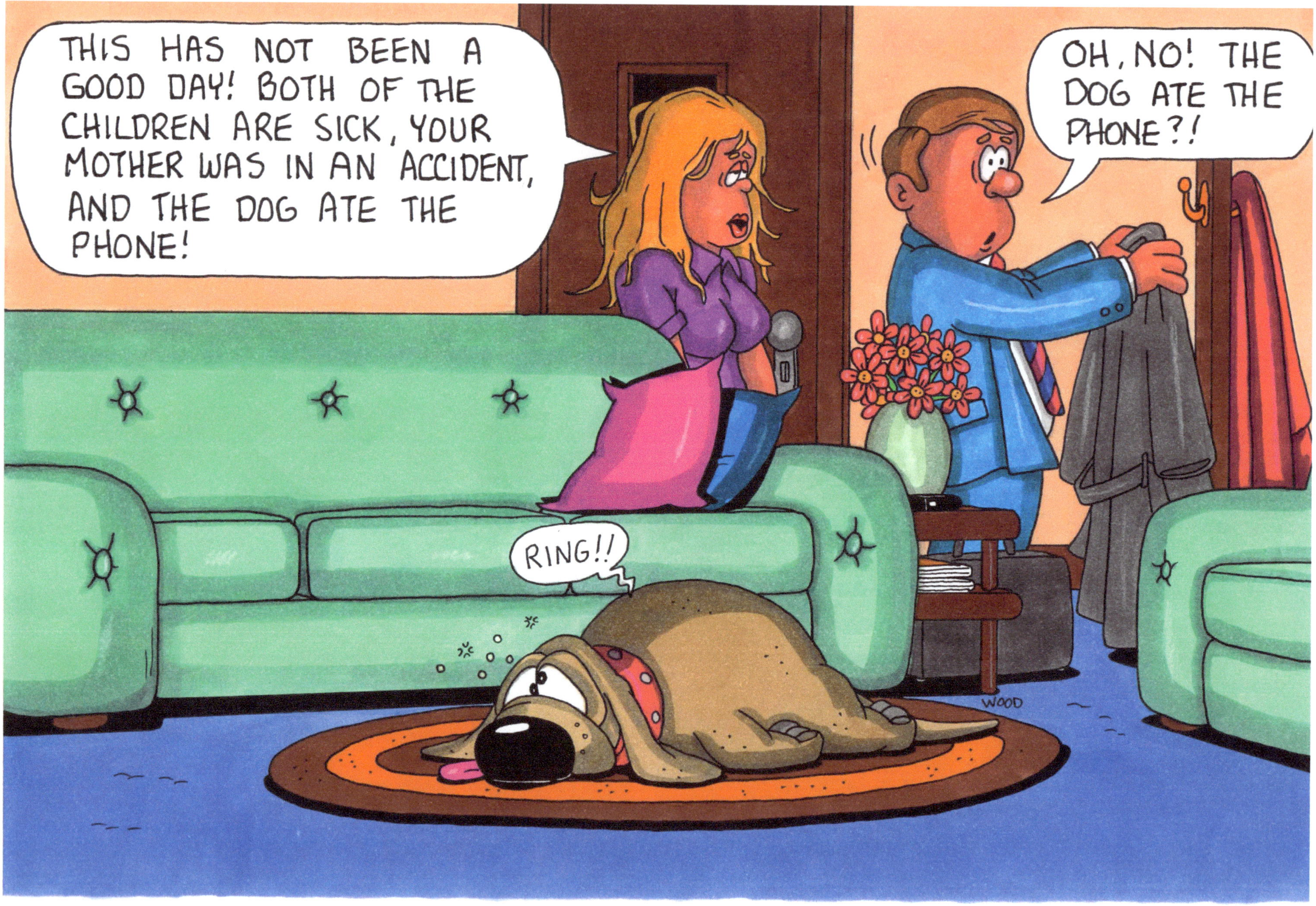
THIS HAS NOT BEEN A GOOD DAY! BOTH OF THE CHILDREN ARE SICK, YOUR MOTHER WAS IN AN ACCIDENT, AND THE DOG ATE THE PHONE!
OH, NO! THE DOG ATE THE PHONE?!
RING!!
WOOD

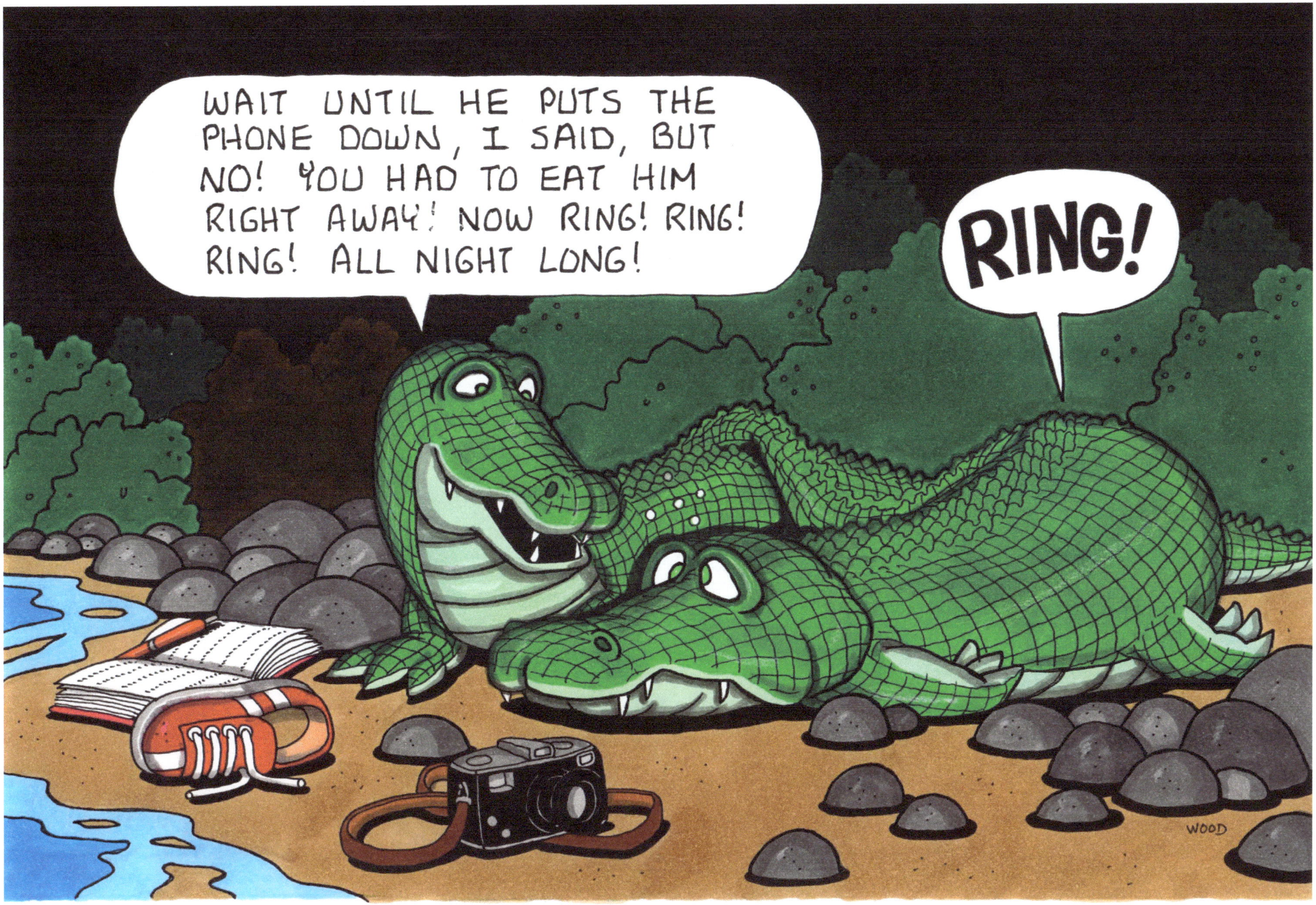
WAIT UNTIL HE PUTS THE PHONE DOWN, I SAID, BUT NO! YOU HAD TO EAT HIM RIGHT AWAY! NOW RING! RING! RING! ALL NIGHT LONG!
RING!
WOOD

The Cell Phone

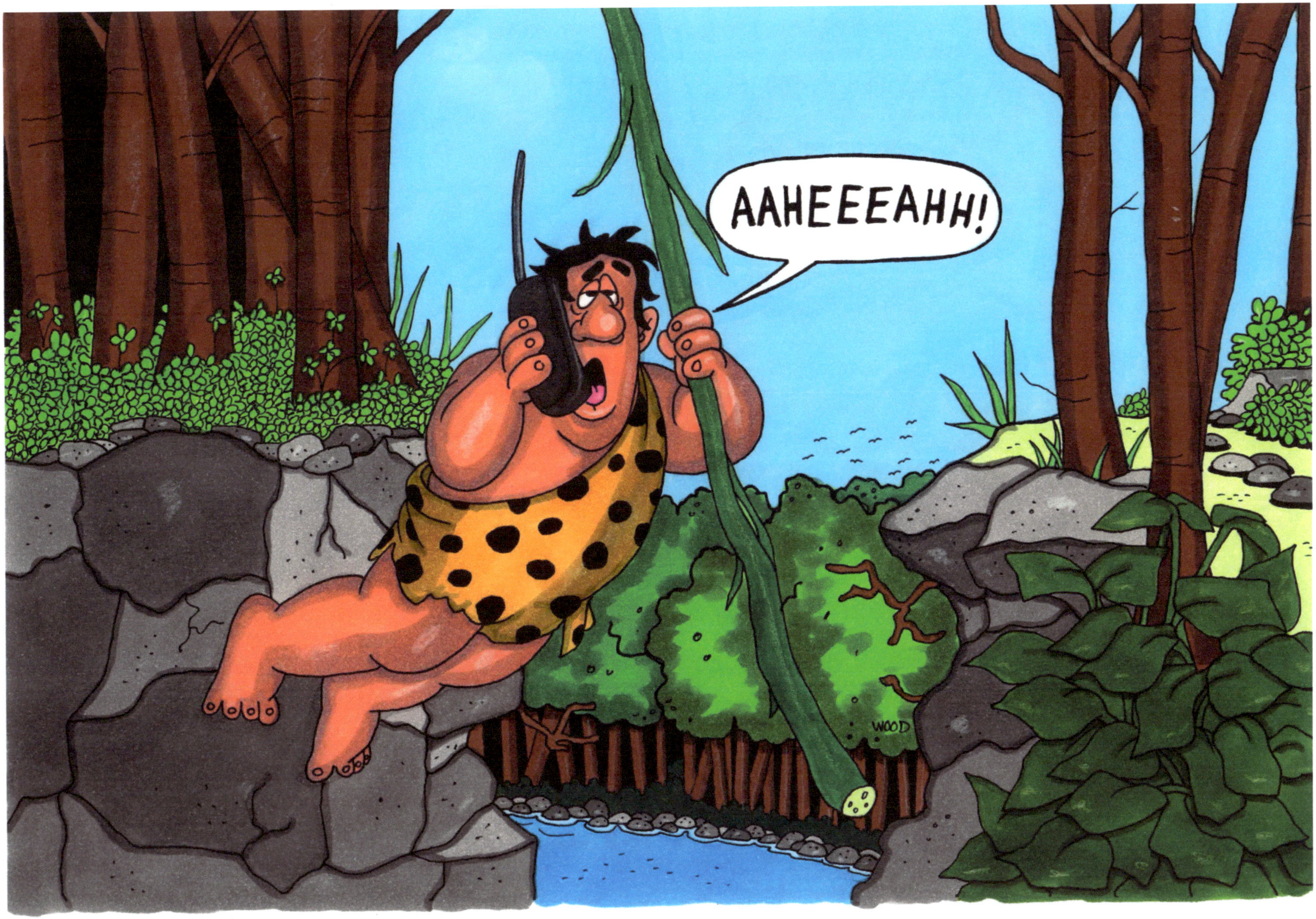
AAHEEEEAHH!
WOOD

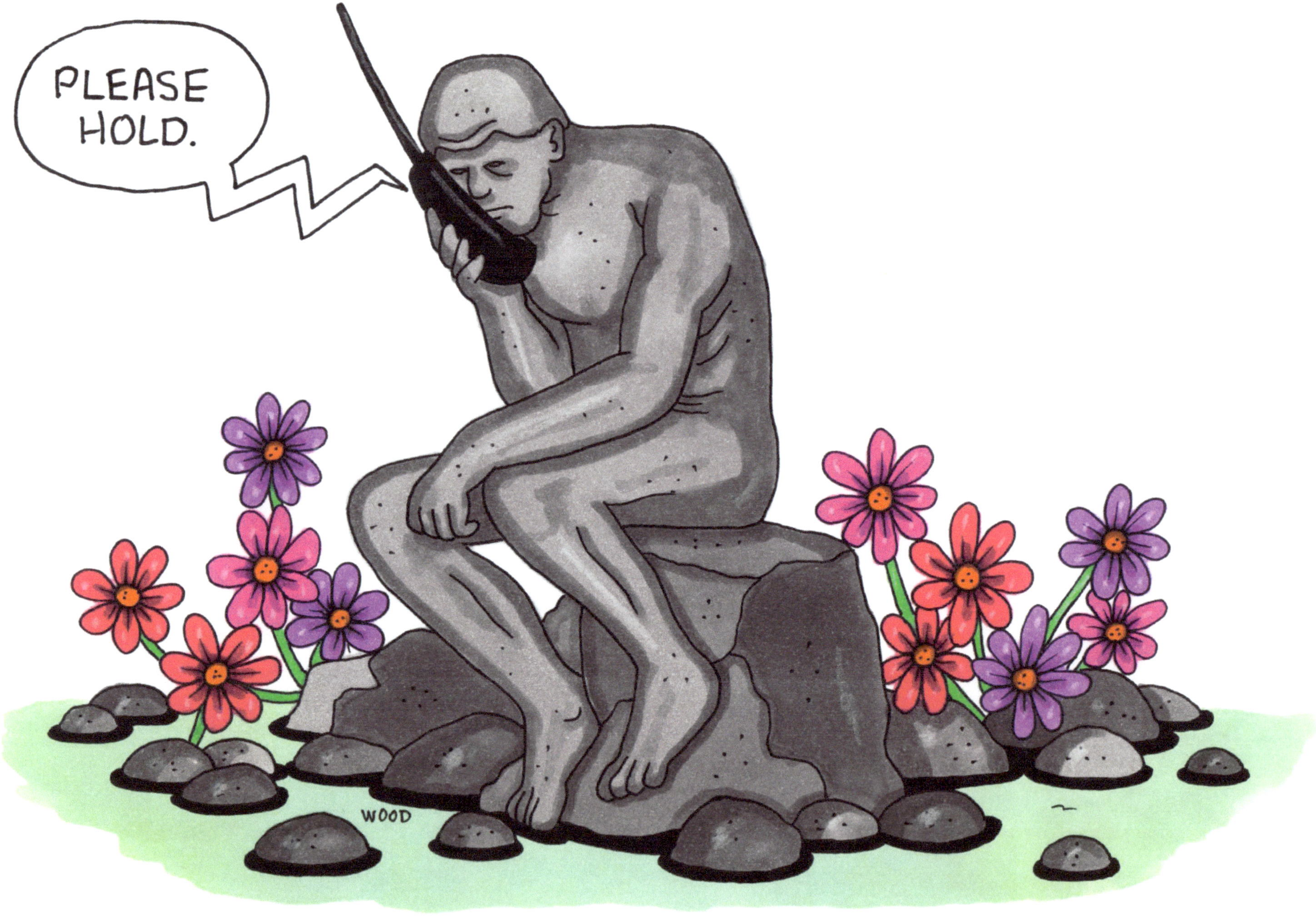
PLEASE HOLD.
WOOD

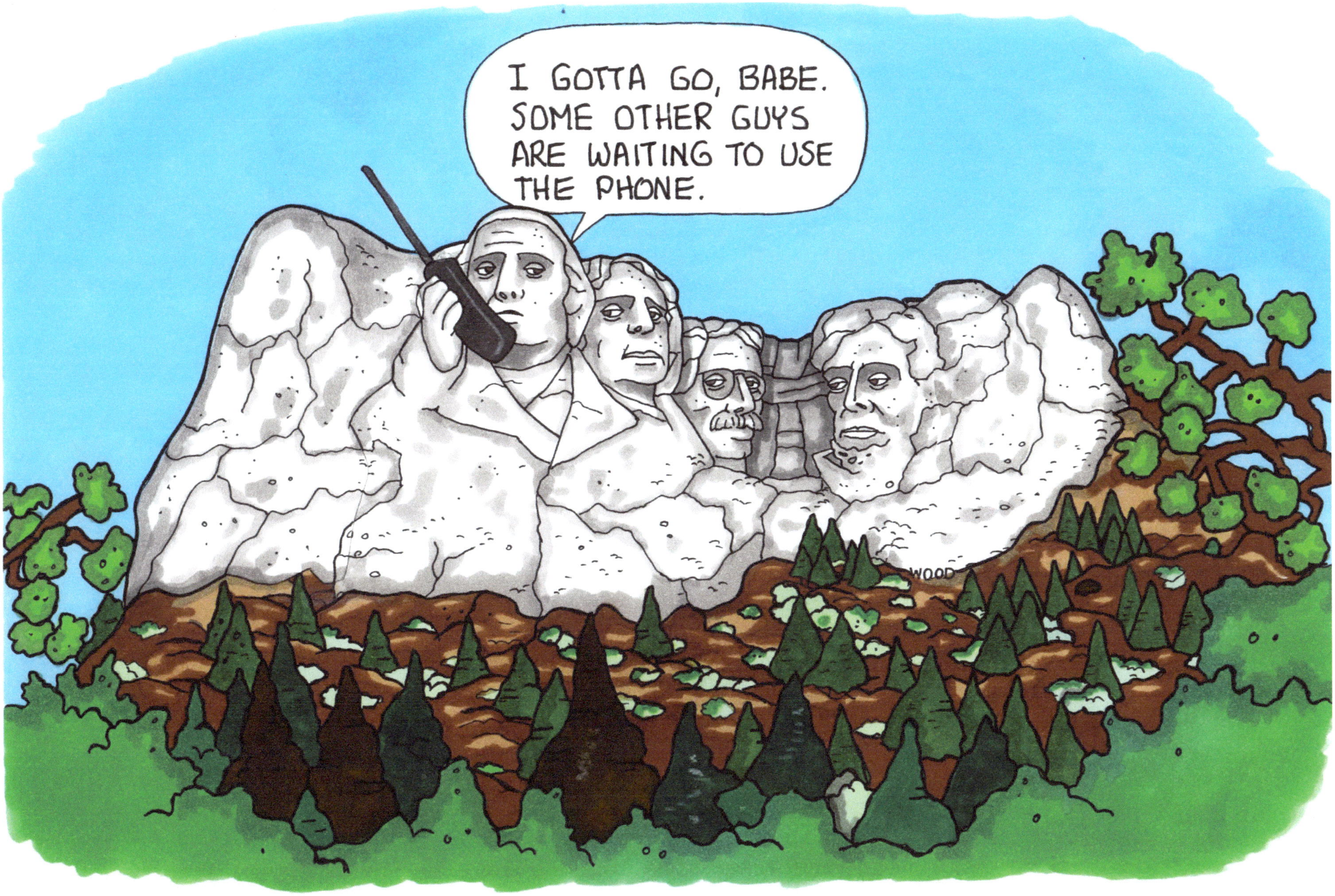
I GOTTA GO, BABE. SOME OTHER GUYS ARE WAITING TO USE THE PHONE.
WOOD

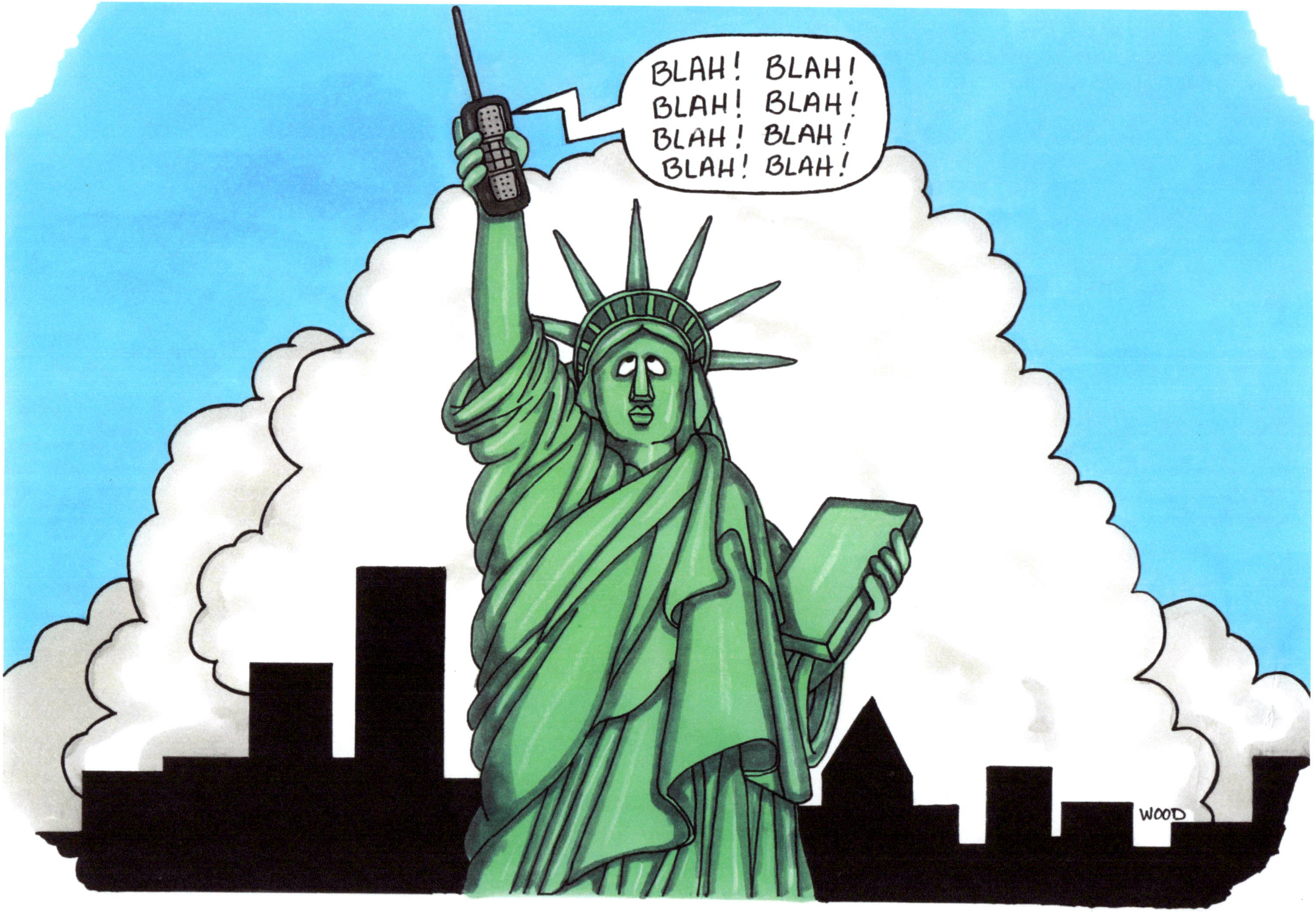
BLAH! BLAH! BLAH! BLAH! BLAH! BLAH! BLAH! BLAH!
WOOD

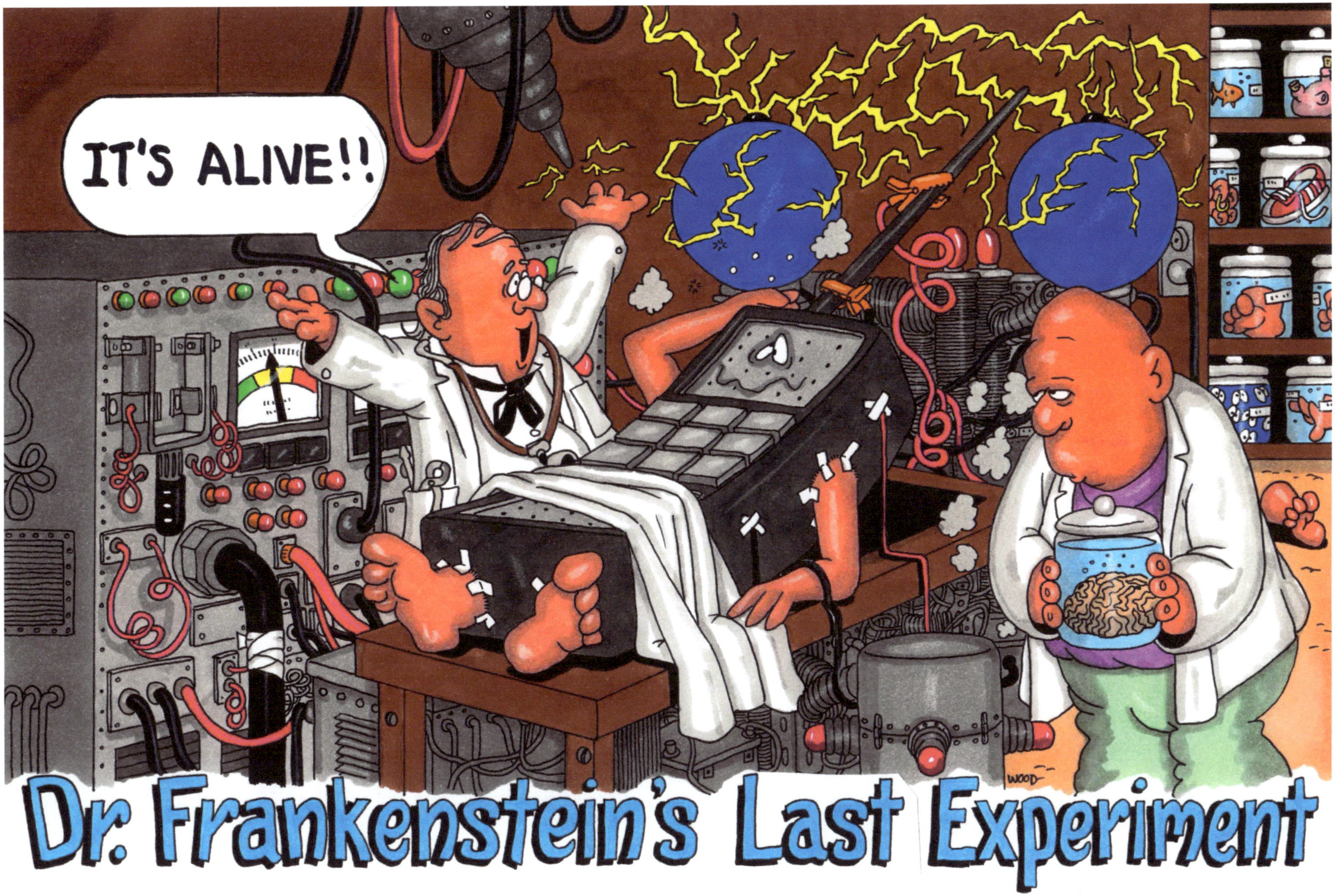
IT'S ALIVE!!
WOOD

Dr. Frankenstein's Last Experiment

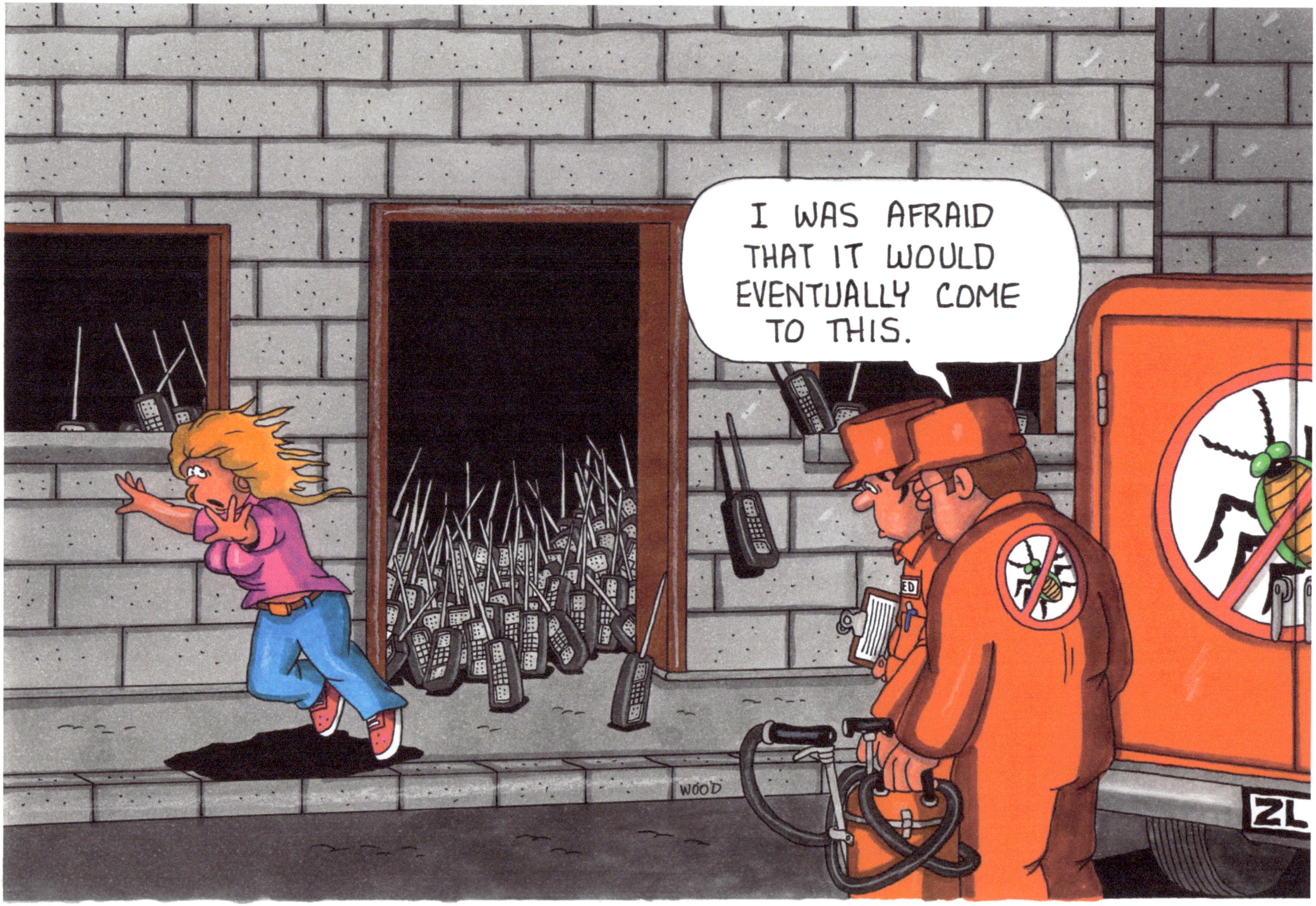
I WAS AFRAID THAT IT WOULD EVENTUALLY COME TO THIS.
WOOD

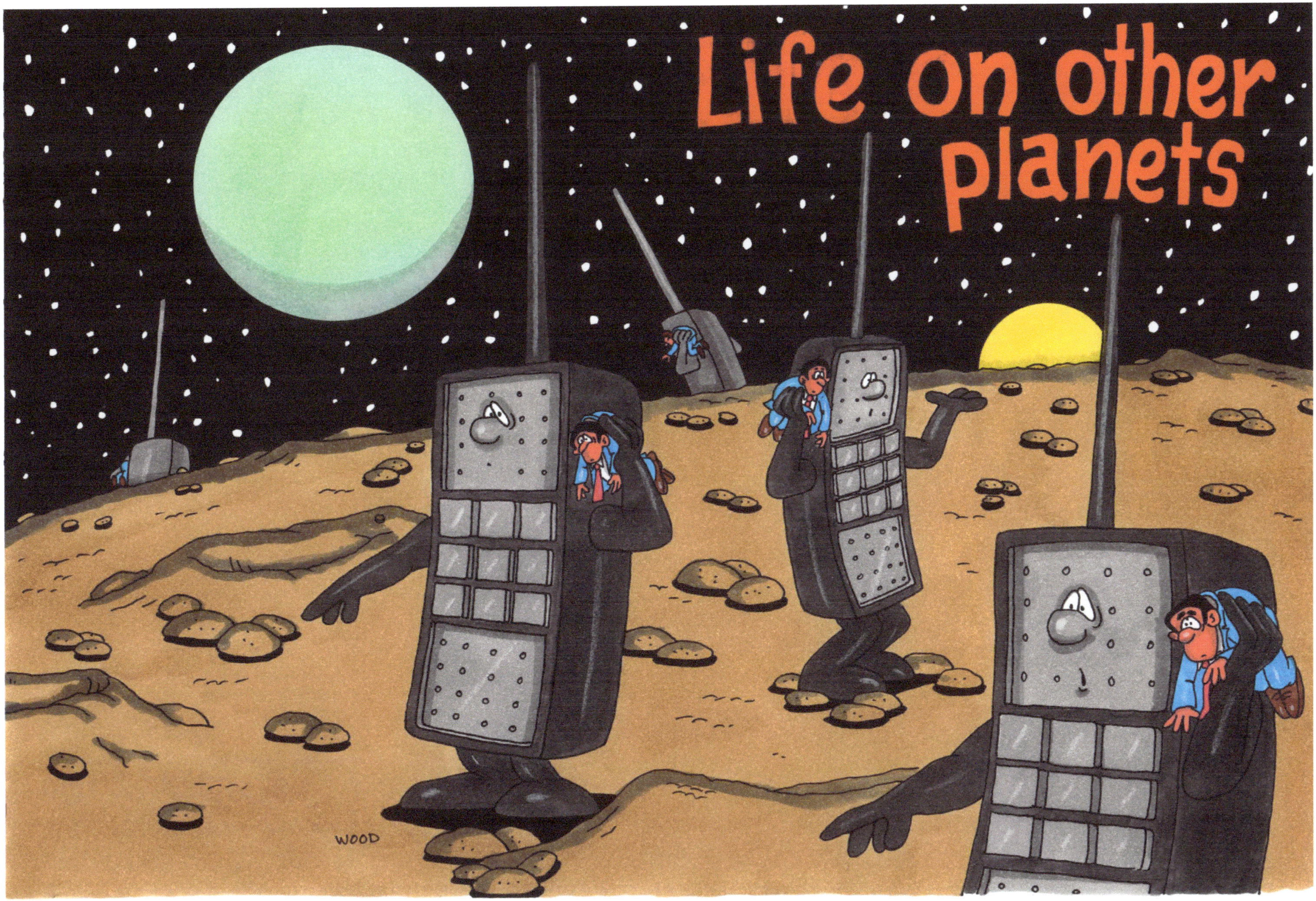
Life on other planets
WOOD

And Finally...

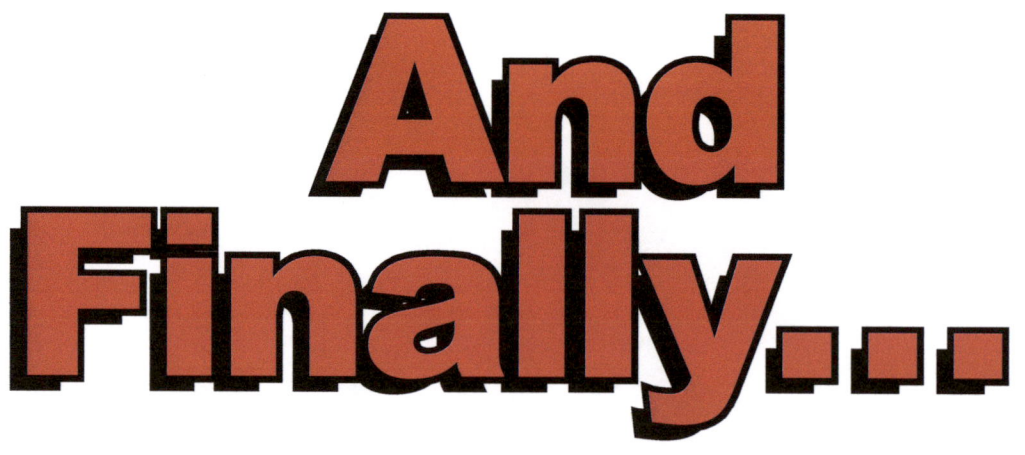

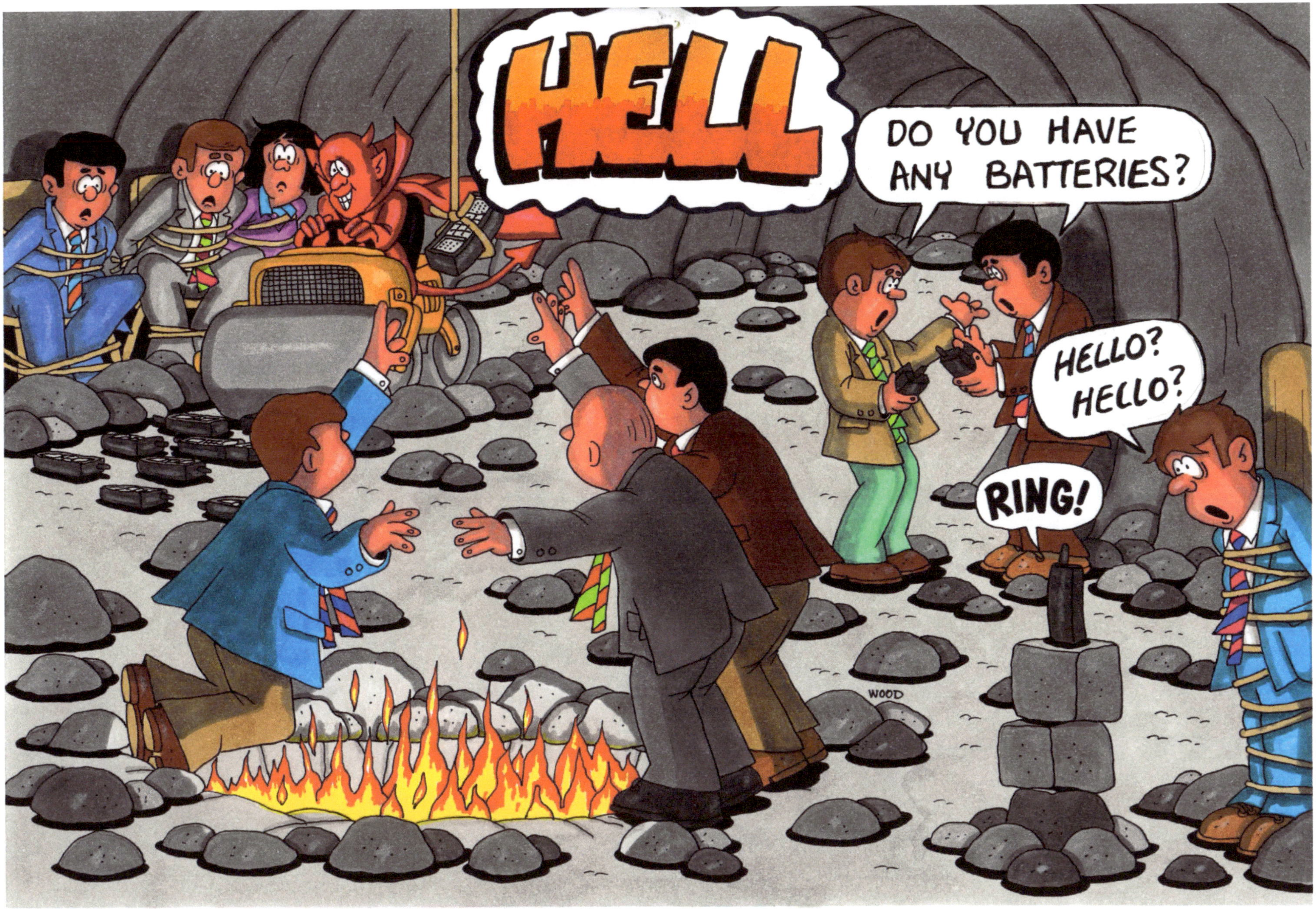
HELL
DO YOU HAVE ANY BATTERIES?
HELLO? HELLO?
RING!
WOOD

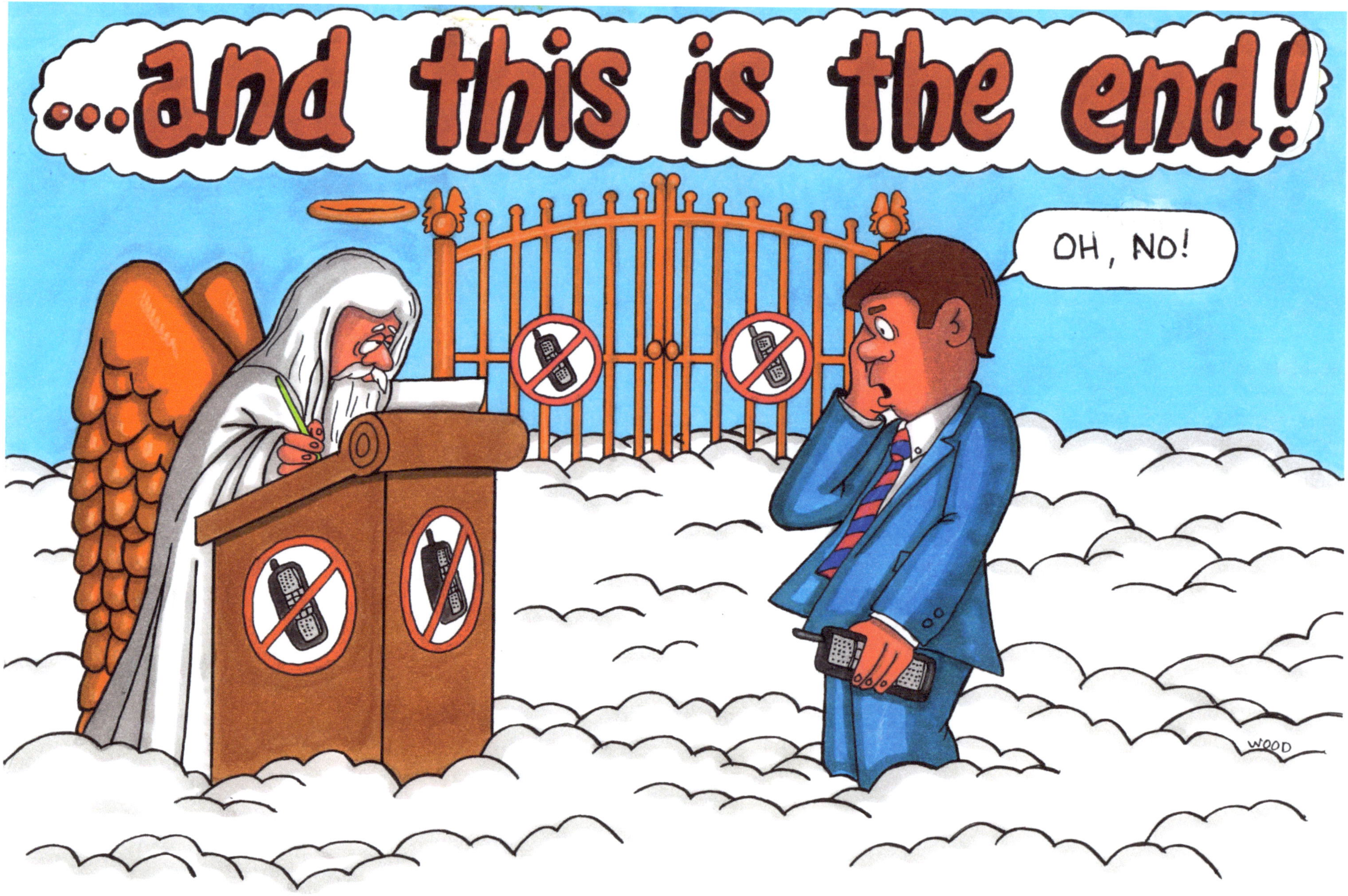
...and this is the end!
OH, NO!
WOOD

SCOTT WOOD

Scott Wood at work with his faithful companion, Comanche

Scott Wood was born in Sacramento, California, in 1943. He enjoyed creating cartoons at an early age, attempting to get his first cartoon published at the age of nine. In high school, he created cartoons for the school newspaper and won a state-wide poster contest highlighting better driving through better vision. Scott attended New Mexico Military Institute and subsequently Texas Tech University on a track scholarship, where he attained a Bachelor of Arts degree in history. After graduation, Scott was commissioned as a Second Lieutenant in the U.S. Army. He served in several posts in the United States and overseas in Vietnam, Korea and Germany as an armor officer, helicopter pilot and instructor pilot. While in the service, Scott obtained his Master's degree in management from Webster University. During his time in Germany, Scott created the popular cartoon strip *Quibbley*, which appeared in the European *Stars and Stripes* newspaper for ten years and spawned eight books and several posters.
The popularity of the comic strip is evidenced by the creation of a *Quibbley* Fan Club with several hundred members. Scott retired from the U.S. Army as a Lieutenant Colonel after 23 years of distinguished service. He continues creating cartoons for a myriad of companies and institutions including educational book publishers, Porsche automotive and the cultural centers of several cities in Germany, as well as for his own entertainment.

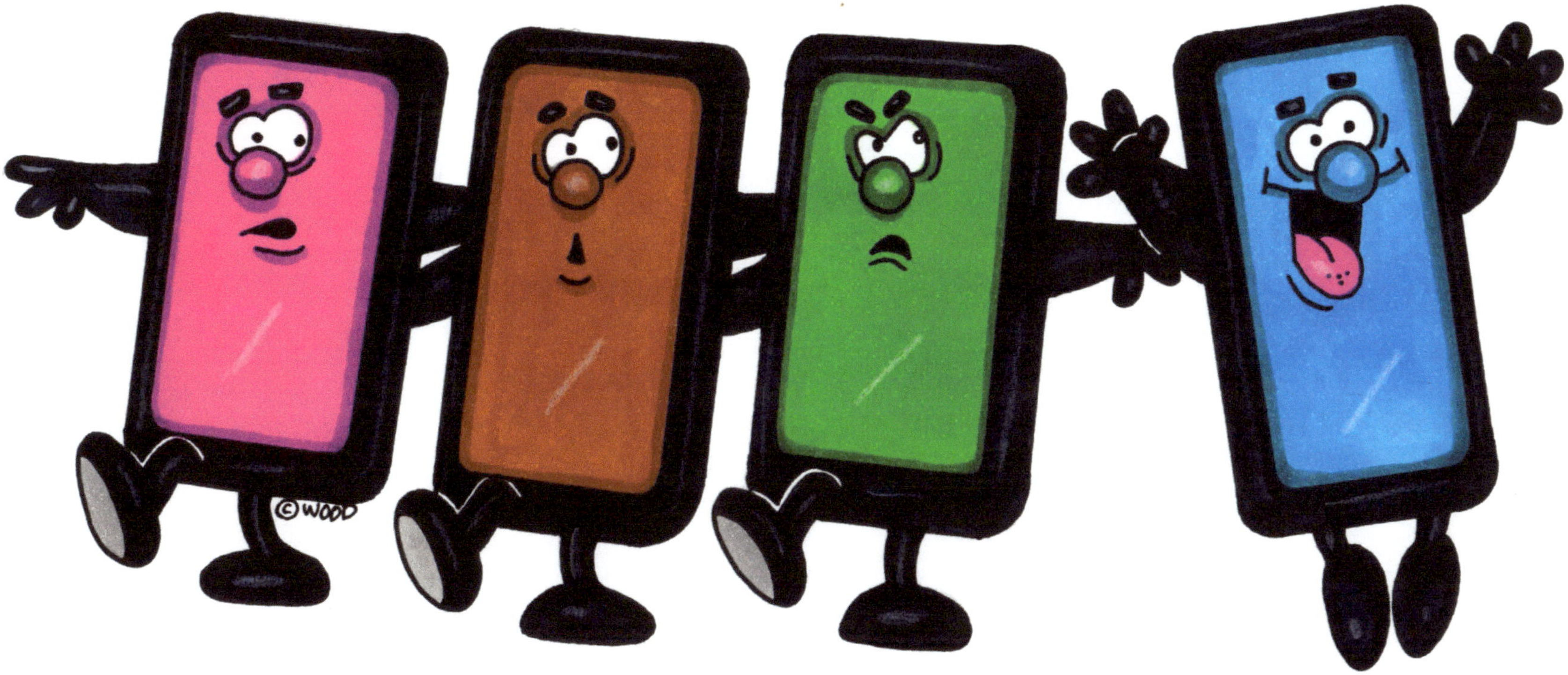
©WOOD

www.ingramcontent.com/pod-product-compliance
Lightning Source LLC
Chambersburg PA
CBHW042108090526

44591CB00004B/43